"In this well-researched Schwartz (*Berkeley 190C* .... rise and slow fall of M. B. Curtis, a Hungarian Jewish actor who thrived on American stages from the 1870s to 1890s, then sank into obscurity . . . Schwartz's intriguing portrayal of celebrity, status, and desperation illuminates the underbelly of an exciting, rapidly changing time."
—*Publishers Weekly*

"An outstanding new biography of one of the most talented characters of his time."
—BARRY MORENO, Bob Hope Memorial Library, Ellis Island National Immigration Museum

"One of the most phenomenal books I have ever read."
—DAN MANLEY, WMST radio

"Making M. B. Curtis's acquaintance is indisputably worth a reader's time."
—TheaterJones.com

"Any modern American will fall in love with Curtis just as their countrymen one hundred years ago did—and get a celebrity murder trial for a little excitement to boot!"
—*History Author Show*

"...Curtis' entire life and his most iconic role typify the American immigrant experience.... Had Curtis not stepped in to keep Lady Liberty's torch glowing, we all might have been left in the dark."
—*The Forward*, P. J. Grisar, Dec. 20, 2018

M.B.Curtis

The Man Who Lit
Lady Liberty

*The Extraordinary Rise and Fall
of Actor M. B. Curtis*

RICHARD SCHWARTZ

RSB BOOKS
BERKELEY, CALIFORNIA

Other Books by Richard Schwartz
The Circle of Stones
Berkeley 1900
Earthquake Exodus, 1906
Eccentrics, Heroes, and Cutthroats of Old Berkeley

Copyright © 2019 by Richard Schwartz
All rights reserved.

No part of this publication may be reproduced or distributed in any form or by
any means, or stored in a database or retrieval system, without prior permission
from the author.

Library of Congress Cataloging-in-Publication Data

Names: Schwartz, Richard, 1952- author.
Title: The man who lit Lady Liberty / by Richard Schwartz.
Description: Berkeley, California : RSB Books, 2017. | Includes
    bibliographical references and index.
Identifiers: LCCN 2017002826 | ISBN 9780967820453 (hardcover : alk. paper) |
    ISBN 9780967820460 (pbk. : alk. paper)
Subjects: LCSH: Curtis, M. B. | Actors--United States--Biography. | Producers
    and directors--United States--Biography. | Real estate developers--United
    States--Biography. | Jewish philanthropists--New York (State)--New
    York--Biography. | Immigrants--United States--Biography. | Statue of
    Liberty National Monument (N.Y. and N.J.)--History. | Statue of Liberty
    (New York, N.Y.)--History.
Classification: LCC PN2287.C7 S39 2017 | DDC 792.02/8092 [B] --dc23
LC record available at https://lccn.loc.gov/2017002826

Front cover photo: *TCS 1. Houghton Library, Harvard University*
Frontispiece photo: *Pen-and-ink poster from the 1880s. (Private collection)*

Visit www.richardschwartz.info
Interior design by Lisa Elliot
Cover design by Ashley Ingram

Printed in the United States of America
5 4 3 2 1

Hardcover ISBN: 978-0-9678204-5-3
Paperback ISBN: 978-0-9678204-6-0

To my father, Milton Schwartz, who has the patience and understanding and determination of a very wise man and who happily went on research forays for me; to my late mother, Mildred, who taught me perseverance and persistence and a respect for learning; and to my late sister, Maxeen, who became my best friend and showed me how to follow and respect one's dreams

Stand on stage and hold the hearts of men in your hand.
Make them laugh with a gesture, cry with a word.
Make them love you. And you will know what power is.
—Jennifer Donnelly, Revolution

The theatre is certainly a place for learning about
the brevity of human glory.
—Iris Murdoch

CONTENTS

Introduction, *ix*

Prologue, *1*

CHAPTER ONE
An Actor Prepares
7

CHAPTER TWO
The Stage Is Set and the Leading Lady Enters
17

CHAPTER THREE
The Role of a Lifetime
31

CHAPTER FOUR
The Trojan Horse of Change
45

CHAPTER FIVE
Staying Center Stage
55

CHAPTER SIX
The Sequel to Success
75

CHAPTER SEVEN

A Hungarian Hebrew in King Arthur's Court

111

CHAPTER EIGHT

Trials and Tribulations

143

CHAPTER NINE

A Troubled Comeback

217

CHAPTER TEN

Down Under and Back Again

243

CHAPTER ELEVEN

A Long, Slow Fade

261

Acknowledgments, *283*

Index, *289*

INTRODUCTION

⁓

I met M. B. Curtis quite by accident in 1996. Curtis had been dead since 1920, but that didn't seem to matter at all.

There he was, radiating like a high-energy particle as I stared at one of the first photos I had ever seen of the man. He was not identified in the photo. But I recognized him as I would myself. His mustachioed face looked at me directly, his right foot propped up on something, his hand resting on his thigh. Curtis stood at the center of the photo amid a sea of people. He was brilliantly dressed in a grand suit and vest, a white shirt with a high collar, and a fine-looking top hat. Standing next to him was his beautiful and elegant wife, Marie, his big wonderful dog Carlo at his side. Curtis was of average height but broad shouldered. His dark expressive eyes drew me in.

I knew why Curtis was in that photo. It was the October 2, 1887, opening of Posen Station in Berkeley, California. Curtis, a hugely successful actor, had donated a large sum of money to help West Berkeley get its first train stop and had asked that the station be named not for himself but for his famous theatrical character.

I had come across this photo during the course of researching Berkeley's early history, a project that had started with my saving a stack of old newspapers from the trash. What began as a spontaneous gesture ended with the publishing of several books. But I couldn't get M. B. Curtis out of my mind, and I began to seek the man out.

What I found out fascinated me.

With each new article I found about his life, I became

A cartoon published in Puck *showing politicians as Sam'ls of Posen importuning the figure of Columbia. (Private collection)*

more astonished at this man's talent, his dreams, his accomplishments, and his perseverance. The other part of the man — his limitations and his foibles — balanced my understanding of him, but his struggles and successes made him even more real and interesting.

His troubles drove him to drink. He suffered from the effects of his celebrity. His finances collapsed. But he kept getting back up. When everything else failed, Curtis always returned to performing, and audiences flocked to see him again and again.

We can only surmise how M. B. Curtis established his magical gossamer connection to audiences across the country. This charismatic and energetic actor and his seemingly foolish greenhorn immigrant character who triumphed against all odds caused an almost overnight sensation with American audiences. Those audiences were living in a country struggling to deal with the biggest wave of immigration to ever crash onto its shores. With the power of his portrayal of Sam'l of Posen, Curtis single-handedly affected the trajectory of

American cultural growth in the late nineteenth century. Everything from Barnum & Bailey's midway to United States senators were compared to Curtis's Sam'l of Posen character. Cigars and boats and writing paper were named after Sam'l. Stores employed quotes from Sam'l to sell their products. And no one would argue with the fact that Curtis paved the way for the next generation of ethnic immigrant comedians as Curtis was the first Jewish actor who portrayed a male Jewish character on stage and endowed him with humanity.

How this man and his life and cultural influence were ever forgotten is beyond me. But he was. How did this happen? In his day, the entire nation watched and wrote about his every move. I needed to know what made M. B. Curtis tick. I needed to study and share this man's life. The endeavor took twenty years.

While I learned enough about Curtis to try to tell his story, I also learned that the research never ends. It never will. There is always something more—a pen-and-ink poster of Curtis found in a wall of an old farmhouse, a poster for one of his plays found in an attic, a brief handwritten autobiography requested from Curtis by an institution I had never heard of until recently.

Even though Curtis's stage career might seem like a historical footnote today, Curtis's dramatic rise and fall, and his continual struggle to reinvent himself, still resonate in modern America. His life reads like a classical Greek tragedy that encourages us to dream big while warning of the dangers of success. No hero is invincible, and the life of M. B. Curtis serves as both an inspiration and admonition to modern readers.

I hope this book will be M. B. Curtis's bell. His lantern. His voice. I hope this story will take you on a journey of incredible human talent and fame and suffering and perseverance and dreaming.

A mature M. B. Curtis posing as his signature character, the immigrant traveling salesman Sam'l of Posen. (TCS 1. Houghton Library, Harvard University)

PROLOGUE

The French steamer *Isère* glided into New York Harbor on June 17, 1885, bearing an unusual passenger. Deep in the ship's hold were the crates containing the disassembled pieces of the colossal neoclassical sculpture *La Liberté éclairant le monde* designed by Frédéric Auguste Bartholdi. Work on the statue had begun in the early 1870s and sections of the Statue of Liberty had played bit parts at the Centennial Exposition in Philadelphia in 1876 and the Paris World's Fair in 1878. Our leading lady was now ready for her American debut.

As with many joint theatrical productions, the road to the show's opening had been rocky. The colossal structure was a gift from the French people, and while France would pay for the statue, it had been decided that the United States would finance the construction of the pedestal upon which she would stand.

Still suffering from the effects of the Panic of 1873 and unable to understand how the pedestal could be as expensive as the statute itself, many Americans were critical of the project. As a result, Congress had failed to approve an appropriations bill for the $100,000 needed to construct the base. In an effort to jump-start the project, the New York state legislature approved a $50,000 grant, but Governor Grover Cleveland vetoed the bill.

In an effort to push the project forward, publisher Joseph Pulitzer, a Jewish Hungarian immigrant and American Civil War veteran, initiated a fund-raising campaign in one of his many newspapers, the *New York World*. Pulitzer offered to publish the name of every contributor—no matter how small—and announced a goal of $100,000, the total cost of the construction of the base. Pulitzer orchestrated a monumentally successful campaign in which thousands of people gave a dime or a quarter. After five months of daily calls to donate, the *New York World* proclaimed on August 11, 1885, that $102,000 had been donated by 120,000 individuals, rich and poor.

With the completion of the pedestal in April 1886, the stage was finally set for the reassembly of the statue, and the dedication ceremony was scheduled for October 28.

Opening day dawned misty and rainy, but the excitement in New York managed to pierce the gloom. Even the theatres in the city knew they were being upstaged as they delayed performances to accommodate the parade that began at Madison Square and headed to Battery Park via Fifth Avenue.

Though the statue had been officially designated as a lighthouse and Bartholdi had designed Liberty's torch to illuminate the waters of New York Harbor and the faces of hopeful immigrants, no arrangement or appropriation had been made by the U.S. government for the lighting of the Statue of Liberty's torch beyond the opening ceremony. The statue's lighting went dark at sunset on November 7.

A November 8, 1886, article in the *New York World* aptly described the gloomy situation.

> The wind howled mournfully around the Statue of Liberty last night. Not even a flickering ray of light from the torch relieved the Egyptian darkness of the island. No attempt was made last night to have the torch lighted and kept burning another night. The men employed by Hampson & Co. to run the engines

banked the fires, locked up the engine room
and left by the early morning boat. The two
policemen stationed at the landing hugged the
picket-fence for warmth and wished they had
worn their winter coats.

But in what might seem like an improbable plot
device, the man who would come to Lady Liberty's
rescue was being bathed in footlights less than three
miles away from where the statue sat in darkness.

Three days after the dedication ceremony, actor
M. B. Curtis had arrived in New York City with his new
play *Caught in a Corner*. Long accustomed to the spotlight, Curtis must have had immediate sympathy for
the copper lady being swallowed up by darkness every
night. After all, he was once a six-year-old immigrant.

By November 8, the *New York World* reported that "Mr.
M. B. Curtis, the well-known actor, and his manager, J. W.
Rosenquest, will offer to-day to pay the expense of keeping
the statue lighted during the week, while Mr. Curtis is engaged
at the Fourteenth Street Theatre." Curtis even placed a large
ad in the *New York World* stating that he would "not allow Miss
Liberty to be Caught in a Corner. "

Major General John M. Schofield had been in charge of
the statue's inauguration, and he stated on November 9 that
he would not accept Curtis's offer as it was better to wait
for Congress to "take official action." After the government
rejected the actor's offer, Curtis cut through the red tape and
paid $800 directly to the electric-dynamo workers to provide
electricity to light the Lady.

The *Dramatic Mirror* of November 13, 1886, recorded that
"M. B. Curtis is delighting crowds with *Caught in a Corner* at

STRAITS TO WHICH OUR GODDESS OF LIBERTY IS REDUCED.
GODDESS (to captain of passing vessel)—"*Say, mister, give us a light, will yer?*"

A cartoon depicting the struggle to light the Statue of Liberty. (Frank Leslie's Illustrated Newspaper, *November 13, 1886, page 208. From the Collections of the Statue of Liberty National Monument, National Park Service.*)

the Fourteenth Street Theatre. Mr. Curtis is not only supplying merriment to New York's Harbor. Miss Liberty would be shrouded in darkness were it not for the comedian's combined business enterprise and patriotism."

Curtis had not only spared his adopted country the humiliation of an unlit Statue of Liberty, he also encouraged others to come to the statue's rescue. The *Dramatic Mirror* announced on November 13 that M. B. Curtis was "to raise awareness of the need for funds to light the statue at night for all to see." And others noted that the actor took special delight in taking his friends to visit the statue at night during this period and that many people had commended his patriotic act.

With public pressure mounting, Congress quickly changed its mind and on the night of November 22, 1886, the Statue of Liberty was again lit by federal funds.

But every actress needs a good script, and the right words for Lady Liberty would be supplied by poet Emma Lazarus. Born in 1849 (the same year as Curtis), Lazarus had been working with immigrants since the early 1880s. She had written the poem "The New Colossus" in 1883 to help raise funds to build the base of what she called the "Mother of Exiles." A friend found her poem in 1901, fourteen years after her death, and in 1903 that poem was mounted on the pedestal of the Statue of Liberty. The statue's purpose now encompassed the hopes and dreams of immigrants as well as the original announced intent of honoring democracy, freedom, and the abolition of slavery.

As historian Carole Perrault has noted, the battle to keep the Statue of Liberty lit did not end in 1886. The "Bartholdi Burden" raised its head again in 1893 when it came to light that the statue's infrastructure and illumination system had significantly deteriorated. The Lighthouse Board deemed in an 1894 report that it was not necessary to spend considerable funds to light the statue's beacon as it "was of no importance whatever" as a navigational aid. They recommended that Congress authorize the elimination of lighting the beacon for the harbor to save money, and this request was approved.

The *New York World* announced on April 9, 1894, that "today Mr. Curtis will visit the Statue of Liberty. He was the first illuminator of the statue. After the *World* fund had built its pedestal he gave $800 to light it till Congress made an appropriation."

When Curtis was asked about the current lighting crisis, he responded, "If that ever comes to a head I want the *World* to put me down as one of ten to pay $1,000 towards the $10,0000 yearly expense."

By July of 1895, the government had extinguished not only the harbor beacon but all of the remaining lights except for those in the torch. But a suggestion by the Lighthouse Board to replace the old lighting system in order to save the government substantial money seemed to save the day. Within a couple of years, an order was issued to begin the maintenance and improvements for the statue as soon as possible.

Though M. B. Curtis was not the only citizen who demanded that the Statue of Liberty remain lit, he was the only one to actually light her when Congress refused right after its dedication. But the story does not end with one now-forgotten man's effort to salvage the nation's dignity and reinforce the statue's sacred purpose. M. B. Curtis spent his career portraying immigrants on the American stage, and his own life serves as a lighthouse for Americans today, illuminating the night with both welcome and warning.

CHAPTER ONE

An Actor Prepares

An actor's course is set even before he's out of the cradle.
—*James Dean*

There was no towering statue raising a torch of welcome when six-year-old Moritz Bertram Strelinger stood on the deck of the *Lady Scales* early in 1856 to catch his first glimpse of New York Harbor and the United States of America. There wasn't even an Ellis Island. Moritz and his family were instead welcomed to the New World at the immigration depot at Battery Park on the southern edge of Manhattan. One can only imagine how happy Moritz's mother, Bertha, was to feel land under her feet after the long winter voyage from Hamburg during which she had to keep track of Moritz; his eight-year-old brother, Frank; and his three-year-old sister, Gisella, while being pregnant with Charles, the first Strelinger to be born on American soil.

The reason thirty-two-year-old Gyula Strelinger had packed up his twenty-five-year-old wife and young family, and left Budapest is lost to history. Maybe he was enticed by the weathered whispers of the American Dream that had reached

Hungary. Maybe he and Bertha were trying not to be devoured by the memory of recently losing their infant daughter, Rosalie. But whatever their motivation, the family had been on the move. Gyula's parents and brother lived in a rural village in Slovakia called Stianvnica. But little Moritz was born on July 20, 1849, in Nagy Selmetz, a Hungarian town that is now in Slovakia outside of Ružomberok. And Gyula had relocated to the sophisticated city of Budapest in 1855, a year before the family's biggest move.

Bertha Schultz Strelinger. (Courtesy of the Strelinger family)

Julien Strelinger. (Courtesy of the Strelinger family)

And the family kept traveling after landing in New York. Gyula, now going by Julien, the new, more American-sounding name apparently given to him by an immigration agent in New York, settled his family in Detroit, a steadily growing metropolis of 40,000 that had become a major port and manufacturing hub by that time. The family quickly put down roots in the city that was soon to be known as the "Paris of the West" and was similar in size to Budapest. Charles was born there on May 4, 1856, and Julien quickly went to work, opening a vinegar distillery and manufacturing liquor, a trade he learned from several Strelinger relatives in Europe, including his grandparents, who were involved in the distillery business and owned inns, a common pairing in Hungary at that time.

Julien soon opened a tavern and a brewery, and then a greenhouse, in which he cultivated rare flowers. He eventually opened four greenhouses and had "a most extensive variety of plants and flowers, embracing the rare and most desirable in beauty and fragrance. Each of these greenhouses is 22 x 130 feet in size, and among the most handsome and complete in this city," according to Clarence Monroe Burton's *Compendium of History and Biography of the City of Detroit*. The Strelinger family had obviously begun to stand out from the huddled masses of new immigrants, naming their next child, who was born in 1857, George Washington Strelinger, a grateful nod of acknowledgment to their adopted country. On April 16, 1860, Julien Strelinger filed a Notice of Intention with the state of Michigan to become a United States citizen. The Jewish Hungarian family that had traveled for so long and so far had finally found a home.

Although his family had given up wandering, Moritz at a young age began displaying the habits of the footloose touring actor he would become by often running away from home. In an article in the *New York Mirror* on November 6, 1886, a newspaper writer recounted a touching reunion with a local Detroit constable who had helped keep the young Moritz at home.

> During those times he would often run away from home. His father remonstrated with him to no avail. At one time he succeeded in eluding his father and was in a fair way to leave home forever when he was approached by Constable Freeburger, reprimanded and sent home. During the engagement of Mr. Curtis here last week the old constable called at the

ticket office and was purchasing seats when
Curtis ordered the old man to accompany him.
He did so and found himself and wife seated
in one of the elegant private boxes. Upon leaving Curtis exclaimed: Uncle Free, if you had
let me run away from home I wouldn't have
been worth $300,000 to-day, and the old man
appreciated the joke, and the box also.

Not yet a teenager, Moritz, known as the strongest and
most energetic boy in the neighborhood after having rescued
his brother from a bigger boy, ran away from home again to
try to volunteer as a drummer boy with the 15th Michigan
Infantry and the Zouaves after the outbreak of the Civil War.
The Zouaves were a collection of volunteer soldiers who had
adopted the exotic uniform of the light infantry of the French
African Army. Moritz was no doubt caught up in a youthful
desire for adventure at the beginning of the war, but one has
to wonder if he wasn't already showing an actor's taste for
extravagant costumes. As many boys were, he was evidently
rejected as a drummer boy due to his extreme youth.

And this desire to be among the best-dressed soldiers in
the Civil War wasn't the only hint of Moritz's future career.

In the 1860s, a literary club met at the Strelinger saloon
at 113 Bates Street, with some well-established Detroit residents — physicians, businessmen, military men, and historians
— in attendance. One club member had a clear memory of
the club and the young Moritz, which is recounted in Friend
Palmer's 1906 *Early Days in Detroit*.

One of Strelinger's sons, the one that went
upon the stage, begged the privilege from his

> father to wait on this crowd, and was allowed
> to do so. He assigned as his reason for the
> request that it gave him opportunities to enjoy
> the literary treat that was nightly presented
> there. This early experience of his led him to
> adopt the stage as a profession . . . His early
> contact with the members of that club con-
> vinced him that he was fitted for better things
> than running a lager beer saloon.

After dropping out of school at about fourteen, Moritz worked
for three or four years as a shipping clerk at Hanna and Co. in
Detroit, a wholesale tobacco house. In an interview published
in the *Illustrated American*, on February 27, 1892, he explained
how, even at this first job, he was inclined toward the dramatic:
"I used the hogs-heads [large wooden barrels used to store
tobacco] to such an extent as rostrums to spout Shakespeare
from, that I was advised to turn actor. I took the advice seri-
ously, and my first step was to run away."

And run away he did. Moritz's next job was at the Briggs
House in Chicago, working as a bellboy when he was about
seventeen. Strelinger augmented his wages at the Briggs
House by selling newspapers. One cold morning, two boys
mobbed him and ran off with his papers. His employers didn't
believe his account, so he was let go, a rather fortunate firing
as it turned out, because this led him to McVicker's Theatre.
"I then went over to McVicker's and worked for about $13
a month for a long time. I drifted from journalism into the
dramatic profession," he told a reporter for the *Chicago Tribune*
in 1885.

Moritz had hung around McVicker's Theatre after work as

a general hand (a "call boy") and was working in the basement print shop. Soon, through his persistence, he procured an acting job. He first performed as an extra at McVicker's then rose to his first speaking part with about a dozen lines as Alf Mann in *Uncle Tom's Cabin*, a role since deleted from the script of the play.

His hard work and initiative paid off. By 1869, at the age of twenty, Moritz had become a regular member of McVicker's acting company. As time went on, he received a well-rounded education in the theatre, performing parts in serious drama, melodrama, and tragedy, as well as in comedy, a typical experience for a stock company actor of that day. After having achieved fame as an actor, he recalled his hectic schedule from his early days in an interview published in a newspaper article

The old McVicker's Theatre in Chicago where Curtis first worked as a call boy and then began his acting career. (New York Public Library, Digital Collections)

titled "How Curtis Came to Fashion It into a Play" found in the Harvard Theater Collection.

> I was not a full-blown comedian by any means
> at that time; and I can tell you it was not very
> funny work either, being a call boy and an
> assistant treasurer at $6 a week, and then get-
> ting up at 5 o'clock in the morning to turn the
> crank of the theatre bill/poster printing press
> for two hours at a stretch for $2 a week. This
> was hardly enough to live upon and travel com-
> fortably in the provinces, so when I was in Chi-
> cago I increased my $6 a week salary by acting
> as a reporter for the *Chicago Times*, for which
> I got paid $4 a week. By the way, don't fancy
> that I did any very extremely deeply thoughtful
> work for its columns, but I was eminently for-
> tunate in "getting on" to a burning factory and
> a death by drowning, and an overturned cart;
> such items, small but interesting.

At some point before 1871, he changed his birth name, Moritz Bertram Strelinger, to one that might be more help-ful to him in the theatrical world: Maurice Bertrand Curtis, or M. B. Curtis, a very American-sounding moniker. The first instance of Moritz using this stage name appears in a May 1871 review of the play *Eustache* in Montreal. Both Frank and George Washington Strelinger also adopted the last name of Curtis, and all three brothers joined the Episcopal Church. No answer survives as to why they chose this faith, though a desire to feel what it is like to fully belong and participate in the majority American culture is a likely one.

The young actor. (TCS 1. Houghton Library, Harvard University)

But while the newly minted Maurice Bertrand Curtis was
beginning to enjoy some theatrical success in Chicago, all had
not been well with his family back in Detroit for some time.
Bertha Strelinger's heart began to fail, and she had decided to
return to Hungary to be cared for by the well-trained doctors
in her own family. She told relatives in the United States
that she was going home to die. She applied for a passport to
return to Hungary one day before Julien took his naturaliza-
tion oath in 1867. After three years of care in Hungary, Bertha

Schultz Strelinger died on May 25, 1870. We do not know if the news of Maurice's mother's death precipitated his return to his father's home in Detroit or if his return was caused by a lack of work and insufficient income in Chicago. But we do know that the 1870 census, taken two months after his mother's death, shows him residing with his father and lists his profession as "actor." Also listed in the household were his brothers Charles and George; a German girl and a Prussian girl, twenty-one-year-old Albertine Selkie and nineteen-year-old Augusta Siter, probably domestics; and an Irish brewer, Arthur O'Hara; and a Canadian bartender, Henry Zimmerman, both of whom must have worked for Julien. All three of Julien's sons were listed as still using Strelinger as their last name in this 1870 census.

Being surrounded by this echo chamber of different accents and having grown up in a neighborhood that was a veritable United Nations of nationalities and languages must have been excellent training for a neophyte actor who was a born mimic. Young Moritz's ability to bring to life the many characters who filled the teeming streets of an immigrant America would serve him well later in his career.

Although he was no doubt mourning the death of his mother while he spent time in Detroit with his family, M. B. Curtis had to reapply himself to learning his craft, a prologue to his meteoric rise in the theatrical world. Fate's stage was secretly set and waiting for the star's entrance.

The Stage Is Set and the Leading Lady Enters

*Actors ought to be larger than life. You come across quite
enough ordinary, nondescript people in daily life and I don't see
why you should be subjected to them on the stage, too.*
—Donald Sinden

One can only speculate why M. B. Curtis left his home in
Detroit again. It might have been his father's recent marriage
or it might have been a desire to get back in the limelight. But
whatever the reason, soon after Curtis's father married Augusta Jacobs on May 20, 1871, the twenty-one-year-old Curtis
traveled to Toronto and Columbus, Ohio, where he learned
more about his trade from experienced actors, many of whom
were nationally recognized figures in the theatre. It was his
good fortune while he was coming up to work alongside many
of the biggest stars of the contemporary stage, such as Joseph
Jefferson and Maggie Mitchell, carefully studying the movement, speech, and nuances of their portrayals.

While the ineffable connection that Curtis established

A young M. B. Curtis. (TCS 1. Houghton Library, Harvard University)

with his characters and his audience is lost to us, we can glean
reflections of his magic from firsthand accounts. The reviews
of his performances mention how audiences delighted in his
inventive use of dialect. He also used his face, large eyes, hands,
and his distinctive walk as finely tuned instruments of expres-
sion. As the *Atlanta Constitution* stated on April Fools' Day,
1896: "His comical walk across the stage is half the battle, while
his plausible manner and audaciously conceived and boldly
carried out explanations would wean a man away from a twelve

month's worry. Mr. Curtis is magnetic, and if ever amusement was afforded one it is by the drummer, Samuel of Posen."

He even got his costumes into the act in a very magical manner, curling a handkerchief or making sure he displayed a fancy vest or coat lining for expressions of some nuance.

Curtis used everything he had at hand, little and big, to make his characters riveting, expressive, and mesmerizingly memorable. One critic described the evocative way Curtis curled his hand and placed his chin on it, the same mannerism made famous by comedian Jack Benny generations later. There is even a surviving reference indicating that Curtis first introduced oversize shoes to the stage (clowns had not yet employed the technique), and it was suggested that Charlie Chaplin had borrowed this idea from his immigrant predecessor, according to an account found in 1931's *Plagiarism: The "Art" of Stealing Literary Material* by Maurice Salzman.

Curtis's theatrical experience included performances with Edwin Booth, Lawrence Barrett, and many other American stage giants of his day. One retrospective of his career reported that Curtis performed about 125 different roles on stage—tragedies; Shakespearean, American, and European literary classics made into plays; as well as comedies. His roles ranged from Louis XIII to an attorney to a domestic. Curtis also played a number of ethnic roles. When Curtis came to San Francisco in 1876, he portrayed a black character with the California Theatre's stock company in a production of *The Mighty Dollar* with W. J. Florence. Other ethnic roles he took on were of a thickly accented German immigrant and a Dutchman, popular groups to mock as their numbers increased in America. His portrayals of African Americans mirrored issues Curtis himself faced—that some ethnic groups were not allowed to portray themselves on stage, which resulted in stilted, stereotypical representations of many Americans in the theatre.

Reviews of Curtis's early work were favorable. He was typically described as "real excellent" in his portrayals. As a Shakespearean character, he was as "strong." In another play, a review said his character was represented "exceedingly well." In Toronto in 1875, Curtis "made the hit of the season in his imitations of various animals." He was learning to use his talent for mimicry to connect with audiences, and he was getting good press for it.

Even though Curtis was still a supporting player, the "trial by fire" training he received by being a member of touring companies would prove invaluable. And Curtis was showing himself to be an apt pupil. An article in the *Illustrated American* in 1892 recalls how Curtis was becoming a quick study and an actor who could transform himself into many distinct characters. Curtis was a member of the stock company at the Woods Theatre in 1873, touring in *The Boy Detective*. In Cincinnati the leading actor was dismissed by a disappointed manager and Curtis was asked to assume the starring role. Curtis had to assume seven separate characters and know their lines only hours before the play was to go on. Curtis was so convincing that night that he was given three curtain calls (the *Illustrated American*, February 27, 1892).

Much of 1876 and the early months of 1877 found Curtis performing throughout Canada, but concentrating mostly on Toronto. His portrayal of Newman Noggs in *Nicholas Nickleby* was done "exceedingly well," at the Grand Opera in Toronto, according to the *New York Clipper* of January 15, 1876. Curtis took part of the spring off while remaining in Toronto. While he might have remained in Canada during that time to establish himself with a local acting troupe at the Grand Opera House, at some point during the period he turned his attention

Curtis displaying his sartorial finery. (TCS 1. Houghton Library, Harvard University)

to an even more important goal: casting a leading lady.

During the late 1870s, Curtis met a beautiful black-eyed
sixteen-year-old French Canadian named Marie Alphonsine
Fleurange. Marie was born in Quebec and told the U.S. census
that she was born in 1861. Her father was Canadian English,
her mother, an American. Marie was said to have been educated
at a convent in French-speaking Canada.

When the couple met, Curtis must have been attracted by
Marie's bright smile, self-containment, ready magnetism, and
soft, lilting French accent. And the charming and energetic
Maurice must have quickly melted Marie's resistance with
his trademark tantalizing optimism. But just as there is little
or no historical record of their courtship, their marriage also
remains shrouded in mystery. Their statement to the 1900
U.S. census dates that event to 1883, but this was long after
they had been together and had even toured as man and wife.
A city history of Montreal claims that Curtis married Marie
"during his sojourn in Montreal," and Curtis stated to a judge
in 1889 that he was married in Montreal when he was earning only $25 a week. Curtis had first performed in Montreal
in 1871 after leaving Detroit after his father's marriage, and
he worked there regularly during the next decade. Curtis and
Marie were almost certainly married in the 1870s, and one
wonders to what end the couple reported the later date to
the census. A December 22, 1876, *Oakland Evening Tribune*
article announced the overland arrival of Mrs. M. B. Curtis of
Canada, seemingly confirming that the couple was married by
this time. They were also noted as "man and wife" in 1879 by
the *New York Clipper*, but no marriage certificate has yet been
located in either Canada or the United States.

*A pen-and-ink drawing of Marie Curtis (née Fleurange) who performed as
Albina de Mer. (Billy Rose Theatre Division, The New York Public Library for
the Performing Arts)*

Marie was not originally involved in the theatre, nor did
she have any aspirations to act. But after their marriage, Curtis
convinced her to accept a part that a theatre company needed
to fill on short notice. She portrayed Kitty Clover in the play
Mr. and Mrs. Peter White and gave herself the stage name
Albina de Mer, using the maiden name of her maternal grandmother, who lived in France.

Marie first appeared in San Francisco around 1878 in the
"smallest utility parts." Curtis had performed with Maggie
Mitchell in the 1870s and formed a lifelong friendship with
her. Marie appeared alongside Mitchell as Florette in the play

The Pearl of Savoy in March of 1880 at the Academy of Music in Buffalo, New York. A review in the San Francisco *Examiner* (June 4, 1882) goes out of its way to mention that Marie had grown tremendously as an actress. The *New York Herald* said they wished they could put on paper "Mrs. Curtis's delicious accent and merry laugh."

In an interview with the *San Francisco Chronicle* (February 27, 1889) later in her career, Marie said of her first stage role:

> I did not know my part well. I was not so good
> in the English, and I said I shall only fail. But
> Mr. Curtis, he only laughs at me and he said,
> "Now don't you mind. I will be there, and if
> you forget, I will tell you what to say." Well, I
> went on and as I stepped out on the stage, ev-
> ery word went out of my head. I just rushed up
> to my husband and said, "Now what do I say?"
> Well, he told me. I said it and everything went
> on well enough until I had to make an exit. I
> forgot where I was to go, and I ran against the
> scenery and nearly knocked it over. Oh, how
> the people did applaud me! I suppose it was
> because I was so awkward and so funny, but I
> thought it was because I had made such a hit.

When Marie began playing the adventuress Mlle. Celeste in the play that would make her husband's career, she wore many memorable articles of clothing, which raised as many eyebrows as did her powers of delineation and forceful presentation. Her costumes changed with every act. She wore a gray gown in one act, which was actually her grandmother's.

Marie dressed in her trademark wardrobe. (Private collection)

In another act, she wore a hundred-year-old hat. One review of her magnificent wardrobe described a cherry and blue velvet brocade and a bodice and shoulder pieces that "radiate with lace." After he had achieved success in the theatre, Curtis bought Marie diamonds and a very valuable ruby ring said to be worth $8,000. Her jewelry, much of which was antique, was as notable as her gowns.

One story regarding Marie actually involves none other than Marie Antoinette. Marie Antoinette was supposedly given a huge ring—a topaz surrounded by diamonds—by a duke in 1783 at her home in Chantilly. A few weeks before her execution, Marie Antoinette gave this ring to her wine merchant's wife, Felice de Mer, as a token of their friendship. Felice was Marie's great-grandmother. Marie wore the ring occasionally, for good luck she claimed, but only on the stage, according to the article "Caught in a Corner," found in the Ford Collection at the New York Public Library for the Performing Arts, Billy Rose Collection.

Whether it was due to Marie's good-luck ring or through his own drive and talent, M. B. Curtis was soon to become one of America's leading actors even during hard times. According to an article published in the *Sketch* on July 10, 1895, Curtis got a big break when the famous comic actor Robert Pateman decided to return to his native England and Curtis was chosen to replace him on tour—a job that eventually brought the actor to San Francisco, where he played light comedic roles for the California Stock Company. However, later in his career, when he was asked in a *Chicago Tribune* article on June 15, 1885, how he got to California, Curtis provided an entertaining and humorous (and possibly fictitious) alternate version of what propelled his first visit to the Golden State.

> I was in New York getting along somehow at a cheap boarding house when a miner from California came to visit my landlady. His stories, which grew bigger every day, made me think I could pick up gold anywhere out there. I got wild. I could think of nothing else but becoming a miner. I raked up all the money I could get. It was just $137, and with that I started out, going steerage. Two days of that was enough, and I bribed the steward to sneak

me into a cabin. The first night I found a game
of poker, and the ship's officers were all in,
having just been paid off. My! They were soft
marks, and by the time we reached the isth-
mus I was $1,000 ahead and was the biggest
man on board. With that I went cabin to San
Francisco you can be sure. I found out in a day
or two that gold was not lying around loose;
a man had to work for it. I soon ran across
John McCullough, who asked me what I had
come out there for. I couldn't own up what a
fool I had been, so I told him I had come for
my health, my lungs were bad . . . I joined the
stock company in which John was then playing, and which has turned out more stars than
any other company in the country, and staid
[*sic*] there until the press of San Francisco
broke it up, crying for something new.

While we don't know if Curtis headed for California to
pan for gold or came there as part of a touring company, we
do know that by 1877 Curtis had teamed up with producer
and playwright David Belasco at the California Theatre, one
of the great stock theatre companies in San Francisco. Curtis
is listed in the cast of Maggie Moore and J. C. Williamson's
Struck Oil when they performed with Belasco's company on
July 9, 1877. Critics touted the troupe of the mid-1870s as a
company probably never equaled in any other American theatre up to that time, and indeed for years later, for this famous
organization was managed by Lawrence Barrett and John Mc-
Cullough. Almost all the members went on to great careers on
the national stage. Belasco left the California Theatre troupe

in January 1878 but returned to San Francisco the following year and became manager of the Baldwin Theatre, where Curtis appeared as Snake in *The School for Scandal*. Actors from the Baldwin and California theatres were to be a fertile source of talent for Curtis when he later formed his own company. The bonds he made in these early years proved strong and enduring, and the Bay Area became Curtis's de facto base of operations.

San Francisco in the 1870s, like the rest of the nation, was struggling through an economic depression. California felt the full effect of this economic downturn in the summer of 1875 when the mighty Bank of California failed. The cloud of bad times billowed and darkened until, in 1877, San Francisco was economically moribund and money became a rare commodity. That year, the effects of a silver-mining crash were felt over the West, and conditions grew even worse in the theatrical industry, which by definition is a problematic economic venture. San Francisco's Bush Street Theatre closed for a couple of months. The Baldwin, Alhambra, and others followed suit, according to the San Francisco *Examiner* on June 4, 1882. The *New York Clipper* (August 11, 1887) described the theatrical venues of San Francisco as "dull, flat, and unprofitable, and they possess the appearance of continuing so for some time to come. The riotous amusements of a lawless mob, the depressed state of the times and the poverty of attraction at the different theatres have been potent reasons for the mighty beggarly army array of empty benches."

Despite the economic downturn, Curtis continued to find work throughout 1877 in two plays at the California Theatre — *Gif* and *The Mother-in-Law* — and in a "low comedy" at the

Grand Opera House, where "M. B. Curtis gave excellent imitations of famous actors," according to the *New York Clipper* (September 22, 1877). At the Bush Street Theatre, the renowned Joseph Klein Emmett performed in *Our Cousin Fritz*, a play about a German immigrant, "well supported as the following names bear witness: Mr. and Mrs. Harry Courtaine, M. B. Curtis . . . business very good" (*New York Clipper*, November 3, 1877). And in early 1878, Curtis returned to the play that gave him his first speaking part, playing Marks the lawyer in *Uncle Tom's Cabin* — quite a step up from being an extra. According to the *New York Clipper* of February 23, 1878, "His efforts were repeatedly applauded."

In the winter of early 1879, Curtis was offered a role in the Broadway Theatre production of *King Lear* in New York. His experience was broadening, and his reviews were very complimentary, often recognizing the special reactions he frequently received from the audience. During the Christmas season of that same year, he gave a special comic performance to eight hundred children at a matinee performance in San Francisco, where he played Julien Krantz, "a Dutchman with difficulties." Curtis was "especially meritorious," reported the *New York Clipper*.

In an article written well after he had become a star, the *Examiner* of San Francisco summarized Curtis's early career.

> After a time [Curtis] made an attempt to get on
> the stage, beginning in small parts, but he had
> a great deal of perseverance in his makeup,
> and despite the lack of education and despite
> almost every disadvantage that an embryo
> actor could labor under, he succeeded in at
> least attaining ordinary rank as an actor. His

strong commercial instincts stood him instead,
and he soon saw that but little money was to
be made by a man of his severe limitations
working for others.

While the *Examiner*'s mention of "his strong commercial instincts" is likely a veiled slur against Curtis's Jewish heritage, his instincts would serve him well as he worked his way toward the role that would propel him to stardom. However, as in any tragedy, those instincts that had helped him achieve so much would ultimately prove to be disastrous after a time.

The Role of a Lifetime

*Preparing a character is the opposite of building — it is
a demolishing, removing brick by brick everything in the
actor's muscles, ideas, and inhibitions that stands between
him and the part, until one day, with a great rush of air,
the character invades his every pore.*
— *Peter Brook*

Like most creation stories, the origins of the play and the role
that would catapult M. B. Curtis to national prominence are
murky and various. And like all good creation myths, there are
several competing versions and more than a few people who
jumped on the bandwagon to take credit for the play after its
enormous success. And Curtis himself was no exception.

While the playwright and former newspaperman George
Jessop is credited as the author of the full-length play that
was initially titled *Isadore Plastrick*, the seeds of the charac-
ter that would eventually emerge as Sam'l of Posen began in
San Francisco, according to Curtis in a later interview in the
Sketch, July 10, 1895.

There was a very funny drummer here at that
time, a man called Wolf. He was, perhaps, one
of the most comical men I have ever met; and
for the life of me I could never refrain from
giving imitations of him. I am a member of the
Bohemian Club; and whenever I wanted to
create a laugh I would just give them Wolf. It
came to be well-liked. W. Mestayer was so particularly pleased with it that I eventually wrote
one act, which I used at a Bohemian low jinks,
and on the occasion of benefits. It was not till
I was East that John Warner, Nat Goodwin's
manager, advised me to make a regular play of
it, assuring for me a great success with it. I did
not pay much heed to him, but when I was in
Texas I showed this act to Rodney Wires, and
while we were roosting upon the fences, waiting for the trains to come along, Rodney and
I planned out the play. Well, we broke up in
Texas [because] our leading lady captur[ed] the
affections of some cattle-king, and somehow
or other I got back to New York with nothing
in my pocket, though with *Sam'l of Posen* half
written.

Curtis was indeed a member of the Bohemian Club, whose
members ranged from artists to entrepreneurs, from January
3, 1877, until November 29, 1878, according to the club's historian, Matt Buff. Membership during this period lends much
credence to Curtis's account.

But after the play became an unprecedented success,
there was no shortage of sources claiming to be the origin of

the character Sam'l of Posen. Charles Dickson, an actor and writer who had a long-standing relationship with Curtis in the theatre, recalled in an interview with the *Mansfield* (Ohio) *News* on June 11, 1904, that he had known Curtis in 1880 when he was living at the Clarendon Hotel in New York. One night, Curtis and he were smoking together, and they started telling stories of characters, and Sam'l of Posen was born from that conversation.

> I had a relative named Plastrick who kept a store on the east side. He was a man whom I had never liked and I remember that I asked Mr. Curtis to name his character Samuel Plastrick.
>
> He did so, and I felt delighted at having held my relative up to public scorn.
>
> My pleasure did not last. Curtis made such a success that his play acted as an ad for my relative and both men made fortunes.

Although we don't know whether the germ of Curtis's Jewish traveling salesman began with the funny Wolf in San Francisco or the disliked Samuel Plastrick in New York, we do know that at some point the outlines of the play were handed to George Jessop to convert into a full-length play for the reported sum of $750. Jessop initially titled the play *Isadore Plastrick* and there was some contemporary mention that it was to premiere at the Star Theatre in New York, with Curtis playing the role of the Hebrew drummer. (A drummer is an early form of traveling salesman who often had a display case.) However, there is no existing evidence that this actually happened.

While it is disappointing to modern readers that there is no record of the first moment M. B. Curtis stepped out on stage as Sam'l of Posen, Curtis does provide us with a very entertaining version of his first performance of the play in an interview found in an undated newspaper article titled "How Curtis Came to Fashion It into a Play." He had been traveling around with different troupes and was opening in Richmond, Virginia, in a play called *Fun on the Pacific*. Curtis's manager at the time was John T. Ford, a good friend of John Wilkes Booth and a former manager of Ford's Theatre where President Lincoln was assassinated. Ford asked Curtis what else he could do.

> I answered, I had a MS play in my trunk, and read him the first act. He said, "Great. Will open in this to-morrow at Athens, Ga."
>
> "This was Sunday," I said. "It can't be done; why the parts are not even written out. It is impossible; we have no wigs, no costumes!"
>
> "Bosh!" was Ford's reply, "I'll soon settle that," and away he went. An hour or so afterward he was back in the hotel with six clerks from the railroad office, who were friends of his, and whom he got to copy out the play. By 1 o'clock that night the parts were distributed, and at 10 o'clock next morning, when in the special car on our way to Athens, we held our first rehearsal. No, it was not called *Sam'l of Posen*, then. Samuel was Isadore and I named it *Isadore, the Commercial Tourist*. It was only after a great many changes that it came to be called what it is now.
>
> Well, we opened on Monday night. The house was an immense one.

Despite this rather rushed and improvised opening—
according to Curtis at least—the show soon hit the road and
was an almost overnight success. In the same interview about
the opening in Athens, Georgia, Curtis went on to say:

> We had great luck with the piece in Charlotte,
> Raleigh and Petersburg, and when we came
> back to Baltimore it was the "Sesqui" Cen-
> tennial, and the receipts of our first week's
> play were $7,300, of which I got $75 for the
> use of the play, $80 for my acting, and $25 for
> my wife, making a total of $150 a week. After
> my engagement was over, I made a proposal
> to him to continue the play, but Ford said the
> success was owing to the influx of strangers in
> the city, and refused it.

After his manager's refusal to continue the play after its
initial success, Curtis relates that he hit the road in search of
financial backers.

> I then offered *Sam'l of Posen*, which by this
> time had been christened and rechristened, till
> it finally resolved into this, to every manager. I
> chased each one in New York from theatre to
> theatre, and from their house doors to stage
> doors, with my play under one arm, and a
> scrap-book containing notices in the other.
>   Finally, my brother Frank, who was in
> Portland [Maine], came to my assistance. He
> mortgaged his theatre for $3,000, came to
> New York, and we engaged Haverly's Theatre,

and in twenty-one weeks from the opening
I banked $47,000 . . . My first week's income
from the play was $2,800—different from
$150, was it not?

Curtis obviously knew a good thing when he saw it, and
even though he had no luck in persuading New York producers to back him, his persistence and ability to persuade his
brother to join forces with him kept *Sam'l of Posen* on the road
before its New York opening. Now partnered with Frank, Curtis headed north to Albany, New York, where he repeated his
previous success. The play opened at the Albany Opera House
in December of 1880 to large crowds. In particular, Curtis's
portrayal received rave reviews. *The Albany Evening Journal*
(December 9, 1880) called his performance "very clever" and
mentioned how the audience laughed throughout the play.
The *Albany Argus* (December 10, 1880) found his performance
"quietly, originally, and intensely funny. There was something
actually mellow in his acting. It was capital throughout, and
we must say that the genera, make-up and by-play of Mr. Curtis was artistic, refreshing, and unique."

The *New York Mirror* reported that when the troupe
arrived in Curtis's hometown of Detroit, they were warmly received, and this account gives us yet another possible real-life
inspiration for the character of Sam'l. "The character of Sam'l
of Posen is understood here to be a copy of a well-known
commercial traveler of this city, whose pleasant face and affa-
ble manners have graced the counters of the leading jewelry
firms in Detroit for many years back."

The production eventually traveled to Boston where *The
Boston Daily Journal* announced on December 13, 1880: "The
attraction at the Park [Theatre] for the current week is a new

Curtis outfitted as the immigrant drummer Sam'l of Posen.
(TCS 1. Houghton Library, Harvard University)

comedy drama by George H. Jessop, entitled *Sam'l of Posen . . .*
Mr. M. B. Curtis, who sustains the title role, is peculiarly
adapted to the part and he has already scored a success in it
in Baltimore and Albany." It was here that Marie Curtis (acting
under the stage name Albina de Mer) shifted from portraying
Sam'l's love interest, Rebecca, to Celeste, the scheming adventuress, giving her a juicier part to sink her teeth into (and, no
doubt, a better chance to display her jewels and gowns). Carrie
Wyatt came east to play Rebecca. Wyatt had performed with
Curtis in 1877 in the play *Gif* in San Francisco, and she would
remain with Curtis and his company for years.

Late January of 1881 found Curtis making what must have
been a nostalgic return to the theatre in Chicago where he
had gotten his start on the stage. One can only wonder if he
permitted himself a pilgrimage to the basement print shop of
McVicker's to visit the hardworking teenage ghost of himself.
The Daily Inter Ocean of Chicago confirms on January 29, 1881,
what we already know about our hero's abilities: "Mr. Curtis
is a young actor of very decided ability, with a clever appreciation of the delicacies of humorous impersonation, and
makes a wholly good performance of this new conception of
character." This must have been a very satisfying homecoming
for Curtis, but he was not one to rest on his laurels as he then
headed for New York via St. Louis, Indiana, and Pennsylvania.

Convincing his brother Frank to produce his play wasn't the
only smart financial move Curtis made. At some point, Curtis
bought the rights to the play from George Jessop for $650.
According to New York's *Spirit of the Times* (May 2, 1881), he
then hired Jessop to help him rewrite this script "to order,"
based on Curtis's concept of making the lead character even

more of a vehicle for his vision.

Jessop agreed to begin a rewrite for $250, and Curtis gave him notes for payment at six and twelve months out. Jessop finished the work in five days. Curtis gave him another $150 at that time. Jessop thought Curtis would perform the play at small variety theatres, as Curtis had never before had a leading role. Indeed, earning $25 a week was good money for Curtis at the time, and he later admitted he had trouble making his $12 board. He confided to Jessop that his payments to him brought him down close to his last dollar, according to an unidentified 1894 newspaper article found in the Harvard Theater Collection. Jessop was astonished that the play wound up being performed by Curtis at so many of the nation's major theatres and that it achieved such a huge success. Jessop stated that, had he suspected the play's sudden impact, he would have asked for a royalty. But no one, including the playwright, could have predicted the monumental response to this relatively unknown supporting actor in a new play about an immigrant drummer.

But we can be fairly certain that Jessop's script did not play a big part in the success of *Sam'l of Posen*. It seems to have been an ever-changing chameleon after Jessop copyrighted the text in 1880 and then rewrote the play per Curtis's specs. By 1883, three years after the opening, Curtis and his friend actor/comedian Edward Stevenson Marble had rewritten the play again. There is a June 1883 copyright of the play, which expands the play's original three acts to four. However, there are many ads proving that the fourth act had been added as early as 1881. Curtis later told the *New York Herald* ("Sam'l of Posen's Varied Career," April 9, 1894) how he rewrote the first act and over a dozen writers polished the balance of the play: "The first and fourth acts are just as they were written sixteen years ago. The second and third acts were rewritten about ten years ago by Mr. Charles Kline. For that service I paid $550. They are played today just as he wrote them."

The obscure origins, the multiple titles, and the numerous real or imagined rewrites are not the only issue with the script. To modern readers, *Sam'l of Posen* seems like a very dated example of a simplistic and overblown melodrama with very little to recommend it.

The play begins with Samuel Plastrick (who has just immigrated from Posen, Poland) entering Mr. Winslow's jewelry store to sell some of his belongings for needed cash. Behind the counter is Rebecca, a pretty Jewish girl who lives with her Uncle Goldstein, the operator of a pawnshop. In one of several somewhat improbable plot devices, Rebecca and Sam'l immediately fall in love.

Goldstein's nephew, Jack, who also works at Winslow's jewelry store, is engaged to Winslow's daughter, Ellen. But Jack loses his wedding ring, which Sam'l finds and returns to him. Jack gets Sam'l a job at Winslow's, recommending the Polish immigrant as "honest, trustworthy and industrious."

As Sam'l's career advances, first working as a clerk and then as a drummer, he and Rebecca get engaged. But before Sam'l and Rebecca can be married, he must deliver $10,000 in diamonds to New York for Mr. Winslow.

Right before Sam'l goes on that errand, he visits a gambling den to warn his friend Jack that Jack's brother, Frank, and the owner of the gambling den, Celeste, are out to ruin Jack's plan to become a partner in Mr. Winslow's business by luring him to Celeste's gambling establishment. In the second act, Frank arranges for Mr. Winslow to see Jack gambling there, and Frank also tells Celeste about the diamonds

Sam'l meeting Rebecca for the first time. From a free booklet given to patrons of Sam'l of Posen. *(Private collection)*

Sam'l is carrying. When Sam'l arrives to warn Jack about the plot, Celeste drugs Sam'l with a poisoned cigar and steals the diamonds.

Frank, it is now revealed, has been secretly married to Celeste, and he threatens to send her to prison for stealing the diamonds if she ever mentions their marriage, as he now wants to marry Mr. Winslow's daughter and become partner at the firm in the place of his brother. Celeste scuffles with Frank, attempting to stab him. In the fray, she herself is stabbed, and Frank escapes with the stolen diamonds. Sam'l regains consciousness and vows to find Celeste's murderer and the diamond thief.

The third act takes place at Uncle Goldstein's pawnshop where Sam'l waits for Frank to arrive to pawn the diamonds. The diamonds are eventually recovered by Sam'l, who uses a huge antique musket to procure them.

"BISSNESS IS BISSNESS!"

The awkward immigrant sells his wares. From a poster for Sam'l of Posen. *(Billy Rose Theatre Division, The New York Public Library for the Performing Arts)*

And with the return of the diamonds, the play ends happily. Jack marries Winslow's daughter and becomes a partner in the jewelry store. Jack offers Sam'l a secure position, and Sam'l and Rebecca are married.

It's not exactly *Long Day's Journey into Night*, is it? But what is important here is not the literary merit—or lack thereof—of the play that put M. B. Curtis in the national spotlight. And it wasn't just Curtis's talent in bringing a somewhat cardboard character to life that was responsible for the phenomenon that would become Sam'l of Posen, although that happy joining of character and actor can't be underestimated. A review in the *Buffalo Courier* on January 1, 1884 (some years after Curtis's initial success), puts it best.

The dramatist did not create the character:
the actor created it. The writer built a skeleton
for the stage; the actor clothed it with flesh,
imbued it with life . . . Mr. Curtis is an artist;
all that he does shows him to be one . . . The
audience sees [Sam'l] grow as the play goes
on, sees him enlarge and gain in purpose and
dignity as circumstances arise.

But this is more than a case of an actor finding the role
of a lifetime. As any actor knows, timing is of the utmost
importance; and M. B. Curtis's timing was excellent. He gave
American audiences something new and heretofore unseen
on the American stage. And they were ready for it.

The Trojan Horse of Change

The theatre is a spiritual and social X-ray of its time.
—Stella Adler

There's a lot to be said for being in the right place at the right time. And M. B. Curtis and Sam'l of Posen were poised at the crest of a wave in a rapidly changing America in the early 1880s. As more and more immigrants followed the American Dream and established themselves in the New World, audiences were becoming more diverse. With both the money and the spare time to look to the theatre for entertainment, audiences were hungry to see characters on stage who more accurately reflected themselves and their experiences.

The history of Jewish characters on stage is not a particularly pleasant one. They were often the figures of cruel fun, notable for their greed and moral and physical weaknesses. As Charles B. Sherlock points out in his February 1902 article in the *Cosmopolitan*, "It required centuries for the Jewish school to get a foothold on the stage. Yet since Shakespeare's time the

Jew has been playing a part in the acted drama. Originally
Shylock was represented as a comedy character, made as
odious as possible by his facial aspect and the garbling of his
lines . . . No greater liberties have been taken with racial peculiarities, real or imagined, than have been taken with the Jew.
He has been mercilessly lampooned by the actors."

One of the reasons for this merciless lampooning is that
Jewish characters were almost always played by Gentile actors.
Few Jewish actors were able to ascend to even minor levels of
success, and when they did, they never did so by portraying
someone of their own culture. Due to the lack of opportunity
on stage, Jews interested in the theatre who wanted a decent
chance at employment generally chose to work in parts of the
trade where they would be subject to better circumstances.
This was usually somewhere behind the scenes, and many
rose through the ranks from stagehands and writers to producers, managers, and eventually theatre owners, with Curtis's
contemporaries Oscar Hammerstein (the grandfather of the
famous lyricist) and David Belasco being noteworthy exam-
ples. M. B. Curtis became one of the first notable exceptions
to this rule when he, a Jewish immigrant, portrayed a Jewish
immigrant on stage.

And the critics were quick to note that something new
was happening on the American stage. *The Boston Daily Journal*, when announcing the first Boston production of *Sam'l of
Posen* on December 13, 1880, stated that the play "brings to
stage a new character, and one which it is claimed will be an
addition to the conventional dramatic personages. Sam'l of
Posen is a young Americanized Hebrew, full of the keenness,
wit and courage of his race." And one of the earliest reviews of
this Boston production also remarked on the character's break
with the past.

> Sam'l of Posen . . . is not "the Jew that Shake-
> speare drew" by any means. Neither is he a
> relative of Dickens' Fagin. He is rather a
> good-natured, lively young Polish Jew, whose
> better qualities of head and heart are healthily
> developed by freedom from persecution which
> he finds in the United States. The novelty and
> boldness of the innovation on the stereotyped
> Hebrew of the modern stage will attract
> attention.

While the Boston critics were focused on the sea change happening on stage, a critic from Chicago's *Daily Inter Ocean* noticed what was happening in the audience on January 29, 1881.

> The character play at McVicker's has created
> considerable interest in the community, espe-
> cially among the people who wish to see the
> modern Hebrew treated with propriety upon
> the stage. It was a happy inspiration that con-
> ceived the idea of Samuel Plastrick. A novelty
> such as this should prove profitable, as most
> new types of dramatic production have . . .
> The Jew of this play is utterly different from
> any former representation of this peculiar
> race, and the caricature is so fair that numbers
> of our Jewish society have sat through the per-
> formance each night in evident enjoyment of
> the humors of the role and its surroundings . . .
> Mr. Curtis is a young actor of very decided
> ability, with a clever appreciation of the

delicacies of humorous impersonation, and
makes a wholly good performance of this new
conception of character.

The success of M. B. Curtis in *Sam'l of Posen* was astounding, and it brought Jewish people to the theatre in droves, as the *New York Mirror* noted on July 23, 1881, a few months after the New York opening.

Curtis draws the wealthy Hebrew families to
the Fourteenth Street Theatre every night . . .
Indeed, if a standing count should be taken
night after night, it would be found that fully
one-half of the audience are composed of
Jews. What greater merit does Curtis's representation require than that of pleasing and
entertaining a race of people, which from the
time of Shakespeare to that of Frank Bush has
been the object of gross caricature and misrepresentation on the stage?

But as we know, caricatures and misrepresentations die hard. And Curtis relied on some time-worn theatrical tricks even while he was creating a different type of Jewish character on stage. In an interview with the *New York Mirror* published on June 11, 1881, Curtis explained that he spent three-quarters of an hour every evening putting on his wax nose for Sam'l of Posen. Curtis does not explain why he chose to cling to this holdover from traditional theatre where no Jew was portrayed without an exaggerated nose. But he does lament the time spent on this rather clichéd convention: "I'd give one thousand dollars to possess my brother's nose. Think what a

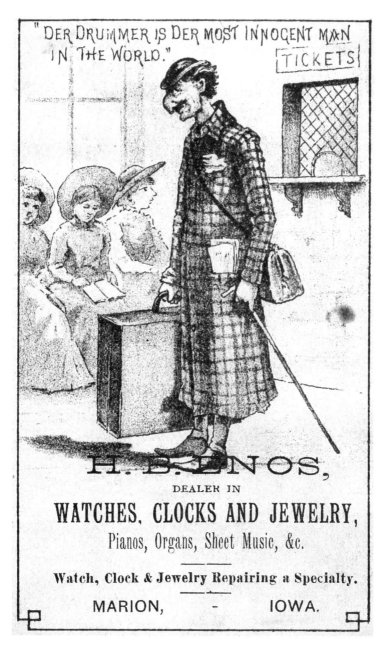

A trade card illustrating the old-school version of the Jewish male with an exaggerated nose and awkward clothing. (Victorian Trade Cards, University of Iowa Libraries, Iowa City, Iowa)

world of time it would have saved."

To complement his augmented facial feature, Curtis had also adopted an exaggerated accent for comic effect, which didn't go over well with some reviewers as this April 5, 1881, *Philadelphia Bulletin* review shows.

> The representation, which is distinguished by many artistic qualities, and which has a right to receive commendation as an ingenious bit of character-acting, is, however, disfigured by the disagreeable personal appearance assumed by the actor, by his too ludicrously broken English, and by the continual introduction of rather low slang, obviously with an intent to excite the laughter of the vulgar.

While this "low slang" upset some critics, Jewish audiences responded with pleasure and laughter as this piece from New York's *Spirit of the Times* describes soon after Curtis's New York opening on May 2, 1881.

> We looked about in vain for a straight nose or a blond beauty. In every direction the view was aquiline and brunette. Yet it was a very jolly and laughter loving audience, quick to take a joke and enjoy a sarcasm. It understood Hebrew evidently, and was fully posted upon Posen. Every bit . . . of Posen slang, every Hebrew catch phrase was taken up quickly by the gallery and emphasized with applause.

But, as with any change, there is always an opposing

reaction from those growing nostalgic for a past that is quickly disappearing. One poster that used Yiddish phrases to promote the play was a cause for debate, some calling it "likely to offend a number of sensitive and worthy people." Who those people might have been is unclear, but there is some suspicion that there were more than a few people who felt left out by the current "in-jokes" being enjoyed by New York audiences.

And there were critics who preferred the well-worn stereotypes over the new persona of the stage Jew being developed by Curtis. A critic from the *New York Daily Graphic* who had attended opening night in New York waxed nostalgic for the Jewish characters of old on May 17, 1880.

> Shylock is one thing, "Sam'l of Posen" another. Shylock, as the great English dramatist drew him centuries ago, is by no means an unworthy representative of a race gifted with great qualities . . . No Christian can leave the theatre after witnessing a true performance of *The Merchant of Venice* without feeling pity and sympathy for the Jew . . . No Hebrew who has seen Shylock performed as Shakespeare presents him can feel ashamed of his race, but from Sam'l of Posen, the Commercial Drummer, angels and ministers of grace defend us! It is very vile in the sense of offensiveness to any person who claims even an approach to refined feelings.
>
> Nothing, not even the faint pretension of honesty, can redeem such a being from his native meanness. The actor, Mr. Curtis, made a wonderfully realistic appearance and

characterization of a miserable type of Jewish
humanity. On that score nothing was wanting;
but to use a paradox, the better the portrayal
the more painful it was to the refined sense.
Uproarious laughter on the part of a crowded
audience greeted his uncouth movements, his
mean "get ups," and his "drummer cant," but
the laughter, which was of necessity deri-
sive, came less from the Christian part of the
audience than from the Hebrew element who
had evidently "been there," and knew the full
meaning of what to a refined American house
would have been as a whole incomprehensible
slang . . . He is made to be gross, coarse and
vulgar throughout . . . and one sickens of him
long before the piece is ended.

While Curtis's "drummer cant" displeased this particular
"refined American," the reviewer inadvertently points to another barrier being expanded, if not broken, by the portrayal
of Sam'l of Posen. By the 1870s, the profession of "drumming"
had grown faster than any other occupation in the United
States, according to Timothy B. Spears's *100 Years on the Road:
The Traveling Salesman in American Culture*. Even though traveling salesmen were a necessary component of the American
economy at the time, bringing new products to relatively
isolated small towns and increasing the sales of big-city man-
ufacturers and retailers, they were viewed with some suspicion
as being outsiders who were beyond the moral influence of
either bosses or wives. Drummers were thought to be free
of family and religious traditions and therefore more susceptible to temptations on the road. But all these qualities

were secondary to the fact that the average traveling salesman mixed charm with business and was thought to easily give up his own "personality," and therefore his integrity, for a sale. Spears posits that the salesman "proved humanly fallible, yet he constantly tried to create himself anew and become something more" (a description that ironically fits Curtis's struggles later in life to a tee) and goes on to say, "Thus drumming reinforced the evolution of a theatrical or liminal self and threatened the conceptions of character—steady work habits and moral uprightness—so vital to republican ideology and the spirit of Protestantism." The drummer's presence in rural America provided a wealth of entertainment, fascination, and fear—not unlike many people's views of actors at the time. Arthur Miller later said that traveling salesmen "loved like artists, like actors whose product is first of all themselves, forever imagining triumphs in a world that either ignores them or denies them altogether."

Curtis's portrayal of Sam'l of Posen enlarged the already theatrical and improvisational character of the drummer in America. He was funny, heroic, and a loyal friend who performed good deeds. And he could love and be loved.

With Curtis's more fully human and charming portrayal of Sam'l of Posen, the commercial drummer, two groups of people who had suffered from being considered "the other" by many Americans could now attend the theatre and laugh at themselves without the sting of hate, laughing with Sam'l, not at him.

All of the figures in this poster are of Sam'l—from awkward outsider to success-ful businessman. The new immigrant is shaking the hand of his future self. (Billy Rose Theatre Division, The New York Public Library for the Performing Arts)

Staying Center Stage

You can't be funny unless you're tragic,
and you can't be tragic unless you're funny.
—Elaine Stritch

⌐

The overwhelming success of the 1881 New York opening
of *Sam'l of Posen* thrust the once-journeyman actor and his
cheerful traveling salesman firmly into the national spotlight.
While a year prior he had been a well-reviewed supporting
actor struggling to pay his $12 board, Curtis was now, within a
year, listed among the biggest theatrical talents in the nation.

As word was blasted across the country about the hit
show, managers around the United States fought for Curtis to
play their theatres. Theatres large and small offered him the
same terms that were offered by the large opera houses. As the
New York World of November 12, 1912, gushed much later, "No
such meteoric rise to fame and fortune had ever been recorded."
In late June of 1881, some two months after the New York
opening, it was reported that Curtis had already made $20,000
in his role. His success, of course, quickly drew two lines of
green-eyed sarcasm from the *New York Mirror* as they offered

backhanded comfort to Curtis on July 12, 1881: "Don't worry, M. B. Better times coming." While this can be read as envious snark, the same comment was applied a month later to superstar Sarah Bernhardt, which put Curtis in rather high-flying theatrical company.

The same newspaper also reported somewhat cryptically that "M. B. Curtis is a young man and a young star to have a bright son and heir." This appears to be an announcement that Marie was pregnant, but no mention of this was made thereafter. Whether this was idle gossip, wishful thinking, or actual fact, Curtis and Marie ended up never having children. And it was one of the first indications that not everything would go Curtis's way after his unique vision put him at the top of his trade.

While the success of *Sam'l of Posen* must have taken New York theatre owners by surprise (especially those who refused to financially back the initial production), there was a humorous harbinger of both the future financial rewards and the audiences' intense involvement with what was happening on stage that occurred on the very spur-of-the-moment opening night in Athens, Georgia, according to Curtis in a later interview.

> Well, we opened on Monday night. The house
> was an immense one; and there is a funny
> thing which happened that night, which nei-
> ther my wife nor I shall ever forget. She played
> the part of Rebecca then, and not the French
> woman [Celeste], and you know that time
> when Samuel says to her, "I have not made
> much this trip." Well, before that time I could

not help noticing an old Hebrew gentleman, and presumably his daughter, who were sitting in the first seats. I saw the old gentleman's head bow lower and lower toward the stick on which were resting his hands, and I noticed him now and then pass the back of his hand across his face, as if wiping his cheek, and when I came to say the words "I haven't made much this trip," he slipped his hand into his pocket and threw fifty cents on to the stage.

Again he threw another half dollar, when the girl who was beside him began to pluck at his sleeve, and try to wake him from his reverie. But the old man so far forgot himself that he rose up and threw a dollar. By this time the house, seeing what was done, began to shower nickels. My wife, not waiting to see what was thrown, and hearing only the clash of coin, became frightened and ran off the stage; as also soon did the heavy villain [the actor playing Frank].

However, the stagehands soon knew what it was, and they being reassured came back again. The heavy villain even so far overcame his timidity that he gathered up $11, whilst my wife and I picked up $13; which sum, in dollars, and quarters and nickels, we have kept as a memento of that occasion to this present day.

But M. B. Curtis no longer had to stoop to pick up loose change on stage. What he knew he had to do was take his hit show on the road, which he did with infinite determination.

The first New York run of *Sam'l of Posen* closed in early August 1881 after three months of full houses. However, it appears that Curtis and Marie took only a very short summer vacation. The *New York Mirror* reported on August 13, 1881, that the Curtises were spending time with their friend the actress Maggie Mitchell in Long Branch, a beachside resort town in New Jersey.

A cartoon celebrating Curtis's financial success. (Billy Rose Theatre Division, The New York Public Library for the Performing Arts)

By August 29, 1881, Curtis and Marie were back performing at McVicker's Theatre in Chicago. After repeating their
initial success there, they packed up their traveling salesman
and embarked on an ambitious and no doubt grueling tour
that took them to theatres in Ohio, Kentucky, Tennessee,
Georgia, Louisiana, Texas, Arkansas, Illinois, Missouri, Indiana,
Wisconsin, and back home to Michigan by December of 1881.

The dawn of the new year found Sam'l of Posen heading
back to New York. In February of 1882 it was announced that
the play would be produced at Haverly's Brooklyn Theatre
"with the original scenery and cast as played at Haverly's
Fourteenth Street Theatre, where it made one of the biggest
hits ever known in New York." And the response to the return
of Sam'l of Posen lived up to this advanced billing as this
review from *The Brooklyn Eagle* of February 8, 1882, shows.

> *Sam'l of Posen* is on the floodtide of success at
> Haverly's Brooklyn Theatre. A full house greeted
> the commercial drummer last night. The con-
> vulsive fun of the principal character ran along
> without a break through the four sprightly acts
> of the play, and there were few among the large
> audience who did not bid goodnight to Sam'l
> with regret. Mr. Curtis has struck a responsive
> chord in the hearts of the playgoing public, and
> there is little doubt that *Sam'l of Posen* would
> draw crowded houses at the Brooklyn for an
> indefinite period. The engagement is limited,
> however, to the current week, and amusement
> seekers will do wisely to early avail themselves
> of the present opportunity of witnessing this
> truly remarkable production.

The production then made a quick tour of other theatres where three hundred people were turned away one night in Williamsburg, Pennsylvania, according to the *New York Mirror* on February 18, 1882. The end of the month found the Curtises crossing the East River to return to Haverly's Fourteenth Street Theatre where, according to the *New York Mirror* on March 4, 1882, "M. B. Curtis has renewed the former success in *Sam'l of Posen*. The houses are crowded and rock with laughter and applause. We heartily congratulate Mr. Curtis upon his double triumph as the originator of a new stage creation and as a new eccentric comedian."

But success, like any major upheaval in the status quo, can bring a new set of problems even while it solves some earlier difficulties. Curtis's brother Frank had been with the production all this time, managing the myriad details of touring so as to allow his younger brother to concentrate on playing the lead character. But by January of 1882, Curtis had purchased Frank's half interest in *Sam'l of Posen*. The two reportedly could not agree on how the business should be run. The stress of constantly touring—and possibly Frank's ill health (he was reported to have contracted malarial fever in Texas during the tour there in October of 1881)—no doubt contributed to the breakup, but one has to wonder if Curtis or Frank (an actor in his own right) had decided that the stage was no longer big enough to hold both of them. And Frank's departure would prove to be the act of a canary in a coal mine as later difficulties and disagreements would attest to. But whatever the reason for their parting of the ways, the brothers would not work together again until some four years later.

Curtis then sold a one-eighth interest in the production to Edward Swett, who had served as treasurer of the company. Swett took responsibility for managing the company, which would now be known as M. B. Curtis's Sam'l of Posen Company.

When Curtis took his newly rechristened company and returned to Haverly's Fourteenth Street Theatre, they were greeted by a full-page story in the *New York Mirror* that commented on how the entire play kept pace with the actor's ascension. And it is here that we find the first recorded instance of Curtis's heartfelt immersion in his character—an immersion that certainly aided in connecting audiences to the character of Sam'l of Posen. Patrons at the Fourteenth Street Theatre received a little card about the play that contained this little elegy written in the melodramatic style of the time.

> Be kind to the traveling man. He has a father; perhaps a mother, who knew him in his innocent youth. Perhaps, even now, in some distant village, fond hearts are beating for him, and sweet lips breathe love's dearest prayers for his welfare. Therefore, lay him down tenderly, fold his hands peacefully on his breast, and close his eyes gently as you put him to rest under the branches of the weeping willow, where the birds carol all through the summer days their softest songs, but PLANT HIM DEEP! PLANT HIM DEEP!

This wouldn't be the only attempt that Curtis would make to generate interest in the play, involve audiences in his theatrical world, and thereby sell tickets. The next year, in 1883, he would offer one hundred dollars for the best joke, gag, trick, or story relating to incidents in the life, trials, and experience of a commercial drummer. Even later in his career, when he wasn't as flush with money or audiences, Curtis would turn to offering free real estate as an inducement to attend his productions. This makes one begin to suspect that the character of the drummer who would do anything for a sale was gradually seeping into the character of the very real actor who played him as Curtis's energy and creativity combined to make innovations on all levels.

Another instance of what would be a lifelong characteristic of the actor who played Sam'l of Posen also occurred during this second run at Haverly's Fourteenth Street Theatre. With a decent cash flow coming in from his performances, M. B. Curtis began displaying yet another one of his trademarks: his generosity. While Curtis was still packing the theatre nightly, this announcement appeared in the *New York Mirror* in March of 1882.

> The event of the season here will be the
> benefit which Mr. Curtis and Mr. Haverly have
> tendered to the Actors' Fund on next Monday
> afternoon. Every professional in New York
> ought to be present, as there are no other mat-
> inees on that day. The auction sale of private
> boxes will take place this Thursday at the the-
> atre, and a grand gathering of the profession
> is expected. This is their own benefit for their
> own Fund. Let us see what they will do with it.

The Actors' Fund had been recently established to benefit actors who were ill, aged, or otherwise in need of assistance. This was a much more reliable source of help than the benefit performances and passing the hat anytime a compatriot fell on hard times, there being no other form of aid at this time. April 3, 1882, was the day many Brooklyn and New York theatres were scheduled to stage special matinees and donate the proceeds

The front page of a pamphlet for Sam'l of Posen. *(Private collection)*

to the new fund. Curtis and J. H. "Jack" Haverly (the owner of the theatre) were anxious to assist this endeavor—and possibly eager to be the ones who received the earliest and best publicity—that they donated all of the proceeds of the March 13, 1882, performance of *Sam'l of Posen* to the new Actors' Fund, becoming the very first benefit to do so. *Sam'l of Posen* boxes went for $25, equal to the highest bid received for any of the other benefit performances. According to a review in the *New York Mirror* of March 18, 1882, "Mr. Curtis enjoyed the distinction of playing before an assemblage such as probably never before gathered inside the doors of a theatre in this city—a company of actors and actresses who are accustomed to sit in front of the footlights only as privileged guests, not as paying patrons . . . At the benefit [Curtis] played with more than usual

THE ACTORS' FUND.

Curtis at the head of the line to donate to the fledgling Actors' Fund. From the New York Mirror, *March 18, 1882. (Private collection)*

care, and the professional audience followed Sam'l's adventures with true pleasure, laughing at his queer Posenisms and delighting at his irresistible sang-froid."

The event raised $366, according to the *Clipper* ($236 according to the *Mirror*), and in mid-June, the state of New York announced the official incorporation of the Actors' Fund of America and M. B. Curtis was listed as a member of this body along with scores of other actors. And while Curtis certainly had to be happy with the success of this fund-raiser, there's no question that he was unaware of how important the Actors' Fund would be to him later in his own life.

Curtis filled out the rest of his successful New York run at Niblo's Garden and then followed that with a week at the Windsor Theatre before heading to Boston and Philadelphia and points west. The *New York Mirror* reported in May 1882 that Curtis's New York receipts in the past twelve months had been $60,000, but this would be dwarfed by what lay ahead. By the end of the month, the same newspaper reported that a one-week run at the Boston Globe Theatre had earned nearly $9,000. Curtis's performances drew larger and larger audiences as word spread, and after May 9, the orchestra at one theatre on his tour after New York had to be moved to the stage so the pit could be filled with more members of the paying public, according to the *New York Mirror* of May 13, 1882.

And if imitation is indeed the truest form of flattery, M. B. Curtis was starting to be flattered by a fair number of his professional colleagues. Shortly after the success of *Sam'l of Posen*, Frank Dumont wrote *My Hebrew Friend* for comedian Dick Gorman. L. Cook wrote *Moses Levy* in 1882. Charles Baswitz penned *Morris Cohen, the Commercial Drummer* in 1883.

Levy Cohen was also written in 1883 by B. Janssen. In 1885, Baswitz also delivered *Levy the Drummer, or Life on the Road*, according to Harley Erdman's *Staging the Jew: The Performance of an American Ethnicity, 1860–1920*. This last play has the lead character going out west where some cowboys trick him into eating bacon, reminiscent of a scene in the 1974 Mel Brooks movie *Blazing Saddles*. And in a sure sign that Curtis and Sam'l had permeated the national consciousness, the famous vaudeville comedian Nat Goodwin (who would later appear in a play written by George Jessop called *A Gold Mine*) added M. B. Curtis to the roster of famous actors he impersonated.

While Curtis and Marie were certainly enjoying the fruits of success and celebrity against the backdrop of their recent humble circumstances, they nevertheless continued to tour relentlessly in 1882, no doubt determined to strike while the iron was hot. The *Brooklyn Eagle* of August 4, 1882, noted that during the 1881–1882 theatrical season, Curtis was estimated to have traveled 18,746 miles—in a day when trains or horses were the only alternatives to walking. He went from Massachusetts to Texas and from New York to San Francisco during that season, and one can only imagine how keeping up with this rigorous schedule was beginning to affect him. Not only was he pouring out his heart on stage almost every night and on more than a few matinee afternoons, he was dealing with travel arrangements, demanding theatre owners, contracts needing to be signed, schedules needing to be finalized, well-meaning well-wishers making demands on his attention, and, not in the least, handling the temperamental actors in his company. In early May of 1882 he was faced with replacing an actor who jumped ship for another company. Although the reason why Edgar Davenport left the Sam'l of Posen Company for another troupe is not known (and he soon rejoined the company), it must have been a difficult task for Curtis to find a replacement while on the road, often performing one evening in a city then packing up the next morning to travel to another city for the next evening's performance.

An incident that occurred in mid-May 1882 at the Leland Opera House in Albany, New York, illustrates the difficulty of running a touring company and hints at the toll the tour was beginning to take on Curtis. Curtis believed that his run at the opera house was done on Friday, May 6, and he was billed to perform the next night in Syracuse. Mrs. Leland, the manager of the theatre, believed that Curtis owed her two more performances on that Saturday. What could have been an innocent misreading of the contract on both of their parts quickly turned into a public battle royale after Mrs. Leland seized Curtis's share of that Friday night's box office receipts. Curtis found out about this after the second act of Friday night's show and refused to continue his performance. While that night's audience never got to see the end of the play, they were treated to an extemporaneous shouting match in front of the curtain when Mrs. Leland appealed to the audience for sympathy and Edward Swett, not to be outdone, appeared on stage and answered her word for word in a "wordy, rich, rare and racy dialogue" while the audience "hissed, cheered, stamped their feet and clapped their hands," according to the *New York Mirror* on May 13, 1882. The newspaper story then moderates its tone and admonishes the combatants.

> The whole trouble seems to be a misunder-
> standing of a contract, which was made by
> telegraph, after much bother, and it is safe to

say that the courts will settle the difference
according to law and the evidence. Mr. Curtis
should have completed his performance, and
there would have been no doubt as to his
getting his share of the receipts. Mrs. Leland
should not have appealed to the audience for
sympathy, and in fact it was very bad taste on
the part of all concerned to make such a public exhibition of themselves, their business and
their troubles.

Curtis soon found himself embroiled in another conflict with a theatre manager in Atchison, Kansas, where it
was reported that he threatened not to go on stage if the
manager didn't furnish the cigars and cigarettes needed for
the performance. This might sound like the petty tantrum
of a newly anointed diva, but remember how important the
poisoned cigar is to the plot of the play. And Curtis must have
had enough to worry about without having to find a tobacco
store in an unfamiliar town just before curtain time. What this
does point out, though, are some of the problems that Curtis
encountered along with his newfound success. He had come
from a humble background and his years as a supporting
actor following orders had given him little experience in the
business of theatre management. His natural streak of stub-
bornness and his being accustomed now to constant accolades
from his audiences probably weren't helping matters either.

One can only imagine the sighs of relief from the Curtises
when they set foot in San Francisco in late May of 1882 to
perform at the Bush Street Theatre. Not only were they back

in one of the places they could call home, but they were scheduled for a long run in the Bay Area so there would be a brief respite from packing and rushing to a train station almost every morning. Although the *Daily Alta California* didn't think much of the play on May 30, 1882, it found Curtis's acting "natural, clever and highly amusing. Not overdrawn, nor strained, nor overdone, it is capital throughout . . . We have rarely seen a better specimen of character acting on the stage, and that Mr. Curtis should have been so quick to discover the bent of his genius and to improve and develop on it is highly to his credit. *Sam'l of Posen* is a rare stage picture and should be seen by all."

From San Francisco, Curtis and company headed to Salt Lake City, Denver, Colorado Springs, and points west, often accompanied by their pet birds. The Curtises' fondness for birds and their bringing them on tour fascinated the press — and provided at least one amusing story for the many readers who followed the Curtises' adventures in newspapers across the country. In July of 1882 the Curtises were staying at the Windsor Hotel in Denver in a suite directly opposite the one occupied by Colorado Lieutenant Governor Horace Tabor. A Denver *Tribune* article reprinted in the *Daily Miner* (Montana) on July 12, 1882, related what happened one night.

> As the Governor was entering his apartments
> he heard what he thought was a female voice
> saying, "Hello baby."
>
> The Governor was a trifle startled. He was
> a very gallant man, but he could not for the
> life of him tell what he had ever done to war-
> rant a female in addressing him so familiarly.
> The situation appeared to be intended for

him, and it came from the transom over the door of the room directly across the hall. The Governor was nonplussed.

"Hello, baby—pretty baby," said the voice again, and the Governor blushed as he stroked his fierce mustache and tried to brace up and look dignified. "Won't you come and kiss your baby?" called the voice again in a deliciously seductive sort of way. Now the Governor seldom takes a dare of any kind! To do him justice, he is a brave man, and at this particular moment he felt big enough to tackle an army. He crept softly over to the door and asked: "Are you talking to me?"

"Nice baby," said the voice, but no sooner had the voice spoken than another voice from inside the room—a big burly man's voice—called out: "Go away from that door and let the parrot go to sleep!" It was Mr. Curtis who spoke, but he had no idea it was Governor Tabor outside. Governor Tabor slid quietly into his room, but he thought it was such a good joke he had to tell the boys about it after supper, and in the Opera-House lobby last night it was all the talk.

After completing their western tour, the Curtises took a short breather in Detroit before the fall season started. But even on vacation, Curtis found himself embroiled in conflict. The *New York Mirror* reported on August 19, 1882, that while Curtis and Marie were strolling the streets of Detroit, a man came up and said something insulting to him, and Curtis "soundly thrashed the brute." This experience must have been difficult for an actor who was used to rave reviews and adoring audiences. The dichotomy of appearing in a play where everything ends happily ever after at the end of every night and then having to deal with the reality of life on the street must have begun to wear on Curtis by this point.

But despite the fisticuffs that marred their brief summer vacation, the Curtises hit the ground running in early September at the start of the fall theatrical season. They played to large and enthusiastic audiences and garnered still more rave reviews such as this one that appeared in the *Fort Wayne* (Indiana) *Gazette* on September 23, 1882.

> Last evening an audience filled the Academy to overflowing, witnessing the production of an American play that has scored one of the great popular successes of the day . . . the plot is skillfully woven and gives the star, Mr. M. B. Curtis, some strong and clever situations. Mr. Curtis, himself a Jew, portrays in an inimitable and delightful manner the fresh and impudent Hebrew drummer stripped of all offensive peculiarities. The humor is keen without broadness, and the entire audience testified their appreciation of it by the most generous applause . . . The audience was the finest of the season, and the "standing room only" card was hung out in ten minutes after the doors were opened. Chairs were in all the aisles and a row of people stood up all around the entire auditorium.

CHAPTER FIVE

Marie as Celeste in Sam'l of Posen. *(Private collection)*

In October 1882, while Curtis was playing a run at the Academy of Music in Brooklyn, a local fireman, Charles Keegan, was killed in the line of duty. A benefit was arranged for October 24, and Curtis volunteered to perform an act from *Sam'l of Posen* as a major draw for the fund-raiser for the fireman's family.

After concluding their Brooklyn run, the company headed to Philadelphia, Baltimore, and smaller cities in Pennsylvania and New York State. They then returned to Brooklyn before finishing out 1882 in Massachusetts and Connecticut.

But it seems the year of 1882 could not end without one more difficulty besetting the Curtises. Marie was taken suddenly ill after a performance in early December. A physician was called for, and after a delay, she was taken back to their hotel by carriage. While Marie seems to have recovered fairly quickly, this would be the beginning of a chronic malady that would affect the actress throughout much of her life. Not only was Curtis a concerned spouse, he was also a company manager who now had to worry about one of his supporting actors' unreliable health. One has to wonder if Curtis was beginning to learn the hard lesson that fame and celebrity and wealth provide very little protection from the vicissitudes of the everyday real world.

The Sequel to Success

The only thing you've got in this world is what you can sell.
—*Arthur Miller,* Death of a Salesman

~

The start of 1883 found Curtis and Marie performing *Sam'l of Posen* in Charlotte, North Carolina, where they had appeared two years earlier. But the actor's popularity hadn't diminished during this hiatus as "Mr. Curtis was called before the curtain after the first, second, and third acts," according to the *New York Dramatic Mirror*'s citing of notices from the Tar Heel State.

But Curtis and *Sam'l of Posen* weren't the only ones receiving accolades. Marie was enjoying success in her own right—the critic Robert Grau thought she was almost as big a hit as Curtis himself. One Indiana newspaper gave a particularly fetching description of the actress playing the French adventuress in *Sam'l of Posen.*

> Miss Albina de Mer (Mrs. Curtis) is an accomplished actress and a clever woman. She has agreeable manners, a graceful stage presence

and a charming voice; yet she is delightfully
unassuming, and has never pushed herself
obtrusively before the public. Her audiences,
however, never fail to recognize her ability and
artistic attainments, and a strong undercurrent
of admiration has already made her one of our
most popular comediennes.

In September 1882, Marie's success in the role of Celeste
had led to other opportunities. She was currently playing the
title role in *Camille*, a play popularized by Sarah Bernhardt
that was now running alongside *Sam'l of Posen* as the Curtises
continued their tour. One paper noted that, according to
her own estimate, Marie's qualifications for the part were "a
$3,000 wardrobe, a few lessons at the Conservatoire and 'a fall
in the last act that is better than Bernhardt's.'" Curtis himself
played the part of Armand in the play, interpreting the young
French provincial bourgeois lover of Marguerite Gautier as
an immigrant Hebrew character—even using some trademark
Sam'l of Posen phrases during the card-playing scene.

Marie was also remembered for her revival of an old
tradition when she performed in Alexandre Dumas's tragedy.
Historically, actors and actresses in successful productions
might expect to be offered elegant buffets featuring wine and
cold meats. But frugal managers had taken to putting out teas
artificially colored to look like wine and other inferior dishes.
During the 1883 season, Marie laid out a memorable table for
her cast. Her backstage feast included the likes of "oysters, raw
and fried, roast turkey and chicken salad, and real wines," according to the *Bismarck Tribune* (North Dakota) on October 30,
1884. And backstage wasn't the only place the Curtises liked
to splurge; they loved to entertain and spent money freely and

Marie posing in one of her elegant gowns. (Billy Rose Theatre Division, The New York Public Library for the Performing Arts)

lavishly in hosting parties when they weren't performing, a trait that would continue during their careers until their sagging fortunes precluded such festive gatherings.

One can only hope that Curtis and Marie availed themselves of the bountiful tables set up backstage as they certainly needed to nourish themselves for their arduous touring. In the early months of 1883, they often played a continuous string of one-night stands, performing in a different city every night as they worked their way across the country. But this difficult schedule was paying off in increased fame and fortune. In March of 1883, Rex, the king of Carnival, bestowed the title of Duke of Posen on Curtis during Mardi Gras in New Orleans, and an April 25, 1883, review in the *Fitchburg Daily Sentinel* (Massachusetts) concisely summed up Curtis's success: "*Sam'l of Posen* is one of the noteworthy stage successes of recent years. It has been widely talked about and praised for its novelty and the excellence of its presentation and it has given Mr. Curtis a name and a fortune within a brief period."

Having reportedly cleared more than $25,000 during the 1882–1883 season, it was now time for Curtis and Marie to take a vacation. They sailed for Europe on the *Egypt* on Saturday, June 16, 1883. While in Paris that summer, Curtis bought an eight-carat ruby ring set with diamonds for Marie, and Marie shopped for new dresses that she intended to wear in the upcoming theatrical season. But even three thousand miles away, the Curtises couldn't avoid the trouble that was brewing in their American theatre world.

In Curtis's absence, his manager, Edward C. Swett, who had done public battle with the truculent Mrs. Leland, received an odd telegram. It was from someone named Bacon in the city of Boston. This unknown man claimed to know of a pirated version of *Sam'l of Posen* that was about to be produced. Bacon offered to stop this production thievery for a fee but provided no specifics as to when and where the play was being mounted. Swett considered the letter a prank and forgot about it. He then received a dispatch from an agent in Chicago claiming that an actor named Lester Franklyn was performing as Sam'l Plastrick in a pirated production of *Sam'l of Posen* at the Halsted Street Opera House, and Swett began proceedings against the thieves.

Upon his return from Europe, Curtis took the next step to protect his interest. On August 12, 1883, in the U.S. Circuit Court in Chicago, M. B. Curtis filed a bill against five men, including Lester Franklyn and two owners of the Halsted Street Opera House, to restrain them from infringing on his copyright of *Sam'l of Posen*. Curtis assured the court that the play was copyrighted before its release to the public, that he had owned the copyright for the past three years, and that his copyright protection had fifteen more years before it expired. The pirates had duplicated the dialogue, the scenery, and anything else they could. Curtis contended the materials and lines were "taken" during performances of his play by stenographers and sketch artists or by some other similar method.

A number of theatre people testified to the truth of Curtis's statements. A movement had begun in the industry to put a stop to the many such copyright infringements. The *Posen* pirates did not stop performing even after an application for an injunction had been made; however, when the injunction was obtained and properly served, the play stopped the next day, and Franklyn and his manager were perpetually enjoined from performing the play. On August 29, Curtis had to file again in U.S. Circuit Court to restrain the copying of his play by yet another company that included Edward Horan, proving that imitation might not be the sincerest form of flattery.

The opening of the 1883–1884 season found Curtis and Marie performing *Sam'l of Posen* at Hooley's Theatre in Chicago. From there, they toured cities in Wisconsin, Michigan, Missouri, and Ohio, where the *New York Mirror* (October 27, 1883) reported that "Sam'l of Posen, the famous creation of M. B. Curtis, drew large audiences. He is a great favorite here [Cleveland], and the past week only duplicated the success of his former engagements."

The end of October found M. B. Curtis's Sam'l of Posen Company back in New York at Haverly's Fourteenth Street Theatre. Reviews credited Curtis with elevating the stage Hebrew in the estimation of the public while provoking unlimited mirth and hilarity. Other company members also received excellent reviews, including Marie (as Albina de Mer), Harry Eytinge, Rachel Booth, and Edgar Davenport. But the company soon left for theatres in New Jersey, Pennsylvania, Illinois, and Missouri, with Marie, a "special feature of her husband's tour," continuing to do matinee performances of *Camille* with much success.

On November 11, 1883, a clock that was used as a prop in *Sam'l of Posen*—a set piece that occasioned Sam'l's line: "When one hand pointed to twelve, the other to ten, and it struck two, it was exactly twenty minutes past seven"—was reported stolen from the property room of a theatre in Lancaster, Pennsylvania, and Curtis offered a twenty-dollar reward for its return.

In what was a masterful public relations move—or a marvelous example of Curtis's vivid imagination and storytelling ability or possibly the truth—Curtis recounted the clock's history to a Philadelphia reporter.

It looked like a cheap, no-account thing, and I

imagine it may have been taken by a couple of boys who were helping my property man, and who stole it, not because they thought it was of any value, but in a pure spirit of mischief. It was a small eight-day machine, such as you could get brand new for $1.50, I guess, and it had its face broken, was pendulum-less, and had a hole through the back. To look at it you wouldn't think it worth carrying away, but my property man had instructions to guard it as carefully as he does the forty-three pieces of solid silver we use in our jewelry store scene in the first act.

You will understand my interest in the matter when I tell you that the clock was owned by the celebrated Barbara Fritchie, and came from her now historic house in Fredericktown. On the eventful day when Barbara succeeded in immortalizing herself, the little clock was standing on a mantel, striking the hour very possibly, when a soldier's bullet went through it, carried away the pendulum, and left its hands fixed at 10 o'clock, where they have been kept ever since.

Buchanan Read first owned the clock, but he gave it to John W. Norton, manager of the Grand Opera House at St. Louis, who made me a present of it three years ago. I carried it carefully packed away in a padded box, and was going to give it, after this season, to the Smithsonian Institute . . .

Right at this moment, Curtis's younger

brother George Washington Curtis sauntered
up with a big smile and roundly handed a telegram to his brother. "By Jove, they've found it.
The manager at Lancaster telegraphs me that
he's got it, so B won't have to get a new clock
for my engagement at the Arch Street Theatre
next week."

Despite the recovery of the clock, the 1883 tour was encountering more difficulties that weren't solved so easily. In
mid-November, Marie was taken off stage for at least the second time due to severe illness during a performance of *Sam'l
of Posen*, and she did not appear in her *Camille* matinee on
November 16. Ironically, the actress who spent her Wednesday
afternoons performing Marguerite's agonizing and heartbreak-
ing death scene at the end of the play was now herself beginning to suffer from ill health.

November 1883 was a challenging month for Curtis in other
ways as well. Edward Swett's contract was up for renewal. It
was rumored that he wanted to buy a larger interest in Curtis's play or perhaps sell his current share. Within the month,
Swett chose to retire from the stage and move to Chicago.
Curtis again assumed the role of manager, which, in the past,
had not worked to anyone's advantage.

But despite these difficulties, Curtis and Marie and their
company continued to perform in various cities on the East
Coast until they took a brief rest in December before returning to the boards in various venues in New York State and
Pennsylvania.

The dawn of the new year of 1884 brought along with it the

debut of a new play featuring Sam'l of Posen. Whether Curtis was beginning to sense a slight slackening of interest in his hit play after three years of continual touring or whether he was getting restless saying the same lines night after night we don't know. But Marie hinted at the frustration that many actors feel when they are locked into playing the same character night after night when she was interviewed later in an undated *Boston Globe* article titled "In Celeste's Dressing Room."

> There is so much about Mr. Curtis and his power of acting that the public does not yet know. They really know but one of his many phases.
>
> Then, too, I want the new play to have a good opportunity for me. I am tired of playing the part of the adventuress. I want something different, something with which I can win the sympathy of the audience. I cannot in Celeste.

The addition of a new vehicle for his talents didn't solve any of Curtis's problems in managing his company. Early in March 1884, Harry Eytinge was fired from the company for "mischief-making," according to Curtis. Eytinge was an old actor reputed to have been a pirate in the Caribbean before walking the boards. Later that month, George Washington Curtis, Curtis's younger brother by eight years, resigned as the treasurer of the company, probably to join their brother Charles's new tool company.

The two resignations were in addition to the four others who had left the company in a three-week period. Meanwhile, as if trying to contain this bad publicity, Curtis wrote the *New York Mirror* from Illinois in March to state that his business was booming, unlike most other productions at that time.

And, indeed, business was good for Curtis. Curtis debuted the new play, *Spot Cash*, in mid-February as Buffalo Bill was ending his role in Ned Buntline's *Scouts of the Prairie* and retiring to his ranch in Nebraska, where he would begin to develop his own Wild West show. The *New York Dramatic Mirror* (February 16, 1884) gave the new play a thumbs-up and called it a "worthy successor and sequel to *Sam'l of Posen*. . . . On the strength of *Spot Cash*, Mr. Curtis has already booked time far into next season. Many have attempted to follow in his steps, but all have failed. He now holds the undisputed possession of the field."

The plot of *Spot Cash* has Curtis's Sam'l going to Chicago for the wedding of a rival drummer, Fred Jerome, played by William Morris. Jerome's bride is Hortense Larivandier, played by Marie, appearing as Albina de Mer. While in town for the wedding, Sam'l passes some bad checks, is blown out of the hotel's safe where he is hiding, and is caught by his wife, Rebecca, played by Josie Wilmere, with three beautiful women coddling him.

Not all critics liked Curtis's new piece, although they generally agreed that Curtis had found a good vehicle for the unique skills he had developed while portraying Sam'l. Curtis closed his preview season in Toronto on May 24, 1884, having enjoyed respectable crowds at his performances. He and Marie returned to New York to rest, staying at the Clarendon Hotel at Eighteenth Street and Fourth Avenue. All of the 1884 performances of *Spot Cash* up until now had been preview performances as Curtis was preparing for the following season's official launch of the play on August 18, 1884, in St. Paul.

Back in New York, however, ads for *Spot Cash* began to appear by June 1884 in the *New York Mirror*. Curtis, it was

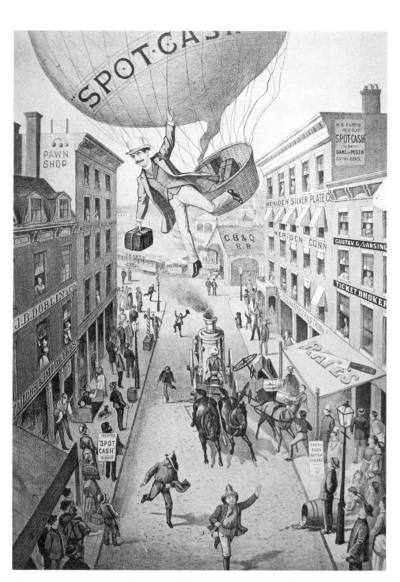

A rare poster promoting Spot Cash *found in an attic more than one hundred years after it was printed. (Private collection)*

announced, had "a sumptuous wardrobe prepared for Sam'l of Posen to wear in the new comedy . . . The plaids are the largest and the silks the gaudiest ever manufactured" (June

Curtis displaying his new plaid suit used in Spot Cash. *(TCS 1. Houghton Library, Harvard University)*

28, 1884). Sam'l was always "up to date."

In addition to commissioning a new wardrobe, Curtis had hired a new manager, Joseph Gulick, according to the *New York Times* on July 31, 1884. The article goes on somewhat optimistically: "Each of the managers who assumed the duties connected with this post ultimately retired under a wrathful contemplation of what they regarded as Mr. Curtis's peculiarities . . .

Gulick's amiability is of that far-reaching type which leads to the general conviction among theatrical people that he may succeed in retaining the position of manager for M. B. Curtis for at least half a season." The *New York Times*'s optimism, however, was to be short-lived as it was announced on August 15 that Joseph Gulick had resigned his new position four days before *Spot Cash* was to open in St. Paul.

But despite suffering a rapid turnover in company managers, Curtis toured *Spot Cash* throughout the upper Midwest to full houses and fairly positive reviews before returning to the East Coast.

By mid-October, *Spot Cash* was ready to open at the Fifth Avenue Theatre in New York. Curtis staged one version of *Spot Cash* on opening night but was not satisfied with it, so he tried a second version on the second night, which went much better despite a few battles backstage among Curtis's company.

As the year 1884 was drawing to a close, Curtis was performing *Spot Cash* at the Park Theatre in New York City. One night, Mrs. Leslie Edmunds, who played Rebecca (and who was the wife of the popular character actor Edmund Law Rogers Jr., who often used the stage name Leslie Edmunds), was making quite a ruckus in the wings. When Curtis retired to the green room, the actress began to level verbal abuse at him. As the *New York Daily Mirror* recounted on December 13, 1884, "She became so violent that Mr. Curtis called in a stage carpenter to put her out. F. O. Savage, who figures in the role of bartender, interfered, and in attempting to quiet the noisy Rebecca, had his facial beauty marred by her nails. The appearance of a burly policeman, called in by Mr. Curtis, finally tamed Mrs. Edmunds, and the play proceeded. Mr. Curtis gave the policeman $5 to stay behind the scenes until after the performance."

Curtis discharged both Mr. and Mrs. Edmunds right after the Saturday night performance. But the couples found themselves on the same ferry home later that night. The husbands wound up in a brief but hot discussion which resulted in a fistfight erupting. According to the *Daily Mirror*, "This raised the dormant passion in the actor's breast, and rising in his might—and in size he towers way above Sam'l—he smote his quondam employer on the nose."

According to the *Mirror* article, Curtis responded in kind and knocked Edmunds out. Then Marie and Mrs. Edmunds got into it as well, pulling each other's hair as they tussled on the deck of the ferry. Edmunds then came to and threatened to have Curtis arrested. The *New York Times* reported that Curtis thought this a real possibility and decided to take the train back to Newark, as the next day his theatre company was off to Scranton.

Edmunds evidently did not appreciate the newspapers' version of events and delivered his side of the story, saying he had kept notes of all the events leading up to the fight and had witnesses and proof of his claims. The actor claimed that he and his wife had been hired on November 20 for a two-week run of *Spot Cash*. On the night of the fight, the stage manager, a Mr. Verner, had asked Mrs. Edmunds not to speak backstage during the performance. She refused to honor the request, saying she could talk if she didn't bother the play's progress or inconvenience anyone. When the couple was told they had to leave the company on Saturday, Edmunds and his wife went to Curtis's dressing room between the third and fourth acts and demanded two weeks' salary. As Edmunds told the *Mirror*, Curtis "then opened on me with abusive language, and called on the stage manager and carpenters to eject myself and wife from his room. As this was unnecessary I dared them to do so, and he used an insulting epithet to Mrs. Edmunds, which, of course, I resented. The people called in begged us not to stop the performance, and I replied that I owed it to the public not to do so, as they had nothing to do with private differences. Mr. Curtis then apologized to us and the stage hands."

Edmunds claimed that the next trouble came when Curtis approached him at the ferry baggage room. He said Curtis demanded an apology from Edmunds, and when Edmunds refused, Curtis struck him. They fought until the police broke the fight up.

Edmunds then rattled off to the *Mirror* a list of everyone fired by Curtis in the recent stretch of time. "I would like to refer you to Edwin Cleary and Davenport Bebus, who have filled the position of leading man to Curtis successively, and whom I replaced, being the third leading man engaged this season. In fourteen weeks he has made fourteen changes, and there are more to follow. These changes speak for themselves."

Curtis wanted his say as well and sent a telegram to the *Daily Mirror* from Pennsylvania telling the paper that Mrs. Curtis did not see the fight between the two men and defending his actions.

> ON SATURDAY NIGHT I PAID THE PAIR IN FULL AND GAVE [EDMUNDS] A LETTER OF DISCHARGE. THIS HE TORE UP AND THREW IN MY MANAGER'S FACE . . . MR. EDMUNDS MIGHT HAVE PROVED AN HONORED MEMBER OF MY COMPANY BUT FOR THE SCANDALOUS CONDUCT OF HIS WIFE. FOR THIS HE REFUSED TO APOLOGIZE, THEREFORE THE THRASHING . . . I NEVER USED ANY LANGUAGE THAT COULD BE CONSTRUED

INTO AN INSULT TO MRS. EDMUNDS OR ANY OTHER
LADY WHO MIGHT POSSIBLY BECOME A MOTHER OF
A FUTURE SAM'L OF POSEN. RESPECTFULLY, M. B.
CURTIS

In spite of positive early reviews (and the replacement of the talkative Mrs. Edmunds and her husband), *Spot Cash* had only moderate success. In February 1885, Curtis was reviewed in his hometown of Detroit. "Our advice is fall back on *Sam'l of Posen*. There could not be a more natural Hebrew Drummer. *Spot Cash* does not give him a chance to please the public." *The Spirit of the Times* had previously said they were "sorry to see such clever acting wasted upon so poor a play."

And Curtis evidently heeded the Detroit newspaper's advice as he began rotating performances of his old stand-by play with the new *Spot Cash*. But Marie seemed to have better success with her new vehicle. Marie had appeared in the new hit play *Elaine* in Fort Wayne, Indiana, where she had appeared many times as Celeste in *Sam'l of Posen*. Marie, no doubt, was enjoying a short break from playing the mean adventuress Celeste.

However, her break proved to be all too brief. In April of 1885, the Curtises returned to *Sam'l of Posen* for a two-week run at Niblo's Garden in Manhattan. The *New York Dramatic Mirror* commented on April 18, 1885, that "M. B. Curtis's wisdom in returning to his old *Sam'l of Posen* is shown in the increased business he is doing down at Niblo's. The original comedy is funnier and better suited to the star than *Spot Cash*, and there is plenty of draught in it yet."

There might have been plenty of "draught" left in the play, but there was now a question of how much draught was left

in its star. Curtis missed the final matinee and evening performances of *Sam'l of Posen* at Niblo's Garden on April 18, 1885.
The entire company was supposed to leave for its Pittsburgh
engagement on April 20, but no one had seen Curtis since the
curtain dropped on Friday night, April 17. He was living at
the Clarendon Hotel as usual, but he now disappeared from
public view.

On Saturday, a number of people came looking for him at
the Clarendon only to be told that Curtis had left town after
a doctor found that the actor had symptoms of pneumonia.
Some people weren't satisfied with the answer and pressed
for further explanation. The main desk said that Curtis had
left town and the group should contact his attorneys, Howe &
Hummel. Marie said that Curtis was sick. A doctor delivered a
note to the theatre saying that Curtis was suffering from nervous fever and his life could be threatened if he performed.

Curtis's attorneys said that Curtis was still in New York,
in seclusion at a private home, waiting to catch the train to
Pittsburgh, the next stop on his tour. He did not want any
more on his plate, which was, at present, spilling over with an
unpalatable array of troubles that he could not dispose of. As
he could neither resolve nor escape from his troubles, they
had overwhelmed him.

Marie offered the management of Niblo's seven hundred
dollars for the broken contract. Patrons who had purchased
tickets to Curtis's shows were offered a performance of *The
Galley Slave* or given their money back.

Marie explained in the undated and unsourced newspaper
article "M. B. Curtis Disappears" found in the Harvard Theater
Collection, "You see, Mr. Curtis is very nervous and excitable,
and he has worried himself that so many accusations should
have been made against him. This morning his doctor called

and took him to a house on East Nineteenth Street, and later they left town. I am just expecting a telegram telling me where they are."

Marie said that her husband had engaged a troupe to perform *Spot Cash* for fifteen to twenty weeks, but that the play "did not suit the public," and Curtis let the play and the cast go, which was provided for in their contracts, and would go back to playing *Sam'l of Posen*. The company of *Sam'l of Posen* was due in Pittsburgh to perform after the weekend and then they would go on the road and eventually end up in San Francisco.

Marie left for Pittsburgh on the nine a.m. train out of New York on August 20, 1885. The scenery and baggage for the company had been shipped two days earlier. When the troupe left New York, five members were left behind: Charles Verner, Walden Riddell and his wife, J. W. Gardner, and J. P. Sullivan. Sullivan had been hired for forty weeks and had two weeks remaining on his contract, which Curtis had paid him for. Sullivan was asked why he was dismissed and answered it was because he was blamed for all of Curtis's troubles. The *New York Times* joked that Curtis left as many lawsuits behind as he did actors.

Other unnamed actors or actresses were interviewed in the Harvard Theater Collection article, and they said that M. B. Curtis's erratic behavior was caused by Marie's fear of others in the company becoming stars in their own right. They claimed that Rachel Booth and others were "gotten rid of because they did artistic work in their parts, and the same may be said of others who have been with 'Sam'l,' but are with him no more."

In May 1885, Curtis suddenly ended his season. A reporter found him, not unexpectedly, at the Clarendon Hotel in New York having breakfast. The reporter sat down at the table and asked Curtis why he was canceling. Curtis, ever the man who wished to give his public something, replied, "Well, although I don't look very ill, I have been ailing for some time, and I concluded that my best course would be to close." When asked about all the lawsuits, Curtis replied, "All smoke, my boy. I am here on the ground to meet any charges, and fear nothing" (*New York Daily Mirror*, May 9, 1885).

By mid-May 1885, Curtis's older brother, Frank, had returned to the company in his original capacity as manager. The two had not spoken since their quarrel in the first season, and we can only surmise that Curtis's somewhat dire circumstances forced the two brothers to settle their differences and work together again.

But despite Curtis's current troubles, he was still getting terrific reviews for his work on the stage. On May 10, 1885, at the Opera House in Dunkirk, New York, Curtis performed *Sam'l of Posen* to a large audience: "From the very first appearance of Mr. Curtis, with his assortment of suspenders and socks . . . until the closing announcement of his Milwaukee store the audiences were kept in a continual roar of laughter," reported the local *Saturday Evening Observer*.

Even though *Spot Cash* did not enjoy the critical or popular success of *Sam'l of Posen*, Curtis kept the play in his repertoire for a while, performing it throughout the country. In the fall of 1885, *Spot Cash* played at San Francisco's Bush Street Theatre to large audiences at first. Curtis received good reviews, particularly in *The Wasp* (San Francisco, September 5, 1885), but by the end of the run, business had been only moderate, with Curtis probably not taking away much after expenses.

A mature Curtis offering his wares as Sam'l of Posen.
(TCS 1. Houghton Library, Harvard University)

There was no doubt that Curtis's Sam'l of Posen had
become a national folk hero. Sam'l, with Curtis in many ways
embracing the character both on stage and in real life, had
become America's definition of the ubiquitous drummer. In
1884, the J. C. Blair Company of Huntingdon, Pennsylvania,
a printing concern, offered Samuel of Posen writing tablets.

The popular *Frank Leslie's Illustrated Newspaper* of November 28, 1885, published an article, "A Drummer's Haven," noting Curtis's character's impact on the nation: "The commercial traveler, or 'drummer,' is known to us, partly through Mr. M. B. Curtis's broad but clever sketch of Sam'l of Posen."

Curtis was warmly welcomed by two hundred drummers who "made the house ring with plaudits on Sam'l of Posen's appearance" at Leubrie's Theatre in Memphis in October 1885. In mid-December of that same year, Curtis announced that he had written a new comedy based on a French Canadian version of *Sam'l of Posen.* The play was titled *Jean Baptiste.* Curtis promised a dialect never before heard on stage, and a play full of good, strong situations with plenty of comedy. In addition, there was to be a scene from a Montreal carnival and the stage's first representation of a toboggan race. No doubt Marie's French Canadian roots had something to do with the creation of this version of *Sam'l of Posen.* Whether American audiences preferred the drummer from Posen over a traveling salesman from Quebec or whether the toboggan race proved too difficult to stage, *Jean Baptiste* appears to have had a short life and was not added to Curtis's repertoire.

Sam'l of Posen was still, six years after its premiere, a very hot commodity across the country despite Curtis's continual touring. As the *Waterloo* (Iowa) *Courier* noted in March 1886:

> Sam'l is alone of his kind and there is but one
> Curtis. No matter how often we see him we
> may trust him to entertain us. There is that in
> his droll looks, in his queer twist of language,
> in his unspeakable assurance, in the laughable
> emphasis of his dress, and in the sharp resem-
> blance to truth which is seen in his broadest

caricature, that makes this impersonation
elemental, human, real. It owes its life to its
many touches of nature, and it will continue to
live and flourish so long as we have a Curtis to
give it breath.

The same paper also reported an argument Curtis had
with the owner of the Irvine Hotel that caused the actor to
relocate to the Central House Hotel. Whether this was an
example of Curtis's need to be treated as an important person
because his magical performances transformed the theatrical
climate of the day or an instance of a tired and hungry actor
only wanting to be served quickly is unknown. And, of course,
Curtis's success and his propensity for conflict made him a
target for nasty rumors. The *Daily Sentinel* published what it
claimed was an inside story about Curtis's confrontation with
a sheriff in Chicago who wanted to arrest him for unpaid
debts on May 10, 1886.

Curtis locked himself in the dressing room
with the courage of Bob Acres [a cowardly
character in Richard Brinsley Sheridan's
The Rivals made popular at the time by actor
Joseph Jefferson], and the villains still pursued him. He escaped through a trap, and
out through the boxes into the audience to
his hotel. There he "made up" with a wig and
beard, donned a long ulster and assumed the
walk of a cripple. The sheriffs were all on the
lookout, but he succeeded in getting himself
locked into the toilet room till the train got
into Indiana.

And one Atlanta newspaper claimed Curtis carried a "professional dramatist" to rewrite lines when a performer other than Curtis got applause. The new lines were supposedly meant to give the "popular sentiment to the star." And it was during this time that stories were floating around that Curtis was not well mentally. The *New York Dramatic Mirror* commented, "Foolish stories are current about the state of M. B. Curtis's mind. Except that it has been exercised by the delay in getting his new piece ready, Mr. Curtis's mentality is in perfect normal state." While a modern reader might think the newspaper was protesting a bit too much, we must remember that such juicy rumors were treated the same as facts in most of the newspapers of the day, not unlike our own tabloid-and-Internet-saturated age.

Curtis must have been encountering difficulties in coming up with a new theatrical vehicle during the 1885–1886 season as he traveled from Iowa to Tennessee and from Nevada to Illinois performing both *Sam'l of Posen* and *Spot Cash.* At the end of May 1886, Curtis returned to San Francisco to the Bush Street Theatre after almost a year's absence. It was announced there that Curtis had added to *Sam'l of Posen* and *Spot Cash* a new play called *General Depot.* But it seems that this new play joined its sibling, *Jean Baptiste*, in obscurity.

The Sam'l of Posen Company spent the summer of 1886 touring California and the Pacific Northwest. By August Curtis returned to San Francisco where the *New York Mirror* announced he was "making preparations for the production of *Caught in a Corner*," yet another new play in the works, but not one that featured Sam'l of Posen.

Despite the middling success of *Spot Cash* and the disappearances of *Jean Baptiste* and *General Depot*, one can almost hear Curtis's characteristic energetic optimism as he described the plot of *Caught in a Corner* and the new character he would portray to the *Dramatic Mirror* on September 18, 1886.

> I shall assume the role of a wealthy Hebrew . . .
> Instead of making him a black-haired, pushing
> young specimen of an Israelite, my audiences
> will see a nice, fat, sleek, good-natured He-
> brew with red curly hair and side whiskers.
> The story deals with an old man who is known
> as "The King of the Street." He makes a very
> good contract with the English Government
> to furnish wheat at ninety-two cents a bushel.
> The French adventuress who acts as a com-
> panion to the old man's daughter, but who is
> actually nothing but a stool-pigeon of Rich-
> ard Sharp, a millionaire grain broker, reveals
> this fact to her master. Without a day's delay
> that operator organizes a syndicate to make a
> corner in wheat, running it up to 110 and 112
> a bushel.
>
> The Hebrew, whom the old man had
> befriended years before, discovers the scheme,
> and the whole action of the play is then devoted
> to the portrayal of his efforts toward breaking
> up the corner, in which he finally succeeds.
> The moral of the young man, throughout the
> play is: "I never tell a lie, and I never go back
> on a friend."

Before the play was to open in New York, Curtis tested it in other states, including Ohio and Michigan. A New York theatre critic, F. A. Duneka, who happened to be in Detroit,

saw *Caught in a Corner* at White's Theatre. He wrote how, as
a self-satisfied New Yorker, he tried not to laugh at the play
but was unsuccessful in the attempt in an article found in the
Houghton Library, Harvard University.

> Everybody in Detroit was rushing to see it and
> the popular verdict in that provincial town
> was that it was the funniest play they had seen
> in many a long day . . . The scene was laid out
> in the weird and hoping West, so the average
> New York man can find out strange and awful
> things about Chicago manners and Illinois
> drawing rooms. It is a kind of farcical melo-
> drama and Curtis himself, in his character of
> Ikie Greenwald, furnishes the fun. Its humor
> is laid on broad lines, just the thing that the
> People—with a capital P—like to laugh at.
> It was not written for the critics, but for the
> public . . .
>
> Curtis himself is half or two-thirds of the
> play. The fun is incessant as long as he is on
> the stage. The character is a happy modifica-
> tion of that of Samuel Plastrick, which all of
> us know so well. There isn't so much in the
> writing, in what the author puts in the mouth
> of his hero, as the way the rogue says his lines
> and acts them.
>
> "My name is Ikie Greenwald, and I never
> told a lie" does not sound funny or doesn't
> look so in cold type here before you. I don't
> know why any sane man should laugh at it, but
> just let Curtis get up on the stage, put his hand

to his ear in that Baxter Street way he has, and
you let sense fly to where it belongs and howl
with the crowd . . .

The fact of the matter is just about this:
The great middle class makes up the play-go-
ing public and the successful actor is he who
tells them of the class to which they belong
and points out the hidden springs of fun that
bubble up all about. We are apt to shrug our
shoulders and shout out that the thing is common, but deep down in our honest hearts and
away back in the woodshed of our souls, so to
speak, we have a sneaking fondness for this
sort of thing.

No doubt optimistic about the audience's "sneaking fondness" for his new offering, Curtis opened *Caught in a Corner*,
written by W. J. Shaw, at the Fourteenth Street Theatre on
November 1, 1886—just a few days after the dedication ceremony that had unveiled the Statue of Liberty.

But Curtis was having more luck helping to illuminate
Lady Liberty than he was getting critics to praise his new
venture. Reviewing the Brooklyn production that preceded
the opening in Manhattan, a *New York Mirror* critic stated on
October 9, 1886, that "Curtis has a weak role. In his endeavor
to be extra funny, he over-acts the part entirely, and makes the
whole affair absurd," but the writer goes on to admit that a
very large audience was present on the night he saw the play
and that a good number of the audience members "seemed to
enjoy it." In early November *Caught in a Corner* was reviewed
by one critic as "not a good play, but it furnishes M. B. Curtis
with a good part." But the writer felt that Curtis would make a

grand success of it and that the new play would be bigger than *Sam'l of Posen*. "The Hebrews, who are among the best patrons of our theatres, laugh at him as the English dandies used to laugh at Sothern's Dundreary [Edward Sothern played Lord Dundreary in *Our American Cousin*]."

But the *Dramatic Mirror* felt very positive about the play. "*Caught in a Corner* is coining ducats for M. B. Curtis . . . The comedy is uproarious, and Curtis's characterization irresistible. It will remain the attraction as long as possible."

Despite some very good reviews and positive audience response, the ultimate fate of *Caught in a Corner* was not the success Curtis had hoped for. It is apparent from reviews that his own performances inspired roars of laughter. But the playwright had failed to give him a play with enough cohesive magical elements to touch the nerve of the public. And yet it is hard to balance this evident failure with the continuing favorable reviews of the play, including statements like this one printed in the *New York Dramatic Mirror* on the occasion of *Caught in a Corner*'s fiftieth performance at the Fourteenth Street Theatre that stated "business still keeps up to high water mark."

Despite steady if disappointing audiences, the Christmas season brought Curtis little relief from his troubles. As one of the most popular actors of his day, Curtis was asked to contribute an article to the 1886 Christmas edition of the *Dramatic Mirror*. His piece was called "The Major's Story." It was soon noted in a number of publications that this work was actually written by Bret Harte and published in the *Sun* a few years prior, and that the articles were identical save for a dozen or so words. Ironically, the theatre artist who had been the victim of plagiarists was now being accused of being one himself.

The *Sun* on December 21 published the following: "It is hardly conceivable that an actor who relies for much of his prosperity upon the favor of the New York public would boldly perpetuate such a fraud as palming off one of Mr. Bret Harte's stories as one of his own. It is more plausible that, being applied to together with a number of other artists to contribute to the columns of the *Mirror*, he hired someone of greater literary experience than himself to provide their desired contribution and then signed it, unconscious that he was putting his name to a production of one of the most brilliant writers of contemporary American fiction."

The *Mirror* stated promptly in its December 25 edition that the last line of the *Sun*'s article was true. The editor of the *Dramatic Mirror* visited Curtis in his dressing room at the Fourteenth Street Theatre, and said, "The actor made a clean breast of the deed."

Curtis was quoted as saying:

> When Mr. Fiske wrote me and asked me to send an anecdote for the Christmas number I replied that I should be happy to oblige him. As the time for sending in the manuscript drew near, I found myself still in doubt as to what to write. One day I met Col. J. F. Milliken, the play adapter, on Broadway. I told him about my promise and he said if I were pressed for time he would do it for me and sign my name to it. A bargain was struck and later when he brought me "The Major's Story" and remarked that it was original, I paid him a good sum for it. Milliken said I had better have

> it copied off as his handwriting was known
> in the *Mirror* office. My stage manager, John
> Queen, made the copy. This was sent to Mr.
> Fiske. I didn't know Milliken had stolen the
> story from Bret Harte until tonight. I thought
> he composed it himself. Mr. Fiske had no
> knowledge whatever that I was practicing a
> deceit upon him. I simply wanted to fulfill the
> promise I had made him. That's all there is
> about it.

When Mr. Fiske asked Curtis if he realized the gravity of the fraud committed upon the paper and its readers, Curtis could only make a joke. "The *Mirror* wanted a story and I sent it one." The *Mirror* took the exact same tack in explaining how the fraud eluded the newspaper's staff, claiming that they did not have the time to read it first. While this incident seems not to have damaged Curtis's reputation with the public, it does provide an insight into how celebrity always comes with a microscope. Curtis was by this time a well-known figure in American entertainment of the period. And he was beginning to pay the price of having every detail of his life minutely examined in public.

The beginning of 1887 must not have given Curtis much to celebrate. With reviews such as the *Chicago Tribune*'s statement that *Caught in a Corner* "is much more forced and extravagant in tone than *Sam'l of Posen* and hence is not likely to achieve the popularity of the latter" no doubt weighing on his mind, Curtis began to explore other possibilities that might reinvigorate his initial success. A particularly disappointing review in the *New*

York Mirror on March 10, 1887 (*"Caught in a Corner*, which has been at the Chestnut Opera House, cannot claim to have met with great success . . . It is only spasmodically funny, though at all times absurd. If it is not bad enough to merit condemnation, it certainly not good enough to praise"), might have been the impetus for Curtis to consider leaving the spoken-word theatre and going into pantomime. He was aware that the use of his body, posture, face, hands, and clothing were major strengths in his theatrical toolbox. As he stated in an untitled and undated article found in the New York Public Library for the Performing Arts, Billy Rose Collection, "Sam'l of Posen as Humpty Dumpty would, no doubt, create a draft at the box office."

Curtis's reference to Humpty Dumpty is not a casual one. In April of 1887 he was also considering joining the famous Bolossy Kiralfy in a pantomime revival. Kiralfy and his brother, Imre, had scored quite a New York hit in 1871 with the pantomime *Humpty Dumpty* and then went on to success with such theatrical spectacles as *Around the World in Eighty Days* and *The Deluge*, where they made it rain on stage. In 1887, the brothers—immigrant Hungarians from Budapest—had a falling-out and parted ways, not unlike two other immigrant Hungarian brothers had done four years earlier. But nothing came of Curtis's brief flirtation with spectacle and pantomime, though; and Bolossy and Imre went their separate ways, producing outdoor extravaganzas such as *Columbus and the Discovery of America* and *Venice in London*, complete with a lake and canals.

As Curtis wrestled with possible new career options, he was also struggling to keep his company on tour and was encountering yet more personnel problems. On April 6, 1887, Curtis was forced to sue an actor in his troupe, the Englishman

Vincent Sternroyd, for $1,000 for breach of contract. Sternroyd was signed to play any part in *Caught in a Corner* "that should be assigned to him or forfeit the $1,000." Sternroyd was given the part of James Holloway and he refused, leaving the company in a bind with performances scheduled. Curtis was annoyed with him and, holding him to his word, had a writ of attachment issued on Sternroyd's baggage. The sheriff came to Sternroyd's dressing room at Havlin's Theatre in Cincinnati and seized all his bags.

But Curtis's luck seems to have taken a turn for the better when he returned to California in the fall of 1887. On October 10, 1887, Curtis opened a two-week run of *Caught in a Corner* at San Francisco's Alcazar Theatre, with the *Oakland Tribune* enthusiastically announcing, "Curtis has struck it rich with *Caught in the Corner* [sic], which fills the Alcazar to overflowing. In it he takes a step higher in his profession, showing powers of wider scope than permitted in his other plays. He is something more than amusing. He shows a carefully drawn character, not easy to depict, but in his hands full of humor, and at the bottom exciting the sympathies of his auditors."

In the Alcazar production, Curtis, Marie, and the noted actor Gustavus Levick were supported by the Alcazar's stock group, the Osbourne & Stockwell's Comedy Co. But even here, in what passed as Curtis's West Coast home base, he couldn't escape some poor reviews. While the *San Francisco Chronicle* complimented Curtis's professional growth as the "petty and at times discreditable peculiarities of the drummer blossomed out into a red-headed speculator with a curious combination of good nature, humor of a broad kind, and the usual shrewdness," the reviewer felt that Curtis did not elicit any feelings "except liking for the eccentricities, which provoked very hearty laughter. The play is not badly written, but the plot is a trifle weak . . . Curtis is the central figure, and one does not feel very deeply interested in anybody else."

It is interesting to note that the grand Alcazar Theatre, the palace of Moorish architecture on O'Farrell Street between Stockton and Powell, would later influence Curtis when he

The Alcazar Theatre in San Francisco. (Courtesy of the San Francisco History Center, San Francisco Public Library)

reinvented himself yet again as a hotelier. The enormous theatre, owned by M. H. de Young, was two years old in 1887. It had seven hundred gas jets that had been converted to electric lighting. The lavish architectural style of the theatre coupled with its having the latest technological advances must have made a deep impression on Curtis.

And it was there at the Alcazar Theatre that Curtis dreamed up a novel way to promote ticket sales of *Caught in a Corner* when he learned of a large tract of land for sale in Tehama County in California's Central Valley some one hundred miles north of Sacramento, six miles from the town of Red Bluff. The land was vacant even though the Oregon and California Railroad ran nearby. There was, however, no stop in the empty tract, making accessibility a problem.

Undeterred by the isolation of the tract, Curtis purchased the land for a reported three dollars an acre, planning to give away a small lot in his future town of Samlposen with each ticket purchased for *Caught in a Corner*. "I propose to give away from ten to 40,000 lots and make Samlposen one of the gem towns of the state," Curtis proclaimed in a speech. About 11,000 lots were platted on a map Curtis had drawn up, which showed spaces set aside for a theatre, parks, schools, and churches. "Yes sir! We have laid out a beautiful town in Tehama County, on the line of the railroad, and possessing all the advantages of soil, climate and water facilities," Curtis enthused.

This novel attempt to increase ticket sales took off like a shot. Audiences were thrilled by this unheard-of opportunity, and many took advantage of it with pie-in-the-sky dreams. The Alcazar made "a good deal of money out of the adventure in town lots as an accessory to Curtis's play. This will be the last chance to see the piece or obtain an interest in the town with the unpronounceable name," warned the *San Francisco Chronicle*. Business was so good that the *San Francisco Post* noted, "If business continues at this rate, some half the population of San Francisco will live in Samlposen."

In order to take legal possession of their free land, ticket buyers had to have their ownership registered and dated at the California Land Association office in San Francisco within two days of the performance. Theatregoers paid the usual twenty-five cents to a dollar for their ticket and then had to pay two dollars to the California Land Association as a registration fee that supposedly went to the county clerk for producing the necessary deed.

Some people speculated that Tehama County, the California Land Association, and Curtis would split the "excess of the fee," but Curtis later responded that the California Land Association was the only entity to make any profit after the county was paid. Although the promotion was harmless, Curtis found himself in trouble because some theatregoers felt deceived by having to pay two dollars to assume ownership of their "free" lot. But despite these grumblings, the Alcazar was filled every night. Within five years, 1,800 deeds were recorded in Samlposen.

Curtis's map of Samlposen shows many familiar names, with streets named Curtis, de Mer, Albina, and Fleurange (Marie's maiden name). There are streets named after Curtis's sister, Gisella; his father, Julien; his mother, Bertha; and his brothers George and Charles. Noticeably absent is a street named after Curtis's brother Frank, who had left the company during the previous year and was evidently not on speaking terms with his famous brother again. Streets were also named after famous actors and major San Francisco figures. Fiske Street was likely named for the manager of the *New York Mirror*, whom Curtis owed a favor to after the 1886 Christmas story incident.

Despite the success of the promotion, the dreamed-of city of Samlposen never materialized. Over the years, most of the lots were sold for back taxes, and it was said that many people did not know exactly where their lots were, as no survey markers were ever set. Some audience members traveled to the site of Samlposen as proud new owners of real estate, but where the map had displayed lots for hotels and stores, only sagebrush and grass grew.

Curtis was almost certainly the first to dream up this novel idea to fill theatres. His strategy was repeated in later decades with Bank Nights, a lottery to draw people to the theatres during the Depression, and in William Randolph Hearst's giveaway of lots in California's Santa Cruz Mountains to spur sales of his newspaper subscriptions. This experience also did not deter Curtis from coming up with other promotional ideas later on. A prize of $10,000 was offered to patrons of the Park Theatre for a poem of two verses on the subject of the popular actor and his latest production.

With his optimistic outlook and fertile imagination, Curtis no doubt actually "saw" the whole town of SamlPosen as he had it drawn, and he expected that the lots would rise in value and that people would easily make a reality of his dream. But as he would later learn, things were often not that simple in real estate development.

A Hungarian Hebrew in King Arthur's Court

Being a good actor isn't easy.
Being a man is even harder.
—*James Dean*

⁓

The idea for the real estate promotion that succeeded in filling the house at the Alcazar Theatre in San Francisco might have occurred to Curtis when he purchased a tract of twelve acres in Peralta Park, just north of Berkeley, in May 1887, just a few months before he bought the land in Tehama County. What might have started out as partial speculation—land in California was underpriced at the time, and investors from around the country would soon take an interest—quickly turned into a refuge and a new vehicle for Curtis's next act of reinvention. Far surpassing Curtis's current problems of declining audiences for his less-than-successful sequels to *Sam'l of Posen* was Marie's increasingly ill health, which was also making touring impossible for the close couple. And it can be safely assumed that Marie and Curtis—who had spent their entire adult life up to this point continually moving around the country together, with only the Clarendon Hotel in New York passing for what might be considered a "home" — were beginning to feel a bit road weary. The itinerant actor who was playing a traveling salesman must have been ready to put down roots, especially now that his number one priority was to care for his ailing wife.

Berkeley had appealed to the Curtises ever since their first visit in 1886. The *Berkeley Advocate* noted on July 31 of that year, "Mr. M. B. Curtis, the famous 'Sam'l of Posen,' and his wife, are the guests of Mr. Passett this week. Mr. Curtis likes our town, and would like to settle here if his profession would allow him to have a home." Although many towns claimed that Curtis intended to settle there, this time the rumor became reality. Curtis soon cut back his touring schedule, taking *Caught in a Corner* to Los Angeles for a few performances, but by November 1887 Frank Howard, an actor in Curtis's company, was playing Sam'l of Posen in Montreal and Curtis was spending as much time as possible in Berkeley with Marie while he established himself as one of the leading lights of the town they wanted to call home. This endeavor enabled him to be there for Marie while staying occupied.

Curtis's Berkeley real estate agent, George Schmidt, reminisced years later about the famous actor's arrival in an article titled "M. B. Curtis Famous for 'Drummer' Characterization."

> I remember Curtis coming to Berkeley. He
> wore a fine big overcoat and an expensive hat
> and he walked away with the town. In those
> days one took for granted that a man who
> could dress like that was a millionaire. He
> didn't have a cent of money, yet he somehow

> or other got that Peralta Park tract. [In fact,
> Curtis did have money as he put an $8,000
> down payment on a mortgage for the tract.] He
> was the greatest promoter I ever saw. He gave
> the biggest lunches and dinners at his home,
> and gathered all kinds of wealthy people from
> San Francisco there. When he finished feeding
> them, they were ready to buy the world.
>
> Curtis was famous as a host. No one ever
> neglected an invitation to his home. He was
> one of the most eccentric, but one of the finest
> men I ever knew . . . He got his money easily
> and he spent it just as easily.

Curtis was planning to build a "fine country residence.
Fish ponds, deer parks and hothouses will be had on a grand
scale"—in fact, as he expressed in the *Oakland Enquirer* on
May 21, 1887, "I will have a home that my friends will be welcomed to, and they will be glad to make the visit." The article
went on to say that Curtis wanted "to see a little life infused
into" the small town of Berkeley. And the *Berkeley Advocate*
was definitely enthusiastic about Curtis's plans, as the newspaper exhorted the actor on June 20, 1887, "Boom 'er up, Samuel!" Who better or more energetic to do just that than M. B.
Curtis?

But Curtis wasn't only interested in building a place
where he could be with his ailing wife and lay his head down
in the same place every night. Curtis threw himself into the
role of promotor and civic benefactor with all the energy he
had brought to his performances on stage. The *San Francisco
Chronicle* noted that Curtis also "helps in the work of intro-
ducing people of refinement and wealth from the East to

come and settle in Berkeley" and that he "attends the meetings of the West Berkeley Development Association [and] heads subscription lists for local needs."

One of those local needs was a railway station in West Berkeley. The Southern Pacific Railroad had initially refused to make a stop in that section of town. Some said it was not worth the stop; others said the "footpads" in West Berkeley made it too dangerous.

People in West Berkeley then submitted plans in hopes the Southern Pacific would accept them if the residents offered to pay for the building of the station. By July 1887, the railroad decided to consider a stop at Bancroft Way, along its Third Street tracks. Subscription lists were passed around at the Neihaus Planing Mill and George Schmidt's real estate office to raise funds for the planned station. After raising $950, the boosters were still $250 short of their goal, and Curtis stepped up to the plate, donating the needed balance for construction to begin. In exchange for his help, Curtis got to name the station and, not surprisingly, he christened it Posen Station.

Curtis spoke to the crowd at the station's opening on October 2, 1887, extolling the beauty and modernity of the new building. Photographers then took over to commemorate the event and people were invited into the station for refreshments. Everyone spent the afternoon riding the train from one station to another, getting on and off at Posen Station "just to see how it felt."

Curtis also agreed to volunteer as president of the Berkeley Light Company, offering to personally pay for the erection and wiring of light poles on Hopkins Street (which bordered his development) and donate them to the electric company. And Curtis helped purchase a bell for the volunteer fire

Opening day at Posen Station. Curtis is in a top hat in front of and to the right of the right post on the porch. Marie is in the white hat to the left of Curtis. (Courtesy of the Berkeley Firefighters Association)

company stationed in the new firehouse in West Berkeley. Through his generosity and civic involvement, Curtis was becoming one of the leading lights of the city incorporated in 1878, which was now beginning to enjoy boom times, thanks in no small part to the man who basked in the reflected glow of Sam'l of Posen.

Curtis's plan was to establish a colony of theatrical artists in Peralta Park near the home he planned to build on Hopkins Street. Forced to end his touring by his desire to be by Marie's side during her illness, Curtis evidently wanted the theatrical world to travel to him. And to that end, he planned to build a hotel around the corner at what is now the north end of Albina Avenue (Curtis was still enjoying the pleasure of naming streets after his family, friends, and associates), bringing in a chef from New Orleans and celebrating his new venture by spending $1,000 on a party for his friends—no doubt a dress rehearsal for when he would become a celebrated hotel owner and host. Newspapers as far away as the *Brooklyn Daily Eagle* reported on Curtis's development plans in Berkeley in the fall of 1887 as New York theatre people began investing in their fellow actor's dreams.

After his engagement in Los Angeles in November 1887, Curtis returned to the Bay Area, where he had scheduled a three-day run of *Caught in a Corner* at the Oakland Theatre, which the *Berkeley Advocate* commented on in a rather blasé tone, "The actor and the play are too well known to require comment from us . . . delighted audiences as a matter of course." It must have been a rare treat for Curtis to be able to go home after each performance to familiar surroundings, with his dogs, birds, and horses. The Curtises had made a home on Sixth Street in Berkeley in a cottage owned by Mr. Neihaus (whose lumber mill would fabricate lumber and trim for Curtis's Peralta Park Hotel) and stayed there until their house in Peralta Park was completed.

In 1888 Curtis formed the Peralta Park Hotel Company to fulfill his dream of an actors' retreat and resort in Berkeley next door to his own home. The hotel would sit on six acres of land on a small hill with a breathtaking view of San Francisco Bay and the hills surrounding it. The *Berkeley Advocate* provided a picturesque description of the actor's plans on February 8, 1888.

> The latest enterprise conceived in the fertile
> brain of Mr. M. B. Curtis is the building of a
> large hotel on Peralta Park, located about half

a mile from Berryman station. It is to contain eighty rooms for the accommodation of tourists, families, students, and all those seeking a delightful home surrounded by unrivaled scenery. Mr. Curtis has informed the *Advocate* that in order to accomplish this great subject he intends to get up a stock company consisting of 6000 shares at $25 per share. He states that the railroad proposes in the near future to form a loupe [*sic*] to connect the east with the west end of town. As a part of the loupe will run near the park it will be a great convenience to travelers who can by this means easily connect with the overland or trains that gridiron the state.

Peralta Park is one of the most beautiful spots in the State, and many advantages will be taken of its natural site to make it most attractive. All night it will be lighted up by electric lights, and for further accommodation of guests Mr. Curtis proposes to build a fine bathing establishment on his property at the West Berkeley waterfront, where guests will be conveyed by bus or car. Boats will also be in readiness for pleasure and excursions.

Construction of the Peralta Park Hotel (named after Californio Domingo Peralta, whose 1841 adobe site was located within the boundaries of the development) began soon after the company was formed, with Curtis serving as one of the directors. The board believed that enough stock had been sold to begin building, and they expected to have the hotel open by October 1 of that year. Plans for the dreamlike hotel were soon drawn up by architect Gustav Behrend, and by April of 1888, engineers were staking out building sites, with excavation beginning a week later.

By late May of 1888, the company had raised $37,775 and the area where the hotel would be built was being graded. A number of bridges were built spanning Codornices Creek, and an electric light tower was placed at the entrance to the park.

Curtis chose to have his hotel built in an extravagant style, which echoed the architecture of his other home, the Alcazar Theatre. It would be surrounded by many stately houses, including Curtis's own beautiful new home located at 1505 Hopkins, which was constructed by Lord & Boynton for

The Curtis home at 1505 Hopkins Street, just outside the entrance to the Peralta Park Hotel. (Berkeley Architectural Heritage Association, Bolton Collection, BAHA Archives)

$4,500 and completed in 1889. It sported a chicken coop, barn, conservatory, and water tank. Four small eucalyptus trees covered in ivy made a green entry to the estate. Behind it was a natural grove of trees with palms and umbrella trees planted in an alternating pattern along the sidewalk.

In the past, when Peralta Park was still open ranchland, local residents had enjoyed themselves there and had grown accustomed to that privilege without the need for permission from the property owner. In June of 1888, Curtis took out an ad in the *Berkeley Advocate* that stated, "Trespassers Beware!" He noted that anyone who continued to shoot or picnic within the park grounds would be liable to arrest and a fine. It was now the Peralta Park Hotel grounds, and construction made hunting and picnicking too dangerous.

Curtis set up his office for the hotel opposite Berkeley Station in the center of downtown. It was quite attractive, but the bigger news was that it was fitted with electric lights, which were turned on at night. Prior to this time, townspeople were accustomed to darkness so extreme that they could see the aurora borealis and needed to carry lanterns to be able to walk safely at night. There might have been giant light masts trying to light the streets at the time, but Curtis was setting an example for lighting in individual buildings and the people of Berkeley recognized this novelty as a step into the future.

Perhaps remembering the difficulties with accessibility that plagued his land in Tehama County, Curtis exerted enough influence to eliminate his Peralta Park project's isolation from town by persuading the Claremont, Branch and Ferries Railroad to extend its tracks from University Avenue up Sacramento Street to Hopkins Street and then to the entrance of the hotel grounds. This line would also connect Peralta Park to the ferries and the Ocean View neighborhood. On May 23,

1888, the Southern Pacific Railroad, with the intention of extending their line around Peralta Park, made a large land purchase. By August 15, Southern Pacific surveyors and engineers were staking out a new rail route to Peralta Park, which would pass through West Berkeley.

But while construction of the new rail route and the hotel proceeded, unexpected costs were mounting, and on August 22 the hotel corporation levied an assessment of $12.50 per share on stockholders. Yet, by October 1888, progress on the hotel was quoted as "surprising" and almost half a dozen new dwellings were going up in the park as well. By the end of the month, Curtis, evidently confident in the progress that was being made, left for the East Coast for three weeks. He also might have felt more confident about leaving town as Marie was finally well enough to take a daily drive, according to the *Berkeley Advocate* (October 11, 1888). She had been reported to be very ill that summer by the same newspaper, and given Marie's doctor's remarks and specialties, it seems likely that she had had one of the earliest hysterectomies performed in the United States.

C. R. Lord, the contractor Curtis had hired to build his dream palace, had finished framing the first floor of the hotel by August of 1888 and was now starting on the second floor. At the end of August, the *Berkeley Advocate* described the building that would soon grace Peralta Park.

> Following up the magnificent driveway
> through rows of stately trees, one soon comes
> in view of the Hotel Peralta. To the contractor,
> C. R. Lord, we are again indebted for facts and
> figures. The building stands on the brow of the
> hill facing due south. It is built on a massive

concrete foundation, is 196 feet long by 60 feet deep, and is four stories high, not including the basement. The roof will be of Gothic architecture, having 2 towers, 8 gables and 12 dormer windows. Surrounding the first and third stories will be broad promenade balconies. On the first floor the main entrance hall is 23 x 24, the dining halls 24 x 43, and 23 x 27; the reading room 25 x 25; ladies' parlor 23 x 25, and music hall 25 x 43.

When completed, the hotel will contain 112 rooms, which will be heated by hot air and lighted by hundreds of electric lights, the plenty for which will be on the grounds adjoining. There is little fear of delay now, and Mr. Curtis expects to have the hotel opened by the first of the coming year.

By September 1888, the grand hotel could be seen from all quarters of Berkeley. The wooden frames of the hotel's towers were piercing the horizon, giving the structure an exotic dignity and an air of mystery. But even as Curtis's grand dream was taking shape, whispers of hard reality were circulating around what was thought to be soon the largest hotel in the West. The *Berkeley Advocate* reported on September 19, 1888, that various hotel magnates had arrived from New York to see the wondrous new hotel being constructed in Berkeley. While they were reportedly impressed by the scope of the project, they were also worried that keeping a hotel the likes of this one open would cost a fortune. And as September turned into October and the Peralta Park Hotel was nearly ready for painting, the *Berkeley Advocate* (October 10, 1888) worried about the project's high payroll each week even though they proclaimed, "M. Curtis, the moving spirit in this large enterprise, has astonished the wiseacres who shook their heads at his proposed venture." But in the end, the "wiseacres" would prove to be more prophetic than Berkeley's leading newspaper.

The hotel was not ready to open at the beginning of 1889 as Curtis had projected the previous August. Instead, the Curtises checked in to the Occidental Hotel on Montgomery Street in San Francisco for an indefinite stay. Marie had become ill again and needed to be near her doctor in San Francisco for constant treatment while Curtis would take the ferry to Peralta Park to work every day, according to the *Berkeley Advocate* on January 9, 1889.

At the end of January 1889, after the Curtises had moved from the Occidental to the Palace Hotel, they received more bad news. It was well-known how much the Curtises loved animals, especially their fine big old dog, Carlo. Because of Marie's illness and the need to move to San Francisco, and though they "were loathe to part with him even when removal made it necessary," they found Carlo a new home with Mr. and Mrs. John Foy. Foy was the manager of the Henry Taylor Lumber Yard, who lived with his wife on Fourth Street in Berkeley. Carlo was partially blind, but still got around, and while he was at the Foys', he ate some poisoned meat that someone had carelessly left lying around and he died within minutes.

In February 1889, the famous actress Maggie Mitchell came to visit Curtis and Marie, possibly to offer support to her old friend and colleague and his ailing wife, whom Mitchell had also appeared with on stage. Born in 1832, Mitchell had been the favorite actress of President Lincoln and Henry Wadsworth Longfellow. Mitchell, like the rest of Curtis's visitors, was given the grand tour. She was very taken by the

The Curtises' dog Carlo attending the dedication of Posen Station.
(Courtesy of the Berkeley Firefighters Association)

location, surroundings, and the evident promise of Peralta Park. "On Friday deeds were drawn up conveying to her five acres of land on Posen Avenue, due north of the hotel, the price paid being $14,000. It is stated that the lady will there build a costly residence," the *Berkeley Advocate* announced.

Painting began on the hotel that spring and graders prepared the grounds for the gardeners. The hotel was wired and electric lights were installed throughout. An electric-light plant, consisting of dynamos, wires, bells, and lamps, had been delivered to the hotel grounds in early April, and many Berkeleyites stood around to gawk at the newfangled marvels.

One night in May when Curtis was taking the ferry to San Francisco, he was shocked to see a multitude of large posters with his likeness on them posted at prominent places around

The Peralta Park Hotel as the finishing touches were being completed in the spring of 1889. From Beautiful Berkeley, *published in 1889. (Photo by O. V. Lange)*

town. A variety actor whose name was on the posters advertised that he was to perform in the city within the month. Curtis handed the matter over to his attorney "who will bring suit against the printers who issued the bills." Many actors and actresses had the experience of being impersonated during this era, and Curtis was no exception as various performers tried to cash in on his fame.

Perhaps motivated by the need to borrow more money to pay his mounting construction costs or by his desire to see Berkeley develop at a faster pace, Curtis realized that the little Berkeley Homestead Loan Association could not meet the demand for loans as Berkeley grew. With his usual well of enthusiasm, he began to explore the idea of opening a new loan association. A subscription letter was soon passed around and fifty-two men signed on for more than seven hundred shares. Curtis wanted fifty, as did contractor C. R. Lord and realtor J. L.

Scotchler. Alfred Leuder, a perfume manufacturer with property in Peralta Park, took some, as did William Kreling, owner
of San Francisco's Tivoli Theatre. The articles of incorporation
of the Peralta Building and Loan Association of Berkeley were
filed April 18, 1889. The corporation subscribed $143,000, and
the capital stock was valued at $1,000,000. Directors were cho-
sen for the new bank, with Curtis among them.

By summer, the sound of the banging of hammers shot
across Peralta Park as many large and elegant houses were
being constructed. The *Berkeley Advocate* noted in early July
that houses "were springing up as if by magic in and around
Peralta Park, and all of them of the most substantial and tasty
kind." The summer of 1889 also found more visitors being
drawn to the site of the Peralta Park Hotel to marvel at the
magnificent structure. A temporary stairway was built from the
basement to the tower, and carpenters, painters, and plaster-
ers scampered in and out of the hotel and up and down the
scaffolding. Work continued vigorously. The Peralta Park Hotel
Company had $25,000 in the bank to finish the project, and
Curtis hoped to welcome the hotel's first guests by November.

"The fertile brain of M. B. Curtis" generated a new idea
in September. He offered smaller lots in the luxurious Peralta
Park development for moderate-income people. Just north of
the Leuder house, which still stands on the west side of Albina
Avenue—a gorgeous remnant of the park's past glory—lots
were divided into twenty-five fifty-foot frontages. Curtis sold
them for five hundred dollars each by accepting twenty dollars
per month until the full amount was paid without any interest
or other charges.

And while Bay Area newspapers breathlessly reported
Curtis's real estate plans, events in his everyday life were considered news as well, as this September 5, 1889, *Oakland Daily*

Evening Tribune article illustrates.

> M. B. Curtis stepped on a rusty nail on Mon-
> day last at his home in Berkeley and has been
> laid up ever since. The nail went very nearly
> through his foot and Mr. Curtis, knowing the
> great danger there was from such an injury,
> did not wait for the arrival of a physician but
> immediately proceeded to cut the wound open
> with a sharp pruning knife which he had in
> his hand. After he had done this he washed
> the cut out with strong vinegar and then he
> cauterized it. The doctor on arriving com-
> plimented Mr. Curtis on his nerve and good
> judgement in the treatment.

In early December 1889, Curtis's brother Frank arrived
in Berkeley, the brothers evidently having patched up their
earlier differences. One wonders if Frank was motivated by
his concern for Curtis and Marie and chose to come to help
them in their time of crisis. Frank was now part owner of the
Third Avenue Theatre in New York, and the owner of a theatre in Portland, Maine, and he had come to see his brother's
development that he had heard so much about. No place, he
said, equaled the beauty he saw in Berkeley. According to the
Berkeley Advocate on December 4, 1889, Frank believed Peralta
Park was the crown jewel and considered buying a lot there.

Delays once again put off the grand opening of Curtis's luxurious hotel. With construction now costing around
$125,000—about 50 percent more than originally planned—
Curtis began to experience financial trouble, having discovered that it was expensive to put the jewel in the crown. On

September 27, 1889, he told the *San Francisco Chronicle* that he, his brother Frank, and Edward Swett all owned a piece of *Sam'l of Posen*, but that he had transferred his interest in the play to Marie to pay a debt he owed her. Now, nine years after its debut, Curtis felt the play had little value, though it might have a few years left in it. Curtis said that he had owned *Spot Cash*, but had returned it to its previous owner after losing $16,000 on the play. He said that after the last time he had performed *Caught in a Corner* he had "burned the manuscript." He related that when he retired from the stage, Marie had about $50,000 in savings and he had about $1,250. By speculating in real estate, he testified, he had lost all his own and some of his wife's money.

In November Curtis was brought before a San Francisco court commissioner to answer questions as to his ability to pay some small bills "incurred for necessities." Curtis's impatience and big dreams, coupled with a cock-eyed and fearless sense of optimism, had always been the basis of his decisions, and his indulgences grew with his success. While Curtis had repeatedly come close to pulling off impossibly huge undertakings, his fortunes were now changing. His wife's illness, his sinking of all their money in real estate ventures, the financial failure of his most recent play, and some shortsighted high living were forcing the actor to rethink his situation. It was time for M. B. Curtis and Sam'l of Posen to get back to work.

The Grand Opera House in San Francisco announced that M. B. Curtis would perform *Sam'l of Posen* there on March 24, 1890. It would be a farewell performance, as the company would open Curtis's new play, *The Shatchen*, at the Star Theatre in New York on April 28. And despite Curtis's long hiatus from the stage, his old magic still glowed brightly, as the *Berkeley Advocate* confirmed on March 27, 1890. "Time has given him only the finer touches which makes his creation of the Drummer a work of fine art. His support is excellent and highly enjoyable." The *San Francisco Chronicle* was surprised to see a large and enthusiastic audience that applauded Curtis heartily. The writer surmised on March 25 that Curtis's "innocence" came from "careful study and attention to the minutest details of the character and a long experience in the part, which makes his acting very smooth and his effects very sure."

The Curtises' comeback certainly got the attention of the theatrical world. In an April interview with the *New York Dramatic Mirror*, Curtis held court.

> They say actors and actresses are pretty much alike in one respect. They say none of them want to leave the stage until they are forced to take that step. As you know, I have been living in retirement at Berkeley, California, principally on account of the illness of Mrs. Curtis, who has now, I am happy to say, been restored to her usual health. I have only acted one week in three years. Meantime I have been kept very active with various business enterprises with which I have become connected at Berkeley.

As planned, Curtis opened *The Shatchen* at New York City's Star Theatre in the late spring of 1890. Perhaps as significant as M. B. Curtis's appearing in a new play was the theatre's novel new air-conditioning system. *The Shatchen* was the first play to offer its audiences "a cooling apparatus, which will make of this house one of the most comfortable summer resorts in the city. Small registers have already been fixed all along the aisles, through which the cool air from the ice chambers will be forced, instead of under the seats, as has heretofore been the case," explained the *New York Times* on May 6, 1890. In the past, theatres had had to close before the heat of summer set in.

The title of the play that was now enjoying the cool comfort of the Star Theatre refers to the character played by Curtis, Myer Petowsky, a Jewish matchmaker known as a *shatchen*. The main character, played in New York by Lewis Morrison (who was staging his own comeback after a period away from the stage), is Joseph Lewis, a moral, hardworking, religious, and proud Jew who disinherits his only son when he secretly marries a Gentile girl. But it was not clear to the *Times* reviewer if the disinheritance was due to the girl's religion, his son's deceitful behavior, or the fact that the girl's father was a wreck of a man. As the growing trend of interfaith marriages was drawing the attention of much of the nation in the late nineteenth century, a number of plays were exploring this topic. But judging from the *Times* reviewer's opinion, this was not among the best of those plays.

The *Berkeley Advocate*, however, reported that *The Shatchen* was an "undeniable, emphatic and instantaneous" hit at the Star Theatre, with Lewis Morrison and Curtis receiving many curtain calls. Morrison was quoted in the same article as saying, "I have been a wanderer for five years, he [Curtis] has been a deserter [referring to Curtis's absence from the theatre while his wife was ill] and I have brought him back." The review goes on to state that the audience was happy to see both of the actors back on the stage.

> The audience . . . gave vent to their feelings in
> great outbursts of applause that fairly shook

the old Star. It was a tremendous ovation, sincere as it was emphatic and one such as few stage-walkers ever receive. Curtis's retirement from and return to the stage has given him an opportunity to know how strongly he is welded to the public heart, and learning as well that it will not tolerate another three years' vacation. We have royally welcomed Messrs. Curtis and Morrison back, and demand that they show their appreciation by staying with us.

And despite the reviewer's confusion over the motivations behind the plot of the play, the *New York Times*'s May 13 notice was happy to see the broad Posen smile and the gorgeous costumes, and the reviewer liked this piece more than Curtis's other vehicles as it was "shorter, simpler and less depressing."

But despite Curtis's relatively successful comeback, he was still plagued by his old problems with his fellow actors. Soon after the opening of *The Shatchen*, Sophie Eyre left the company, furious at what she considered rude treatment. And by June, Lewis Morrison had left the cast as well. During the last week of the run at the Star Theatre with Morrison's replacement, George Osbourne, the box office drew only $1,077. With nothing left to lose, $20,000 worth of tickets were given away for performances in the last two weeks of the run. The future of Curtis's new play was looking very doubtful as the *Oakland Tribune* of June 14, 1890, ominously predicted, "If the following from *Dunlop's Stage News* is true, M. B. Curtis's new play *The Shatchen* will probably not go on the road next season, owing to its comparative failure, and to the fact that when the play was booked it was with the understanding that Lewis Morrison was in the cast. When it was found that it was never Mr. Morrison's intention to go out with it, the dates were cancelled."

This reminder of the difficulties of keeping a theatrical company together might have been one of the reasons that Curtis signed with the managerial firm Locke and Davis on July 3, 1890, for a five-week tour of *The Shatchen* in syndicated theatres, where only the management company's signed talent would perform. The tour opened at the Bush Street Theatre in San Francisco on July 13, and one of the advance flyers for the upcoming production claimed that Curtis was actually a matchmaker and had opened a matrimonial bureau in the lobby of the theatre. Whether what happened before the last matinee performance was actual fact or a clever follow-up story to a rather risky promotional scheme, this account from the *Sunday Morning Constitution* (Chillicothe, Missouri) that was published on November 23, 1890, shows how the line between life and theatre often became blurred for Curtis.

> A buxom-looking girl of decided Semitic features called at the box-office and asked for Mr. Curtis. The polite ticket-seller told her that the gentleman was on the stage getting ready for the matinee. The girl, however, seemed so anxious to see Curtis that the obliging young man in the box-office, seeing it was early, sent around to the stage door for the jolly comedian. Curtis quickly responded, and, on seeing the young lady, supposed it was the usual request for tickets and that the lady was a professional. Raising his hat, he said to her in his suavest manner: "Would you like two?"
>
> "N-n-n-n-o!" stammered the girl, blushing

until her olive-tinted cheeks were like the bloom on the pomegranate. "Von will be enough."

"You can have two if you like," remarked the old-time Sam'l of Posen in dulcet tones.

The girl blushed still more, and turned and twisted in evident embarrassment.

"Give me one good seat," said Curtis to the ticket hustler. This was done, and he presented the coupon to the fair Jewess.

"Oh-h-h! I don't vant a ticket. I er-er-er-er vants a-a-a husband!"

The young man in the office nearly fell off his high stool, and Curtis blushed even more than the Hebraic damsel as he saw the point. He recovered himself, however, and said to her: "I'm awfully sorry, miss, but I have no good bargains in my catalogue. I'm expecting a job lot in a few days and will put you down for the first choice."

Unfortunately for Curtis, this possibly fictional young lady wasn't the only one who was disappointed at what was happening at the Bush Street Theatre that July. The *San Francisco Chronicle* did not like *The Shatchen*, complaining that the serious and comedic elements did not mesh. The San Francisco *Examiner* believed that Doblin and Dickson, the writers of the play, had an excellent theme—the possibility of a deep friendship being shattered by issues of differing religious beliefs—but the newspaper pointed out, as previous critics had, that too much comedy was inserted into this deep and heartfelt theme, reiterating that Curtis's presence did not "dignify" the more serious motive of the play. It is a rather tragic review for Curtis—acknowledging his superb magic, but deeming it out of place. Reviews were mixed, but mostly unfavorable for the play. But despite the disappointing reviews, Curtis and company embarked on their planned tour, performing in major cities as they worked their way toward Chicago and then on to the Grand Opera House in Denver on August 18, 1890.

Curtis then continued performing *The Shatchen* in various theatres on the East Coast. But early in November, he canceled a three-night run in Hoboken, New Jersey, due to his own ill health. An interview with Curtis published in the *Dramatic Mirror* on November 22, 1890, clarified Curtis's condition. "My plans for the future are all unsettled. I have been suffering for some time with catarrh of the stomach, and this is the first time the doctor has let me leave the house. I am getting well and just as soon as I am able I expect to resume work." The *Dramatic Mirror* also reported seeing Curtis on Sixth Avenue around this time. "The report that he was a sick man needed no further corroboration than his appearance. He looked pale and haggard."

One Atlanta paper felt that Curtis should stick to low comedy. "He is certainly out of place in *The Shatchen*, in which a Hebrew merchant disowns and curses his son for marrying a Gentile. The great cursing act is out of time in the nineteenth century and out of place in the United States . . . Curtis as the humorous Americanized Hebrew is as amusing as when he first presented the public with that type in *Sam'l of Posen*. He should try, however, to moderate the serious passages in the play, because at present they threaten to rival his own lines in comicality." And reports were circulating that the large amount of money Curtis had invested in *The Shatchen* and its lack of success were nursing the demon of the actor's excessive drinking.

M. B. Curtis wasn't the only major American artist during this time who was struggling to find a fresh outlet for his creativity —and to make enough money to pay his bills. Mark Twain had found himself in need of income for his family and his other business ventures, and in 1890 he arranged for his old friend Howard P. Taylor to write a stage adaptation of *A Connecticut Yankee in King Arthur's Court*. In July Taylor had a first draft, and Twain wrote to his daughter Clara and told her to keep it a secret that he disliked the adaptation Taylor had produced. However, Twain planned to go ahead with the play anyway despite his unhappiness with Taylor's script and the fact that Taylor had found no takers for the play after approaching almost every producer in New York City.

Taylor soon became nervous that Twain had lost faith in him and was turning to someone else after he read an article in *The World* stating that a certain well-known actor would be starring in the very play Taylor was trying to place. So Taylor wrote Twain on January 24, 1891, with a unique proposal contained in a letter curated by the Mark Twain Project at the Bancroft Library, UC Berkeley.

> I find after canvassing the matter thoroughly,
> that the only way to get a production is to
> allow some prominent star comedian to pro-
> duce it. I am quite sanguine I could make an
> arrangement with someone if you will consent
> to it. I read the piece this week to M. B. Curtis
> (the famous Sam'l of Posen), and he is quite

enthused over it, and says he will produce it
if we will allow him to make a modern American Jew of Morgan, and call the piece *Sam'l
of Posen at King Arthur's Court*, dramatized
from your work, etc., or founded upon incidents from it. He seems to understand the
fine points in the part, and would not make a
caricature of it. He says he would be willing to
spend between $15,000 and $20,000 upon the
production, and get an opening here for a long
run. I do not think his suggestion a bad one,
for, if you have seen him act, you will confess
his Hebrew idiosyncrasies are not unlike those
of such a Yankee as you have made Hank. It is
an opportunity such as we may not have again,
and is well worth considering. We did not talk
terms. The chief thing is, first, to get your consent to the change. That favorable, we would
then come to bushiness [Taylor is employing a
"Sam'lism" here].

One can imagine the great Mark Twain holding this letter,
smiling to himself, and saying, "Well, *bushiness* is *bushiness*."
But this letter also indicates to what extent Sam'l of Posen —
and Curtis's portrayal of him — had penetrated every level of
society.

Twain sent Taylor a telegram, which is also archived at the
Mark Twain Project, Bancroft Library, UC Berkeley and dated
January 29, 1891, that responded to the idea of Curtis playing
his New England Yankee character as a Hebrew in the vein
of Sam'l of Posen. BEEN AWAY. I LIKE THE IDEA BUT SUBMIT THE
TERMS TO ME BEFORE YOU CLOSE. SL CLEMS.

On January 30 Taylor wrote to Twain acknowledging the author's agreement to make the changes Curtis requested. Taylor believed the deal close to fruition and that "it only remains now for Curtis to come to business. He is playing this week somewhere in Pennsylvania, but will be in Brooklyn week after next, when, if he means business, I shall do all I can to settle it, and get the best terms possible." (Mark Twain Project, Bancroft Library, UC Berkeley.)

Getting wind of the plans to transform Hank into Sam'l, the *Dramatic Mirror* of February 14, 1891, reported, "I do not know, however, whether Mark Twain would consent to such a change. But I am sure of one thing—Mr. Curtis would make a great success of the piece."

The idea of pairing Sam'l of Posen and Hank Morgan might make the head spin at first. However, their creators had similar characteristics that might not have been lost on Twain and Curtis. Both Mark Twain and M. B. Curtis had had meteoric rises to success while their lavish spending caused them both money problems. Both men had financial success followed by failure and both were trying to re-create their earlier successes. And Twain was certainly no stranger to the character of the drummer, given his description of the conversation between two traveling salesmen in *Life on the Mississippi*.

And the Connecticut Yankee and the Hungarian Hebrew had more in common than one might suspect at first glance. The characters of Hank Morgan and Sam'l of Posen were both dropped into worlds they had little understanding of and both were obvious outsiders—Sam'l by his foreign dress, language, and manner; and Hank by his knowing nothing of the culture, manners, or political structure of the historical period he was transplanted to. Sam'l was thrown into the future in America, and Hank was transported into the past. Both characters succeeded by relying on their wits, creativity, and determination. Both achieved personal satisfaction on their own terms, even while their choices were limited at each step. Sam'l's desire was to be a part of his new world, to profit within it, and to help others; Hank wanted to profit from his alien environment while helping those willing to confront the culture's medieval ways. Both men maintained a strong sense of self and a clear vision through their many challenges in the brave new worlds they found themselves in.

But American audiences were not destined to see one of America's most popular actors play one of America's best-known fictional characters. By March 8, 1891, Taylor had written to Twain that he had not yet finalized an agreement with Curtis. Curtis had been in the city for a couple of weeks but was so busy with engagements for the short time he was there that he did not meet with Taylor. The two were hoping to meet toward the end of the month when Curtis would return to New York. Taylor had spoken to Curtis's brother Frank, who had assured Taylor that his brother wanted to do the piece and that as soon as Curtis returned to the city he would "give his whole attention to it."

Despite this promise from Frank, Taylor, under increasing pressure to sell the rights to his adaptation for Twain, kept shopping the play around.

On April 25, 1891, Taylor wrote Twain that he had made an arrangement with some managers in New York who had offered 5 percent of the gross for the rights to produce *A Connecticut Yankee in King Arthur's Court*. The managers wanted to open in Philadelphia at the Grand Opera House in the early summer of 1891 for a test run before bringing it to New York City. Taylor informed Twain that he might have to "alter the tournament scene and eliminate the horses, as they can only

be used on very large stages." Taylor advised Twain to accept
the offer as he wrote, "I do not know that we can do better."

Twain responded within a couple of days. "I approve of
the terms proposed in your letter of the 25th instant." On
April 30, Twain responded to Taylor with a signed agreement
for the upcoming production, but the work never made it into
production, and the idea fell into oblivion.

One of the reasons that Curtis failed to meet with Taylor to
discuss his playing Hank Morgan was that Curtis was busy in
court and in various managers' offices as the new year of 1891
dawned. Curtis was so disappointed in what he considered
Locke and Davis's poor management of *The Shatchen* that he
sued them for $20,000 in damages for incompetence and then
signed a three-year management contract with Gustave Kahn.
Kahn told the New York press, "We shall revive *Sam'l of Posen*
now . . . most probably in this city." Curtis was returning to the
play that had given him fame and fortune, evidently seeking a
theatrical life raft in his sea of current rough waters.

The new production of *Sam'l of Posen* opened in Detroit.
Kahn traveled there to inspect his handiwork. "I have just
returned from Detroit, where Mr. Curtis has played a return
engagement to packed houses. He seems to be as popular as
ever as Sam'l of Posen." And the *Detroit Free Press* concurred
on February 3, 1891. "The revival of *Sam'l of Posen* seems to
be one of the happiest theatrical ventures of the season. The
warm reception it received is convincing proof that the public
were ready and eager to welcome it, and the considerable new
material that has been worked into it tends to brighten it."
Buoyed by mostly good reviews, the Curtises played houses
from Jersey City to San Francisco, closing in the middle of

The luxurious interior of the Peralta Park Hotel. (The Bancroft Library, UC Berkeley, BANC PIC 19.xx.040:014 – PIC, Pictorial miscellany of Berkeley, Calif. views [graphic], C. T. Blake residence interior)

March so they could spend the summer in California.

But in spite of new management, Curtis's money troubles continued. And his new manager was having money issues of his own. One of the actresses in the company had reportedly advanced Gustave Kahn about $1,000 and wanted the loan re-paid, and the manager got into a dispute over pay when Walter Harcourt decided to leave the company. In addition to this, the Neilson Lithographic Co. issued an attachment for printing against Mr. Curtis, but found nothing to attach. "The theatrical company was on sinking financial ground," according to the *New York Clipper* on March 28, 1891.

When the Curtises arrived back in Berkeley on April 1, they announced that the Peralta Park Hotel was about to open its doors. But on April 23, 1891, Curtis gave up his grand

dream of running a luxurious hotel when it was announced
that the Peralta Park Hotel would be leased as a young ladies'
seminary for ten years even though much work still remained
to complete the finishing touches.

The school was due to open for business on May 15. In
the meantime, Curtis honored his commitments to finish the
grounds and furnish the interior of the building. Curtis may
have been down, but he was definitely not out. His instinct
for showmanship was as sharp as ever—even when he was
ordering furniture for the hotel. "M. B. Curtis never forgets
to advertise Berkeley whenever an opportunity occurs. Three
days ago fifteen carloads of furniture for the Peralta Park Hotel started from Grand Rapids. On both sides of each rail car
there is posted a large banner bearing the following legend:
Furniture for the Hotel del Peralta, Berkeley, Cal., M. B. Curtis,
Proprietor," trumpeted the *Oakland Tribune* on June 15, 1891.

The hotel, now a school, was finally completed on July 1, 1891.
However, the Peralta Hall School closed after only a year,
and the building was then badly damaged when the Judson
Powder Mills exploded down by the bayshore. A reporter from
the *San Francisco Chronicle* wrote about his walking around
the deserted building on August 26, 1894: "And the actor's
hotel stands deserted. Its empty halls and parlors, with their
remnants of luxury and comfort, look as if in other days they
might have held many a company of revelers, but they never
did. Seminary girls could hardly be called revelers any more
than could the quiet family which now occupies one corner of
the place. The Peralta Park Hotel is simply a white elephant.
Its builder is seeking fortune and obscurity goodness knows
where. Probably he has had enough of the hotel business." In

1903 it was purchased for St. Joseph's Academy, and then by Saint Mary's College High School under the auspices of the Christian Brothers, who affectionately called the ex-hotel the "Palace."

In mid-July, while Curtis was preparing for an upcoming tour of *Sam'l of Posen*, Marie received a letter from France informing her that the grandmother she had taken her stage name from had passed away. The letter also informed Marie that she would receive a portion of her grandmother's estate, and the *Berkeley Herald* informed readers on July 16, 1891, that the Curtises would visit France in September. But they wouldn't leave for the Continent until they saw the world-renowned actress Sarah Bernhardt play Camille, a role that Marie had performed with great success. The Curtises planned to attend a performance in San Francisco on September 10, 1891, with their good friends Dr. and Mrs. Cook—an evening at the theatre that would have tragic consequences off stage as well as on.

CHAPTER EIGHT

Trials and Tribulations

If I had stayed with my poor wife,
this thing would not have happened.
—M. B. Curtis

⁓

Sarah Bernhardt had arrived in San Francisco in April 1891 as part of the longest world tour she would ever undertake. She was traveling with a special eight-car train, which also transported sets, costumes, baggage, her troupe, her huge Great Dane, a Skye terrier, a three-pound butterfly terrier, three cats, and her own drawing room, complete with a piano, Oriental rugs, a substantial collection of bric-a-brac, and so many flowers that the space looked like a garden.

After a short stop in the city, she headed for Australia and was scheduled to return to San Francisco to perform again at the Grand Opera House on September 4. A series of storms and heavy seas delayed her voyage, and she did not arrive back in San Francisco until September 5, giving every crew member twenty-five dollars for bringing the ship in safely.

After a quick trip to the Hotel Del Monte in Monterey and the marriage of two troupe members back in San Francisco,

The actress Sarah Bernhardt. (Private collection)

Bernhardt opened her run on September 10, 1891, with the
Curtises planning to attend the opening night performance as
Marie was a huge fan and performed *Camille* herself.

On the evening of September 10, 1891, Curtis and Marie

and their close friends Dr. and Mrs. Cook entered San Francisco's massive Grand Opera House at Mission Street between Third and Fourth streets to see the theatrical world's most popular female star. By about ten p.m., after watching a good portion of Sarah Bernhardt's performance from box F, one patron grew very restless and had to leave. M. B. Curtis rose from his chair and whispered to his wife that he was going out for a break and would visit his friend William Kreling and return before the play was over.

He left the theatre and walked directly to the Tivoli Theatre on Eddy Street, where his friend Kreling was the proprietor. They drank and talked in the bar with other patrons until about 11:15 p.m. when Curtis suddenly realized that the play must already be over and that he needed to rush back to pick up his wife.

At 12:25 a.m., September 11, 1891, three shots were fired on Folsom Street between Fourth and Fifth streets, about 120 feet from the Mission Street police station. On hearing the shots, the police on duty that night charged out of the station house. Outside, to their sudden horror, they found their fellow officer, Alexander Grant, lying on the sidewalk, dead of a gunshot to the forehead, the bullet lodged in the back of his skull. Death was instantaneous for the forty-year-old native of Nova Scotia.

Upon rushing out, one officer saw a man running in the distance and pursued him down Folsom Street and then Fifth Street. He caught up with him at Shipley Street and discovered M. B. Curtis stumbling drunkenly. Curtis had police nippers (a type of handcuff that tightens its grip if the person resists) attached to his right wrist and kept that hand in his pocket as he ran. The officer placed him under arrest. Curtis strongly denied doing anything and told the officer what had happened.

Curtis said that he was walking from the Tivoli to try to get back to his wife and catch the last ferry home to Berkeley. He turned onto Mission Street and heard something behind him. Before he could turn around, he was hit on the head and knocked unconscious. When he came to, a police officer was arresting him and another man, apparently his stalker, and was in the process of taking both of them to the police station. When the three men were almost in front of the station, the other man pulled out a gun and shot the officer. Curtis said he had been drinking and, thinking his life was in danger, his first reaction was to run.

The intoxicated Curtis was said to have talked "in an incoherent and excited manner" while he was insisting that he had no pistol and had not shot the officer. At times he groaned with "the most despairing cries, wringing his hands and manifesting extreme emotion," according to the next day's *Oakland Enquirer*.

Curtis was taken by a horse-drawn police patrol wagon to the city prison. A group of officers there were surprised to see the dapper actor step to the ground from inside the wagon. He was escorted into the prison, charged with murder, and put in a cell directly opposite the keeper's desk.

Even though Curtis maintained that he was under the influence, some people thought he was acting the part of a drunk. But his face was said to have a look of "utter bewilderment, and his eyes moved about nervously, wonderingly from face to face. He smiled now and then, and walked with an unsteady step to the cell. Once inside he sat down to await developments," said the *Examiner* the morning after the murder. The newspaper quoted Curtis as saying, "I've nothing to state at all . . . All I remember was someone grabbed me, whirled me around and about, and after that, coming in the patrol wagon with handcuffs jabbed on. I tried to explain to the police, but they would not let me." Curtis went on to tell the *Examiner* writer his side of the story.

> I was at the Grand Opera House tonight with my wife in box F. I paid $25 for the box, because I wanted Mrs. Curtis to see Bernhardt in *Camille*. I left the theatre about 10 o'clock to go up to the Tivoli with Billy Kreling. Billy and I had a drink of whisky together, and then I left him to return to the theatre for my wife.
>
> But when I got to the corner of Third and Mission streets, I was tumbled in the gutter and after that I remember nothing, only somebody pulling and jerking me about till I found myself in the wagon with handcuffs on me.
>
> I wonder where my wife is now. She must be wild about me, but she does not know I'm here.

The *Examiner* followed up by stating that Curtis was "generally looked on as a talkative, rather good-natured fellow, and about the last person in the world to commit an act of violence."

But the police were convinced they had their man based on the fact that Curtis was caught running away from where the homicide occurred and the fact that he had a pair of handcuffs dangling from his right wrist, proof that Alexander Grant had arrested him, although Curtis maintained that the nippers were put on him when the police picked him up after the crime already happened. The facts in the case were already becoming murky as some witnesses immediately reported seeing Grant collapse as another man ran off into the night while others reported seeing two men run away.

The police hurriedly commenced their investigation, putting six officers on the case, and they concluded that Officer Grant had not searched Curtis when he arrested the actor and that this failure to follow standard procedure had cost the policeman his life. The *San Francisco Call* reported on September 13 that the investigators could find no witnesses who saw the initial arrest, only the aftermath. However, as the days wore on, many supposed eyewitnesses came forward with wildly varying stories, possibly the result of cash being spread around in preparation for the upcoming trial.

Tivoli Theatre owner William Kreling was one of the first witnesses whose story changed as the investigation continued. He first stated that when Curtis left his establishment at 11:30 the actor was rather drunk and speaking in an excited manner. Days later, Kreling was quoted as saying that Curtis left his bar in a sober condition, though he might have been drinking some. The *Reno Evening Gazette* posted an interview with Kreling the morning of September 11, asking the theatre owner if Curtis had a pistol on him when he visited the Tivoli. Kreling replied, "No, he did not and there was no occasion for such a subject to be mentioned. He seemed to be perfectly contented with life and its surroundings and had no complaints to make."

A rumor began circulating that Curtis had been drinking heavily of late, and some people were even speculating about his general mental state. One newspaper reported that his friends said that he had been acting queerly and had spoken of returning to the stage, but the actor had taken no steps in that direction. The article went on to surmise that the failures of Curtis's last couple of plays were pressing hard on him.

But Curtis had regained his composure by the second day after his arrest and spoke "at times glibly," according to the United Press reporter who interviewed the jailed actor. The September 13 *San Francisco Call* quoted Curtis as saying, "Don't ask me anything about this trouble for my attorneys have insisted upon my saying nothing . . . I am only too glad to see you, and will tell you anecdotes or anything else I can that will be of interest, but don't ask me about this, please . . . I never was considered a blood-thirsty man. I don't think I could kill one of those cockroaches crawling up the wall there. My poor little wife feels terribly about this matter. When she was coming over here yesterday morning, she fainted several times." The article went on to note, "It is apparent that he is still laboring under great excitement, and his confinement in the tank, where he can speak to no one, is almost intolerable."

Pursuing their investigation, the San Francisco police sawed out two fence planks that had bullet holes in them, one low in the gate and another one in the boards above it. The investigators believed the first shot had made the upper hole as the pistol was shot close to policeman Grant's face. They believed the second bullet penetrated his forehead and lodged in his skull while Grant was bending his head down. The last bullet was believed to have been fired at a lower target, possibly after Grant had fallen about eight feet from the fence.

The San Francisco shooting and Curtis's arrest became national news overnight and offered newspapers a chance to indulge in a bit of moralizing about guns and alcohol. The day after the shooting, the *New York Times* reported that Curtis said he did not shoot the officer and was not even carrying a gun. The *Examiner* made the point that when carrying a gun in a city like San Francisco it will be used in a tragic way nine times out of ten, noting that it would be safer to be without a gun. "Especially should a man who ever allows liquor to get the better of him shun deadly weapons as he would a rattlesnake. He never can tell when they will bite." The *Berkeley Advocate* also took the opportunity to espouse the evils of "excessive use of liquor" saying that if something like this befell Curtis then no one is safe.

In Boston, the day after the shooting, theatre people were in shock. F. E. Piper, the treasurer of the Park Theatre, on being informed of the news, exclaimed in an unsourced newspaper article found in the Harvard Theater Collection, "You have astounded me. If it had been anybody but Curtis, I should not have been so astonished. I always found him the embodiment of good nature and sociability—never quarrelsome. He was that sort of man whom, when you had met him once, you always desired to see him again."

While many of his friends were visiting Curtis at the city jail the day after the shooting, San Francisco policemen were

A rendering of Curtis in his San Francisco jail cell the day of the murder of Officer Grant. (The San Francisco Examiner, *September 12, 1891)*

staring with saddened disbelief at the body of Alexander Grant lying on the coroner's table. As the *Examiner* described on September 12, 1891, "Police officers crowded around the body as it lay upon the hospital table and stood silently there contemplating the face with its ghastly pallor and the blood trickling from the wound in the forehead . . . The dead man was dressed as they were, in the rough and heavy clothes worn on morning watches, and a flannel shirt close up around his throat, only the star was not upon his breast."

A newsboy named Ginsburg who said he was arrested and shared the cell with Curtis the night of the murder said that Curtis had talked all night long. The newsboy would not say what the content of the talk was. "But I think Curtis will have to hang," he was quoted as saying by the *Oakland Enquirer*.

Curtis complained to the *Examiner* of deceptions instigated by the police, who seemed determined to establish his guilt.

> Today, three men came to me, and one of them declared that he was greatly interested in my behalf. He spoke in German and told me that that large-hearted friend of mine, Bill Kreling, had sent him to me to see if he could be of service. I told him after he had spoken to me for some time that I could not under-stand German, and then one of his compan-ions commenced to address me in French. They asked me who gave me the pistol with which I shot the policeman, where I obtained my drink that night, where I was arrested by Grant, and such questions as that.
>
> I believed them, and thought Kreling had some special object in drawing from me an

answer to these questions, but before I could
do so, my attorney, Henry I. Kowalsky, appeared
and recognized the men as three policemen . . .
There was quite a lively scene for a few mo-
ments, but Kowalsky ordered them out, and
they went.

That same day, Curtis's defense team, now consisting of
George A. Knight, Colonel Henry Kowalsky, H. H. Lowenthal,
and the firm of Napthaly, Friedenrich & Ackerman, made a
public statement of the actor's innocence. They told the press
that the evidence against their client was strictly circumstantial and that he did not carry a gun. There was also talk that
Curtis would hire the famous defense attorney W. W. Foote to
be a major part of his assembled team of lawyers.

San Francisco Police Chief Patrick Crowley immediately
dismissed the defense statements and promised that when
the evidence was in it would be clear that Curtis killed Grant.
They had witnesses, Crowley said, and the powder marks on
Grant's forehead and the two bullets that missed (and whose
holes were in the fence nearby) suggested a close-range firing.
Crowley thought that Curtis must have been lying in a doorway and that Grant had arrested him for drunkenness.

On September 14 a coroner's inquest with a jury of more
than a dozen people found that Curtis should be held over for
trial. Curtis did not testify or appear, as was his legal right. But
the jury heard from many other witnesses. A man who had
repaired Officer Grant's nippers testified that he recognized
them by the special spring he used in a repair. A tamale salesman spoke through an interpreter about knowing Grant and
seeing Grant and a prisoner at Sixth and Folsom around 12:15
a.m. The witness testified that Grant held the prisoner by his

right hand as he turned down Folsom Street. They passed by
the witness, at which point he closed up the tamale stand and
went home and never heard the shooting.

Then a Mrs. Annie Johnson, who was standing by a window nursing a sick child, said she heard a noise, opened her
window, and saw two men — one short and one tall — scuffling
near the fence with one of the men saying at least three times,
"Come along now." She claimed to have seen the flash of a
gunshot followed by a loud report, which was quickly followed
by two more shots, and the tall man fell. She said she saw the
short man run and the police pour out of the station, some
to tend to their fallen comrade and others to chase after the
running man.

A Mrs. Jennie Holder, who lived across from the police
station, testified that she had company over that night and
was still up when she heard the shots and ran to see what was
happening. She saw two men scuffling, with the smaller man,
who was dressed in a dark coat and hat, trying to get away.
She thought if the police arrested the man who ran off, then
they had their shooter. But no one at the inquest seems to
have questioned this witness about how she could have seen
the scuffle if she had run to see what was happening only
after the shots had been fired and the shooter had run off. As
the inquest proceeded, Mrs. Holder's testimony would not be
the only statement that suffered from questionable logic or
contradictions.

The biggest news that came out in the coroner's inquest
was that a probable murder weapon had been found. But even
the discovery of this vital piece of evidence came with conflicting claims. A mold maker named Edward Toomey testified that
he was across the street from the murder and witnessed it,
later finding a still-warm revolver on Fifth Street near Folsom.

But another witness claimed to have also been an eyewitness to the murder and that *he* had found the gun. This witness, a man named Thomas Mullins of 26 Shipley Street, testified that he was within one hundred feet of Grant when he was shot and saw the incident.

> My friend said to me, "Get on to those two
> drunks trying to take each other home." Then
> I heard three shots. After the three shots were
> fired myself and friend ran toward the car
> track, when we saw a man run away. My friend
> ran after him while I went over to the man we
> saw fall. As I did so, two officers came toward
> him, and one officer [a man named] Bode
> stumbled over him. Then more officers came
> up and sent for the patrol wagon. I helped put
> his body in the patrol wagon and then went
> to the police station and gave our names. We
> started home, and when near the corner of
> Fifth and Folsom I saw something glisten in
> the sand. I stopped and picked up a pistol. It
> was the one shown here . . . The man who ran
> away looked as if he had on a Prince Albert
> coat and what looked like a black Derby hat.

To confuse matters even more, Curtis's attorney Henry Kowalsky would later testify that these two witnesses, Toomey and Mullins, had approached him about "doing business" and claimed they asked him, "How much is it?" Unfortunately, testifying to anything that someone would pay for was not an uncommon practice in the San Francisco of 1891.

The *Examiner* claimed, after publishing the transcripts of

a number of witnesses' testimonies, that "all of the witnesses assert that there was no one else on that side of the street, so that any theory that the shooting might have been done by a third person is effectually disposed of." But the newspaper overlooked some key discrepancies in the various statements made at the inquest. How could so many witnesses on the same street fail to see each other, and why did police accounts not mention the other people on the scene, especially those who supposedly assisted them?

Officer John Allen, the officer who had arrested Curtis, said that the actor began to speak when they reached the body of Officer Grant. "Would that I could recall the last four hours," Curtis supposedly said. "If I had stayed with my poor wife, this thing would not have happened." The officer testified that "at the station I searched him rapidly and found no weapons. Then I went out to look for the pistol. The prisoner kept on making different statements about being at the Grand Opera House and the Tivoli." But Officer Allen said that he did not think Curtis was drunk enough to have been arrested for that by Officer Grant.

Five days after the murder there was still no evidence as to whom the pistol found at Fifth and Folsom belonged to. It was a Smith and Wesson double-action, hammerless, six-chambered gun. Three chambers had been fired. The serial number was 48,705, giving police the hope they could discover who purchased the gun. In spite of an intensive search, the police did not find the two bullets that went through the fence. Two detectives stated that they were told a day or two after the murder that two men who were not from the police force had come around the scene offering neighborhood boys $1.50 for each bullet recovered, but no evidence of this or bullets were offered.

One of Curtis's visitors in jail was John E. Boyd, a popular Berkeley moving man who had many friends in both high and low places. Boyd returned to Berkeley and reminded everyone that although Curtis was charged with a crime he was not convicted. He asked in an *Advocate* editorial, "Where is the man who has done more for our town? Who made a commodious park out of a cow pasture? Who has induced a desirable class of people to build fine residences in the same neighborhood? Who engineered the grading of Hopkins Street through the town board and who pays for a large part of the work? Who was head and front of the Peralta Hotel? Who sunk every dollar in property in town?"

But even in Berkeley, opinions about Curtis's innocence or guilt were mixed, as this September 17, 1891, article in the *Berkeley Advocate* shows. "He has been genial, jovial and hospitable, with a merry smile and kindly word for everyone, and it was deemed impossible that he could commit so fearful a deed. Many have full faith in his innocence, believing he is the victim of some dreadful chain of circumstances, and that he must be cleared. Others fear that, under the influence

The revolver purportedly used to murder Officer Grant. Despite having a serial number on it, no owner was ever discovered. (The San Francisco Examiner, *September 12, 1891)*

of liquor, and suffering from the torture of the nippers in the hands of a too zealous guardian of the peace, he may, in self-defense, have fired the fatal shot . . . The cursed liquor was at fault."

And some people were suspicious of the police force's desire to quickly arrest the killer of their colleague. Known as a good-natured and kind man, Alexander Grant had been one of the most popular men on the San Francisco police force, having served the city as an officer since July 1886. When a police captain was asked about Curtis, he sounded very sure of Curtis's guilt in an unsourced newspaper article found in the Harvard Theater Collection. "Well, I think it was a cold-blooded murder. I think that Grant arrested him because he was drunk and disorderly. He went along quiet enough until he got to Folsom Street, where he thought he could kill the policeman and affect his escape."

A United Press reporter went to Dr. Cook's home on Post Street in San Francisco and found Mrs. Cook weeping. She was horrified that Curtis was being charged with this crime as she felt the actor was always "such a harmless little man who would not break Mrs. Curtis's heart."

While the reporter was still there, Marie arrived at the Cook home. Marie answered the reporter's questions by saying that Curtis "was not intoxicated as the papers seem to say. In fact, I did not know that he drank to excess." She told how she had just made the last ferry at 12:15. "He could not be found. I thought that he was talking to friends on business and I would meet him on the train, but he was not and I had to ride home alone in our carriage, which was waiting for us at Berkeley. I thought he had missed the boat and thought no more of it until I saw the papers in the morning," the *Oakland Enquirer* reported her saying.

When asked if her husband carried a pistol, Mrs. Curtis replied, "No, at least not that I know of. I never knew him to carry a weapon except when he went hunting. I think there must be some mistake about the whole thing."

Public opinion was swinging back and forth with every new revelation, rumor, or published opinion. And on September 15, 1891, the *Philadelphia Inquirer* kept the theory alive that there was a third man who killed Grant.

> There has developed a remarkable change of public sentiment, and half the people now believe that M. B. Curtis, the comedian, is an innocent man. The theory of Curtis's friends that another hand than his fired the shot which killed Officer Grant gains support from a story told by Eli Denison, who has charge of the news matter distributed on trains of the Southern Pacific Company.
>
> Denison, who lives in Oakland, makes the following statement: "On the ferry boat, Sunday, I met a man I know by sight."
>
> "This talk about Curtis having done the killing is all a mistake," said the stranger. "I met a man to-day who says he saw the tragedy, and he is ready to take oath that Grant and Curtis were accompanied by a third man, who did the shooting and then ran."

One New York columnist wrote that Curtis would enter a plea of insanity and argued that his behavior when last in New York City demonstrated that mental state. The writer said he saw a "good deal of him, and so did a number of my friends

Officer Alexander Grant. (The San Francisco Examiner, *September 12, 1891)*

who from time to time told me of his remarkable conduct. I must say it did not impress at the time as being at all the behavior of an insane man, but that of a drunken rowdy. Those who have known Curtis longest and best are fully aware that when he drank liquor he became turbulent, offensive, and belligerent."

Officer Grant's body was placed at the Masonic Temple on September 14, 1891, for those who wished to view him one last time. Thousands gathered on Post Street trying to get into the building. There were many floral arrangements, and a Reverend Smith offered a heartfelt eulogy.

At three p.m. that day, Grant's casket was carried to its final resting place. There were forty-eight uniformed policemen on duty in the procession and it was reported that almost every policeman not on duty was present wearing street clothes, their stars cloaked in black crepe to mourn the fifth policeman killed in the line of duty in the city's history.

On the day of Grant's funeral, the coroner's jury charged Curtis with murder despite hearing some conflicting testimony and not being presented with any evidence that the gun found on Fifth and Folsom was Curtis's.

Other papers around the country followed the goings-on in San Francisco concerning Curtis. The *Chicago Tribune* wrote on October 25, 1891, "It is charged by certain journals on the Pacific coast that the police of San Francisco are in a conspiracy to convict M. B. Curtis (Sam'l of Posen) for the murder of a policeman. It is claimed that two or three witnesses have already admitted that the testimony which they had given against the actor was secured by intimidation by the police. Although there is circumstantial evidence against Mr. Curtis, there are also many facts in his favor and he certainly should have fair play even if he is an actor."

While Curtis was stuck in jail, Marie and his defense team were scrambling to prepare for the upcoming trial. A week after the murder, an ad in the *Berkeley Advocate* offered a "handsome suburban residence" for sale at "great sacrifice." The owner was M. B. Curtis. The Curtises were now attempting to quickly sell about one hundred lots in Peralta Park in addition to their own residence, which was sold at about half its value, to raise money for the actor's legal defense.

The upcoming trial of M. B. Curtis was being touted by many newspapers (including the *Manitoba Daily Free Press* on December 30, 1891) as "one of the strangest in the court annals of San Francisco, and it may be said, without any exaggeration, that when the trial comes off it will be as sensational as any criminal trial of recent years." Much of the sensation was attributed to the anticipated role of the San Francisco Police Department. A Berkeley newspaper commented on the prevalence and influence of police corruption in San Francisco at the time. "The victim of Curtis's pistol was on the force—and in a policeman's eyes, the killing of a policeman is something more than murder. It is sacrilege. If, therefore, policemen stand ready to perjure themselves . . . to secure conviction, merely as a matter of principle, in ordinary cases, almost any development in the line of crooked testimony is to be looked for when it comes to the trial of Curtis."

Henry Jeransen, Curtis's former gardener at Peralta Park, had taken the stand in a preliminary hearing after the coroner's inquest and stated that he had personally seen Curtis with the pistol that was identified as the murder weapon. Following a weekend where he must have been tormented about the consequences of what he had said, Jeransen voluntarily took the stand again to tell the court that his previous testimony was not true. He stated how he had never seen Curtis with a pistol and that he had said what he did the previous week because the San Francisco police had threatened him severely. He said that he was scared and did what they requested of him, but that he found he could not live with himself and

wanted to tell the truth (*Arizona Republican*, October 6, 1891).
There were a number of articles about other prosecution witnesses who were coerced—or worse—by the police for their
testimony. A writer for *The Wave*, a San Francisco magazine,
stated in an undated opinion piece, "There is no testimony
against Curtis; the circumstantial evidence is in his favor;
and the character of the witnesses for the State will hurt the
case. Two of the principal witnesses wanted to know what the
defense would give them to leave town; the police have shown
a bitterness of feeling that will destroy the value of anything
they say, and the array of legal talent, W. W. Foote, George
Knight, and J. N. E. Wilson will be hard to beat. Curtis will not
be found guilty."

At the preliminary hearing before the trial, Curtis sat with
Marie and his attorneys in Police Court in Judge Alfred Rix's
courtroom. Curtis reacted to some of the testimony by shaking
his head or whispering something to his lawyers or his wife.
When the testimony got to an important event, Curtis would
"chew vigorously on some gum-drops which he had before
him in a paper bag. Curtis bears his confinement well and
does not appear to be much worried at the final outcome of
his case," the *Morning Call* opined on October 11, 1891.

A number of people testified who had already spoken at
the coroner's inquest. Officer Bode (one of the policemen who
had rushed to Officer Grant's body) testified about witnessing
the scene after the shooting. Bode was cross-examined and
admitted that he came to Curtis's cell in civilian clothes the
morning after the shooting. But he denied that he had tried
to extort a confession from Curtis by fraud and false damning
statements.

Curtis's attorney W. W. Foote accused the police officers
present, especially Officer Newman (who had transported

Curtis from the crime scene in a patrol wagon), of making signals to the witnesses and the court went on alert to stop any such actions. In another blow to the prosecution's case, Officer Allen admitted that he had allowed a witness to testify at the coroner's inquest even though he knew the witness was lying and that he had not informed the court or the defense of this fact (*San Francisco Chronicle*, October 11, 1891).

Then a new "eyewitness," a Joseph Denny, took the stand. He testified that he had witnessed the entire crime from a doorway across the street. Upon cross-examination, it was learned that Denny had had to resign from the post office due to drunkenness and that when he had been arrested for burglary, Officer Grant had helped to get the case dismissed.

Despite the dubious testimony presented at the preliminary hearing, Curtis was denied bail and was sent back to jail to await his trial, which would be presided over by Judge James Morris Troutt. This left Marie to run the couple's real estate dealings even though Curtis's brother Frank had rushed out from the East Coast to help in any way he could. In order to raise money for her husband's increasing legal expenses, Marie put more Peralta Park property up for sale, saying that she would accept $175,000 for land valued at $250,000. Two men, James P. McCarthy and M. W. Connor of San Francisco, supposedly representing interested parties from Los Angeles and the East, approached Marie with an offer. The *Berkeley Advocate* reported that Marie "recorded" an agreement for the sale of "a large portion of Peralta Park, including Peralta Hall, for the sum of $125,000." But the deal proved fictitious and Marie had to file suit against the two men who were demanding their commission anyway. Marie alleged fraud and conspiracy that put a cloud on her title to the property, and she demanded a $100,000 judgment against them, according to

Judge James Morris Troutt, District Attorney William S. Barnes, and Defense Attorney W. W. Foote. From an undated Wave. *(Private collection)*

the *Berkeley Advocate* on November 19, 1891.

Curtis again asked to be released on bail, but the Supreme Court denied bail and stated that the evidence, if not contradicted, would justify a conviction and the law read that if proof of guilt is "evident or the presumption great," no bail should be given.

Even before the trial started, some disturbing rumors arose about Judge Troutt's standards. The *Wave* commented in its December 26, 1891, edition that "W. W. Foote, one of the defendant's attorneys, asked that the case be postponed until January 15, alleging indisposition and weariness—the results of his labors in the Howell case in Oakland. Judge Troutt refused. In his determination to proceed at once with the empanelment of a jury he was absolutely inexorable. Nothing would induce him to grant a further stay of proceedings." But Judge Troutt ended up delaying the trial after Foote's second request. The *Wave* speculated that this delay was obtained from Troutt after J. N. E. Wilson was added to Curtis's defense team.

> Much put out, for his physical condition was
> the reverse of vigorous, Mr. Foote prepared to

go ahead when someone whispered that were
J. N. E. Wilson given a retainer of $1000, the
continuance could easily be obtained. It may
be explained that the Judge and Mr. Wilson
were partners prior to the former's elevation to
the bench. The suggestion was acted upon, Mr.
Wilson was retained and when, on the following day, Mr. Foote again preferred a request
that the trial be postponed, the Judge courte-
ously asked him how long he desired to recu-
perate and set the case for the day in January
that best suited his convenience . . . Curtis's
attorneys, George A. Knight and W. W. Foote,
have evidence to show who shot Policeman
Grant, and they will also demonstrate that the
police have known from the first day who did
the shooting, but that they preferred to work
up a case against Curtis rather than reveal the
name of the man who committed the murder.

While rumors were floated that Curtis's defense team was
obtaining mounting evidence that the police were railroading
Curtis, jury selection began in January of 1892. Empaneling
a jury proved to be as difficult as the rest of the proceedings.
One potential juror was dismissed after he revealed that his
two previous jury duties resulted in hangings, an admission
that caused repressed laughter in the courtroom. Another
potential juror was dismissed when he responded, "No, sir, I
never place any reliance upon the evidence of police officers,"
which again elicited chuckles in the courtroom.

Other potential jurors were released due to a variety of

reasons: living out of San Francisco, a sick wife, a conviction that the death penalty was vile, defective hearing, and being more than seventy years old and unable to endure the rigors of the trial. A man who stared blankly after every question, including if he understood English, was laughed at and excused. As soon as the judge stated that he was excused, the man jumped up and quickly pushed his way out of the courtroom, which brought even more uproarious laughter. The judge dryly said, "I see he understands that much English," according to the *San Francisco Call* on February 2, 1892.

After fifty-one of the first fifty-three prospective members had been rejected, a jury was finally empaneled on February 3, 1892, and the trial immediately began in Judge Troutt's courtroom, Superior Court Department 8. The room was packed to "beyond its doors and into the corridor, as in fact, it has been ever since the tedious process of getting a jury began . . . No one would know from his demeanor that he [Curtis] was anything more than an unimportant witness in the trial." Curtis's three attorneys seemed "cheerful and confident as ever," the

Augustine Marcoval testifying that he saw Grant and Curtis right before the shooting. (The San Francisco Examiner, *September 16, 1891)*

San Francisco Chronicle reported on February 4, 1892.

It wasn't long into the first day of the trial before the credibility of some of the prosecution's witnesses was called into question. When the prosecution put Augustine Marcoval on the stand (the tamale salesman who had testified at the coroner's inquest), he needed a Spanish interpreter. After some questioning, Foote, one of Curtis's attorneys, who knew something of Spanish, stated the interpreter was not phrasing the questions correctly and the interpreter was admonished.

On cross-examination, Marcoval testified that he wasn't sure of the statement he signed and that the police had written it out and told him to just sign his name.

"I think it was below what they had written. When they got through writing, they told me to sign my name. When they told me to sign my name, I signed it," Marcoval said through the interpreter.

"Did they read the paper to you?" asked Foote.

Marcoval responded that he couldn't remember if they had.

After the police surgeon who had done the autopsy on Officer Grant and several other witnesses had testified, the court was adjourned for the day.

The following day, the prosecution presented some of its most important evidence. The circumstantial evidence did not seem to disturb Curtis or Marie, who was always by his side in the courtroom. "Curtis wore a smiling face and a little bouquet of pinks. He and his wife frequently chat in a pleasant way, and in the courtroom, before and after the sessions, Curtis jokes with attorneys, reporters and other acquaintances, tells stories and tries to make things pleasant generally for those who have to attend his trial . . . He displays a good deal of confidence in his defense, which, whatever it is, has not yet been given to the public," said the *San Francisco Chronicle* on February 5, 1892.

Maurice and Marie maintained a visceral closeness.

On February 9, 1892, Officer Bode took the stand and denied that he took any special interest in procuring witnesses and denied "bullyragging" Curtis in his jail cell the morning after the murder. He also denied yelling at Curtis, "You dirty little Jew ***, you are in a hot box!"

When asked why he went to the jail the morning after Curtis's arrest, Officer Bode said that the police surgeon had ordered him there as Curtis was claiming that hoodlums had attacked him. Bode testified that he had found no bruises on Curtis's body save for his right wrist where the nippers were attached.

When Officer John Allen took the stand, he stated that Curtis was not drunk when Allen arrested him even though other prosecution witnesses had testified that they had seen a very drunken man running with difficulty.

Allen testified that "Curtis commenced to stagger, and I said to him: 'You did not stagger just now when you were running. You need not do so now.' Then he straightened up."

"Do you mean he pretended to be drunk?" asked Foote.

"He was simulating drunkenness. He was not drunk."

The prosecution then objected to the next few questions Foote posed to Allen, and Foote pounded his desk and exclaimed, "We want to show that not only is the defendant a victim of unfortunate circumstances, but also of the venom and malice of police officers."

At this, the prosecutor jumped to his feet, and the two lawyers had a vociferous exchange in which Foote asked his opponent to "please stand a little further from my elbow; I sometimes gesticulate."

The examination of Officer Allen resumed with Foote asking him if he heard Curtis say the murder weapon was not his.

"I never heard him say anything of the sort," the policeman responded.

On February 15, 1892, defense attorney J. N. E. Wilson, Judge Troutt's former partner, outlined to the jury what the defense team intended to show. He announced that Curtis would testify even though this was a rare occurrence in a murder trial. This possibly showed the defense's confidence that Curtis had nothing to hide and that he would charm the jury when he was on the stand. Throughout the trial, Curtis had nodded and smiled to the many folks he knew, his unshakable pleasure in interacting with his audience still functioning despite his being on trial for murder.

Wilson stated that the nippers on Curtis's right hand would have definitively prevented him from firing a gun because he was right-handed. A gunsmith from Oakland had earlier testified for the prosecution that he knew Curtis was left-handed, but the gunsmith would later admit to being induced to lie by the police. Attorney Wilson also pointed out that from the first time Curtis was shown the murder weapon by police he had denied ownership of the gun. This evidence, Wilson maintained, had been suppressed, according to the undated and unsourced newspaper article "Left His Pistol at Home" in the Harvard Theater Collection.

Defense attorney Wilson then went on to outline the defense's case as transcribed by the same article.

> We will prove further by Attorney Kowalsky
> that Toomey and Mullins, two of the princi-
> pal witnesses for the prosecution, went to his
> office and told a story wholly conflicting with

their evidence for the prosecution, and we will show that they told their story on the stand for coin.

The fact is, Curtis is not left-handed, he is right-handed. We will prove there were two or three men there. One ran across the street and the police were informed of that fact, but they have suppressed that testimony. On the night of the shooting, Curtis came to this city from his home in Berkeley and left his wife in the Grand Opera House. He had $240 with which he intended to pay a bill, but missed the man to whom he owed the money. He remained with his wife at the theatre until about 10 o'clock. Then he went to the Tivoli Theatre. He had $240 on his person, but no pistol. He was under the influence of liquor, we must confess.

Near the corner of Third and Mission streets a man met him that used to play with him in Atlanta, and walked along with him. At Sixth Street he made up his mind he would get rid of the man by going down Sixth to Howard. He had gone about half the length of the block when he heard a step behind him. As he turned around, he was knocked down. A policeman came up and arrested both men. The policeman started with the two, and the other man started to run when the policeman put the nippers upon the wrist of Curtis. Curtis did not then know that he had been robbed, nor did he find it out until he got to the police station.

The policeman took the two men across Folsom Street. The next thing Curtis was startled by a shot. He then felt himself drawn toward the building and then two other shots were fired. Believing he was being shot at, he broke away and ran. The night was dark, and it was impossible for a person on the opposite side of the street to tell whether there were two or five persons there.

A man residing in the house at the corner of Folsom and Fifth streets was ill, and up when he heard the shots. He saw a man run rapidly up Fifth Street. He saw three people, a policeman and two others, whom he had under arrest. We will prove by Mrs. Abbott that there were three persons present when the shots were fired.

Two ladies who were coming from the Tivoli saw a man, not Curtis, run up Fifth Street immediately after the shooting. We will prove that Curtis did not have a pistol upon his person that night, and that he is not in the habit of carrying a pistol. Curtis does not know how the bottle of whiskey, if it be whiskey, found in his pocket came there. We will show you, by Rev. W. W. Davis, that the bruises found upon Curtis in the police station were made when he was jumped on by the robber. We will show that Curtis had no possible reason for shooting Grant and that the man who fired the fatal shot had a reason for firing . . .

The time has arrived when the defendant

in this case has the right to speak in his own
behalf—a time and place when his words will
not be misquoted or misunderstood.

Curtis was then called to the witness stand. He stated
that he was thirty-nine years old and that he had never been
arrested before and had never been charged with a crime. He
told his recollection of the events, which matched Wilson's
account. In a most emphatic manner, Curtis proclaimed, "I did
not kill Policeman Grant. I did not fire my pistol that night. In
fact, my pistol was at home."

Curtis was then shown a white-handled pistol and he
identified it as his own. It was the one he had bought to use as
a prop in *Sam'l of Posen*.

The prosecution then grilled Curtis but shook neither his
testimony nor his composure.

After the cross-examination of Curtis was concluded,
attorney Henry Kowalsky was asked to testify. He stated that
he had met Curtis on the morning after the shooting and that
Curtis had solemnly assured him that he did not shoot Officer
Grant and asked, "Can't you get me out of here? I want to get
to my wife."

"In answer to my questions," continued Kowalsky, "Mr.
Curtis said he did not know when he was arrested, and at the
same time complained of a pain in the head and asked me to
see if the back of his head was bleeding. 'No,' said I. 'There is
a lump, but whether it is a natural lump or not I cannot tell;
there is no blood.' I asked him if he had any money and he
said, 'Yes, over $200, but the police have taken care of it.' I
went to the desk and saw that Curtis was credited with only
85 cents. Then I ordered coffee for him and left to hunt up Mr.
Foote and Mr. Knight."

Kowalsky then spoke of the visit that witnesses Mullins
and Toomey had paid him to ask the attorney what money was
in it for them. "I told them I could not do anything, and then
one of them said that they saw the row and heard the shooting. Then two men, one with a light overcoat and one with
a dark overcoat, ran away." The prosecution objected to this
statement being admitted to evidence, but they were over-
ruled.

After Kowalsky stepped down from the stand, other witnesses testified to Curtis's good character and the court was
adjourned for the day. The *Boston Herald* reported, "It was a
field day for the actor, for, if he can sustain his story, he cannot
be convicted."

Mrs. Cook, the wife of Dr. Cook, was the first defense
witness to be called the next morning, Tuesday, February 16.
She testified that on the night of the murder she saw Mrs.
Curtis give Mr. Curtis a sum of money and had previously seen
a white-handled pistol "like the one produced by the defense" on Curtis's bureau at his home. When cross-examined,
Mrs. Cook stated the gun was the only one she had ever seen
owned by Curtis and never saw him carry a gun on his person.

Dr. Cook was next in the witness box, testifying that he
had heard Marie tell Curtis to be sure to pay a "certain bill"
and saw her hand Curtis some gold pieces. Dr. Cook also identified the white-handled pistol owned by Curtis as the one he
had seen in Curtis's bedroom and that it did not match the
murder weapon.

Berkeley baker and hotel owner Fred Fonzo then testified
that two policemen came to his restaurant to see his employees Frank Spencer and Harry Jefferson (who earlier had testified that the gun the police found was Curtis's). He witnessed
a policeman say to Jefferson, pointing to a pistol, "This is the

one Grant was killed with." Fonzo told the court that Jefferson
came to him afterward and confided that he was not sure the
gun he identified in court as belonging to Curtis was actually
Curtis's.

One of Curtis's character witnesses was the Reverend W. W.
Davis, the rector at St. Luke's Episcopal Church, who had
played tennis and hunted with Curtis. The reverend testified
that when he visited Curtis in the city jail the morning after
the murder he saw Curtis's head was bruised, which must
have left the jury wondering who was lying about Curtis's
injuries—the policeman or the minister?

The defense then produced another eyewitness, W. E.
Harrington, who said he had had a toothache and was looking
out his window on Folsom Street the night of the murder. He
stated that he saw three men on the opposite corner and one
man said, "Let me go, I have done nothing," and the other
man said, "Let him go, I will take him home." After they
crossed Folsom, Harrington heard three shots and one of the
men ran toward his house and up Fifth toward Market. That
left two other men in the middle of the curb on the far side
of Folsom (policemen who rushed out of Southern Station).
One of them said, "For God's sake, hurry up; there he goes!"
Harrington said that the man who ran up Market was gone
before two more men arrived on the scene.

When the prosecution asked Harrington why he did not
tell this to the police, he answered, "I did not see fit to . . . and
I did not think it wise to tell everything to a policeman. If you
want to know, I'll tell you. I did not want to have anything to
do with the case."

"Ah, indeed, how did you get into it?" asked the prosecutor.

"A detective hunted me up," Harrington responded, saying
that he did not realize the importance of his evidence.

A Mrs. Abbott, who lived in the same building as Harrington, testified to hearing shots and seeing from her window a man dart out of the darkness on Folsom and run toward her house and then turn up Fifth. Her husband also testified to the same information but added that he saw a second man run down Fifth toward Shipley (evidently Curtis). He said that when he told a policeman what he saw the policeman said it was odd how he was the only one who saw three men. Mr. Abbott ended his testimony by saying that he didn't want to be dragged into the case and had asked Foote not to involve him.

On cross-examination, Mr. Abbott was asked if he had paid a $1.50 bill at the Cosmopolitan Saloon with a "twenty-dollar greenback" and he replied that he had.

"Did you say you received the money in the Curtis case?" asked the prosecutor.

"Yes, I did."

"Where did you get the money?"

"From Mr. Foote."

Murmuring immediately bubbled up in the courtroom until Foote exclaimed, "Here, I'll clear up that twenty-dollar business. Now, Mr. Abbott, did you not say that you were a poor man and that you could not afford to travel back and forth between this city and Lathrop?"

"I did."

"Did I not tell you that if that was the case I would see His Honor?"

"Yes, you did."

According to the *San Francisco Chronicle* of February 17, 1892, "Judge Troutt, J. N. E. Wilson and Mrs. Curtis were all sworn and testified that the money was only paid after due consultation and to secure to the witness the necessary funds for traveling back and forth," though no mention was made of why Mrs. Abbott was living in San Francisco and Mr. Abbott was traveling from Lathrop, California, to testify.

George A. Knight summed up the case for the defense in an eloquent speech. He showed how the case had grabbed international attention because Curtis was an actor who was lauded all across the United States. Knight listed the relevant points for the jury: the murder weapon did not belong to Curtis; Officer Grant was in street clothes; the last witness had seen a third man in the street; and there was strong evidence that the police had used nefarious tactics to suppress or contrive certain evidence to convict Curtis while knowing he did not commit the crime. He also tore into the character of many of the prosecution's witnesses. When Knight reached his dramatic crescendo, Marie fainted dead away onto the floor, while Curtis's face reflected tears, according to the article "Summing Up for Curtis" found in the Harvard Theater Collection and most likely published by the *Boston Globe* on February 23, 1892.

Knight finished his closing remarks the next day to a packed and feverish courtroom. "You will be told by the court that you must start with the presumption of innocence. It is your duty to reconcile the facts in the case as far as possible with this presumption. You must deal only with facts that are proved."

As Knight reviewed the evidence, he pointed out that it was all circumstantial and some of it very peculiar. How could Mrs. Johnson lean out her window and see a man running but not see Mullins and Toomey, who testified they ran to the victim just after the shooting? Knight asserted that the police had made Augustine Marcoval (the tamale vendor) sign a statement they themselves had written.

Knight then forcefully proposed, "What motive could Curtis have had to kill Officer Grant? Is it reasonable to suppose that a man of his standing in life would descend from the position of a gentleman, which he has always held, to that of a brutal murderer? There was no homicide in his heart that night. Suffering as he was from his wounds, from the effects of liquor and the terrible charges against him, it is no wonder that he was incoherent and that he exclaimed at the police station, 'O, that I could recall the last few hours of my life!' Now, you must remember that the law has thrown the mantle of innocence over the defendant, and that the prosecution must tear that mantle from him shred by shred before he can be adjudged a guilty criminal."

As applause broke out from many of the women in the courtroom, Knight continued his summation. "The district attorney has called your attention to the fact that Curtis sits

Marie and Curtis listening to the final arguments. (*The* San Francisco Chronicle, *February 25, 1892*)

here with a smile on his face and surrounded by flowers. I think the remark ill-timed and somewhat flippant. Is it against him that his devoted wife should bring to him every day flowers from their beautiful Berkeley home? ... Do you think for one moment that this defendant who in his whole life never did a wrong act, so far as the prosecution have been able to ascertain, cruelly killed a man at midnight? Let your verdict be not guilty." (The *Examiner*, February 25, 1892.)

As Knight lowered his head and sat back down, the courtroom broke out in another round of applause.

W. W. Foote followed Knight with a fervid appeal. "I am not here to make a coward's plea for mercy, but to lift my voice that justice may be done this defendant." He called Officer Bode a "black-hearted perjurer whom every decent man ought to lash through the town," claiming the whole case reeked of perjury hatched by the police.

> The prosecution of the defendant by the police department has been shameful. This man who sits here on trial for his life has suffered torture and torment at the hands of these detectives. One would think we were living in Russia. You listened to the stories told by Allen and Bode. They repeated them like parrots. How carefully the police department guarded the statement made by Curtis ... that he had been set upon and beaten by footpads. It was not until this trial that we ever heard it ... Oh, these policemen are curious cattle ...
>
> Curtis, I say, is the victim of the police department ... The evidence for the prosecution reeked with perjury and was manufactured

by the police. They wanted to send this man
like a sheep to the shambles . . . The murderer of Grant is not here in this room. He
escaped that night, and the fact that he has
gone unpunished is due to the neglect of this
bogus police department . . . We have called no
witness here whose testimony has been drilled
into him. I ask you to give a verdict in favor of
the defendant. I leave the case with you, in the
belief that the day and hour of his delivery has
come. (The *Examiner*, February 25, 1892.)

In the afternoon, it was the prosecution's turn to make
their final pleas to the jury. Walter Hinckle made sure the jury
understood that the witnesses had only seen one prisoner
with Grant and that no prosecution witness had seen a third
man run from the scene. He said that if Grant had arrested a
well-dressed gentleman and a footpad he would have hand-
cuffed the footpad. He reminded the jury that they had only
Curtis's word (and the word of several of the defense's witnesses) to contradict the six witnesses for the prosecution
and that if Curtis had been arrested along with the footpad
who had shot the officer he would have told this to the other
policemen immediately instead of waiting until after he had
consulted with an attorney.

Hinckle continued his arguments for more than an hour,
according to the *Examiner*.

The defense has been surrounded with all the
sympathy that could be procured by wealth.
When I heard the lawyers for Curtis level shaft
after shaft at the district attorney and the police

department, and heard the applause and laughter that greeted each fresh attack, I fully realized the sympathy that was with the defendant. And that is what I want to warn you against. You must decide the case on its merits, and not from sympathetic reasons. If Curtis had been knocked down and robbed, upon whose wrist would the nippers have been found? Do you think Grant would have put it upon Curtis instead of the robber? There were six witnesses who saw the shooting. All those testified that there were but two men at the spot when the policeman was murdered. Their testimony has been absolutely unimpeached. Only one man ran away from the scene of that killing. They caught him in full flight.

Contrast Curtis's conduct all through with what an innocent man would have done. It was several hours after the shooting before Attorney Kowalsky told him never to talk to anyone about the case. Is it not strange that in all the time that intervened this man told nothing of what he testified to here yesterday? Is that the manner of a guiltless person? Do you for one moment believe these statements of the defense that the police department has conspired to send an innocent man to the gallows? I do not think you do.

When Hinckle concluded his summation, he was met by silence in the courtroom, and Judge Troutt called for a recess. People remained in the courtroom and the atmosphere was

Curtis shaking hands during a recess. (The San Francisco Examiner, *February 25, 1892)*

almost festive. Curtis's legal team seemed happy with Curtis's prospects, and there was a sense that things were going Curtis's way. Bets were placed that Curtis would be free by that evening, and the odds given for a hung jury were 2 to 1.

When the recess was announced, a large crowd surrounded the Curtises. One reporter thought the throng stared at the actor "as though he were a caged curiosity." Curtis and Marie struggled through the people and made their escape to the judge's chambers.

When court resumed, Judge Troutt gave orders to the jury

about following the law, which mandated the presumption of innocence, and he reminded the jurors about the significance of reasonable doubt and circumstantial evidence.

At 4:10 p.m. on Wednesday, February 24, 1892, the jury retired to deliberate in "the nicest jury room in the new city hall." Curtis's friends stayed in the courtroom, thinking the jury would not take long to decide Curtis's innocence.

As nine p.m. approached, the crowd increased in numbers and intensity. The sheriff arrived and stated that the jury had no news to report. At eleven p.m., the jury was sequestered for the night.

Curtis and Marie entered the courtroom the next morning in a cheerful, optimistic mood. Curtis's counsel had told him they thought he would be a free man by nightfall, but so far there was only more nerve-wracking waiting.

Later in the day, the jury bell rang and the judge mounted his bench. The room was filled to overflowing with apprehensive spectators. Friends crowded around Curtis, while Marie laid her head on her husband's shoulder. The judge's voice rang out, adjourning the trial until nine that evening, and everyone was off to supper.

But the jury was still deliberating when everyone returned later that evening. Judge Troutt informed the sheriff that if the jury made any decision before midnight he should be informed and he would come back to court that night. Curtis was taken back to the jail for the night, but Marie could not bring herself to leave the building in spite of the protests of her friends who wanted her to get a good night's sleep. She could see the deliberating jury through a window in the second-floor corridor, and she stood rooted to this vantage point.

A number of people lingered and waited for news even though it was getting late. The *Examiner* said there were as

many people waiting that evening as there were in the day-
time. As the night wore on, Marie was the only person remaining and her worried pacing echoed on the marble floor. No
verdict was reached that night.

On the third morning of jury deliberation, as the *San
Francisco Call* reported on February 26, "Mrs. Curtis and Mrs.
Davis of Berkeley were early on the scene and held whispered
conversations with the sympathizing friends who surrounded
them. The court-room, indeed, was crowded with members
of the theatrical profession, and when the prisoner himself
arrived, he was met by a host of old acquaintances, who gave
him words of cheer to sustain him in the trying ordeal he was
passing through."

With each passing minute, more people filled the hallway,
and the police held the crowd back from the doors of the
court where they pressed in aggressively. It was reported that
Marie looked drained and haggard. Curtis entered the courtroom about five minutes after his wife. His eyes were bloodshot from lack of sleep and his countenance anxious. Next to
arrive was Judge Troutt who, upon taking his seat, immediately
asked, "Has the jury reached a verdict?"

"They have not, Your Honor," stated the deputy sheriff.
Curtis flopped back in his chair, and Judge Troutt adjourned
the court until two that afternoon. Curtis and his friends took
that as a sign that acquittal was more likely, and Curtis bright-
ened. Marie told her husband that she would prepare for an
oyster celebration lunch at two thirty.

The judge was seated promptly at two, ready for the verdict. The twelve-man jury filed in as Curtis and Marie did their
utmost to read their faces. The jurors' eyes were bloodshot
and their countenances stern.

Judge Troutt asked the jury if they had reached a verdict

The foreman announcing that the jury could not reach a verdict.
(The San Francisco Examiner, *February 26, 1892)*

and the jury foreman said no. Curtis's muscles relaxed; he slouched and exhaled. When asked if they thought they could reach a verdict if they deliberated more, the foreman replied that he doubted it but that some of the jurors thought they might. The foreman asked for further instructions on some matters. The jury was told again that when part of a witness's testimony was found to be false it was up to their judgment whether they should dismiss all the witness's testimony.

After one more adjournment of about two hours, the jury foreman announced that there was no possibility they could agree on a verdict. "We have got no nearer a conclusion than when we appeared before you two hours ago. I don't believe it is possible for us to agree," the *San Francisco Call* quoted him as saying on February 26, 1892.

Judge Troutt said the law required them to deliberate for a reasonable time and that they had done exactly that. As it seemed useless to continue, the trial was declared over with a deadlocked jury. Judge Troutt dismissed the jury and called for a continuation of the case until Saturday with Curtis remaining in custody.

Suddenly, hundreds of people attending the trial charged directly at the jurors to learn their story. It turned out that ten jurors had voted for conviction and two for acquittal.

According to news reports, Curtis "kept perfect command over his face" and showed no disappointment with the results. But Marie paled perceptibly when the decision was announced "and looked as if she would like to have a good cry."

Curtis's attorney J. N. E. Wilson was stunned. As the jury filed out, a tall man with sandy whiskers came up to him, shook his hand, and said the lawyer had done his best for Curtis. The crestfallen attorney shook his head silently in agreement. As Curtis was led out of the courtroom on his way back to jail, he was followed by Marie, the Reverend and Mrs. Davis, and a large crowd, all walking solemnly. A few minutes later, the courtroom looked like an empty disheveled stadium after a ball game.

It was later discovered that the two dissenting jurors were W. J. Hurley, a saloonkeeper, and S. C. Porter, an insurance broker. The *Examiner* asked Hurley, "a large, pleasant-faced man," to give a written statement about his vote.

> I will say that when the jury retired to deliber-
> ate upon their verdict at 4:20 p.m. on Wednes-
> day afternoon, the first ballot was seven for
> conviction and five for acquittal. Of the five
> who voted for acquittal, three claimed that

they would not vote for murder in the first
degree, but were in favor of either a verdict of
murder in the second degree, imprisonment
for life, or manslaughter. Mr. Porter and myself
were in favor of acquittal, and we were the
remaining two of the five who voted for an
acquittal on the first ballot.

On the second ballot it was ten for murder in the second
degree. It stayed that way all night. After receiving instructions
the next afternoon that they could dismiss a witness's entire
testimony if part of it was believed to be false, there was one
final ballot. The jury cast their final votes six for life in prison,
two for manslaughter, two for second-degree murder, and jurors
Hurley and Porter voting for acquittal, as they had consistently
done in every ballot.

Hurley said that he was sure the testimony that the gun
was still hot ten minutes later and that a prosecution witness
heard Officer Grant at a distance of one hundred and fifteen
feet with the window down must not be true. Hurley said he
fired his own gun a number of times at the beach and then
put it in the sand. He picked it up six minutes later and it was
cold. He believed that Toomey and Mullins were vindictive in
their testimony and that made him suspicious. Then, when
Henry Kowalsky said that these men approached him for a
bribe, it made Hurley not believe their testimony at all.

Hurley's recollection of policeman Bode's testimony was
also revealing. Bode kept speaking so softly on the stand that
he could not be heard. Even the prosecutor had asked him repeatedly to speak up. Finally, Foote asked the officer if he had
something in his mouth. Bode said, "Yes, I have. I've got some
tobacco," and pulled the quid out of his cheek and angrily

Saloonkeeper W. J. Hurley. He was one of two jurors who held out for acquittal in the first murder trial. This pen-and-ink drawing was done while Hurley was in jail after being charged with jury tampering in another trial almost two years after Curtis's trial. (The San Francisco Chronicle, *January 29, 1895)*

offered Foote a chaw. Hurley believed Bode's conduct showed all he needed to know about the policeman's testimony.

Hurley gave Curtis the benefit of the doubt on the testimony of Harrington and the Abbotts. They said a man was running toward Shipley Street after the shooting and a man was running toward Howard Street. Curtis could not be running in both directions at once, Hurley reasoned, and he felt those witnesses were good people and credible, so it proved to him that there was a second man involved. Hurley said the jurors were friendly in their differences, and some had acknowledged that they believed Hurley was honest and voted his judgment. But this experience wouldn't be Hurley's only encounter with the judicial system in San Francisco as he was arrested three years later on a charge of jury tampering.

Another juror described his experience to the *Examiner* on February 26, 1892.

> "I think I shall enjoy my sleep tonight. The room we had last night was well supplied with chairs and comfortable enough fixed otherwise, but the only place where one could lie down was on the floor. I tried to sleep, but only did so about an hour, as there was altogether too much talking going on for slumber. However, what with playing cards, telling stories and smoking we got through the night very comfortably. Altogether the whole business was pleasant enough, but I'm not sorry it's over with. There wouldn't have been an agreement if we had remained out until the crack of doom."
> Yet another juror related that nearly all the panel was composed of '49ers, so the storytelling about "old times" was quite lively.

It was revealed that by the final afternoon of deliberations nearly thirty votes had been taken, most with the 10–2 result. One juror, R. Husband, was a talented musician who recited and then sang a moving spiritual song, which brought some of the men to tears, but not to an agreement on a verdict.

On February 27, 1892, Curtis came with a gloomy countenance to the hearing that would set a date for his new trial. It must have sunken in that what he had just been through was about to be repeated, but the setting of the second trial date was postponed for two weeks on a motion by the defense.

Judge Troutt finally agreed to release Curtis on a $50,000 bond on the morning of March 25, a month after the first trial had ended. Marie and Foote left the courtroom immediately in search of a bail bondsman. By two p.m., they returned with a $100,000 bond. It was double the required amount, probably because real estate, not cash, secured the bail. Marie put up the lion's share, $50,000. Foote put up $15,000 as an act of faith in his client's innocence, with others contributing the balance required.

Curtis must have felt a great oppression lift as he left his jail cell at about five that afternoon, accompanied by his wife and friends. "Before leaving the prison he was lavish in his expressions of gratitude to his keepers for their kindness toward him during his incarceration and bade each of them adieu in turn. He intends to immediately devote all of his energies to securing an early and speedy trial, and also to straightening his business affairs," according to the *San Francisco Chronicle* on March 26, 1892.

The Curtises arrived at their Berkeley home the next day at two p.m. Two weeks later the Curtises registered at San Francisco's Occidental Hotel. They then moved into the house of a Mrs. Sarah Lewis on Hopkins Street in Peralta Park.

Curtis's second trial was scheduled to start on September 25, 1892. In the meantime, Curtis traveled to his new Sanger Junction property near Fresno. He had acquired the ranch by trading his interest in the Peralta Park Hotel to a Fresno vineyardist who took over the mortgage on the park by paying the balloon payment that was due.

Conspicuous even in his absence, Curtis was missed

in Berkeley while he was in Fresno. The local papers were wishing Curtis would commence some new endeavor in town. "The town is not tired of Mr. Curtis. No other man in the world could have built and contemplated the hotel building. We hope he will start another colony in some other part of town." (*Berkeley Daily Herald*, June 3, 1892.)

Jury selection for the second trial began in mid-September of 1892. Curtis looked tan and rested from the sojourn on his ranch when he joined his same defense attorneys for the new trial.

There was a pool of one hundred prospective jurors to choose from, and Marie, dressed simply and sitting by her husband, was said to listen to the questions and responses with deep interest, acting as an integral part of the legal team in picking and questioning prospective jurors, according to the *Examiner* on November 11, 1892. Despite the complication that many potential jurors had formed opinions as to the guilt or innocence of Curtis by reading newspapers during the previous trial, a jury was finally empaneled and the second trial began in Judge John Murphy's courtroom on October 14, 1892, but the testimony phase of the trial was delayed due to a juror's case of tonsillitis.

On November 12, 1892, a periodical called *The Sporting Life* noted that "M. B. Curtis is so confident of acquittal of the charges of murder for which he is now under indictment in San Francisco and awaiting a second trial, that he has commissioned Edward Marble, of Baltimore, to rewrite the manuscript of *Sam'l of Posen*, which he intends to revive if he is allowed to return to the stage."

On November 25, 1892, Department 12 of San Francisco Superior Court finally began hearing witness testimony.

Curtis, in a fine navy-blue suit, sat next to attorney J. N. E. Wilson and looked in "splendid physical health." Marie, wearing a little, flat, seal-brown-and-white hat, sat next to her husband with a veil over her face, looking more relaxed than the last time they were in court. Her hat was evidently worthy news, as the *Examiner* thought it was the same one she wore at the trial last winter. Walter Hinckle was joined at the prosecutor's table by District Attorney William S. Barnes.

Many of the witnesses had testified at the previous trial, but the prosecution introduced a new witness, John A. Parker, who corroborated the testimony of previous prosecution witnesses, which elicited surprised looks from the defense attorneys. When Foote asked Parker if he was a periodical drunk, Judge Murphy interrupted and advised Parker not to answer.

The jury heard from tamale salesman Augustine Marcoval again, but there were rumors circulating in many national papers that the prosecution would bring a new witness to court. They reported that an ex-policeman from Idaho named John Cann, who was visiting San Francisco on business, was headed home the night Officer Grant was killed and witnessed the murder but was claiming he didn't tell police what he had seen because he had to leave San Francisco the next day.

Cann, a large man, seventy years of age, was reportedly being kept in seclusion by detectives even though his late appearance on the scene would probably cast doubt on his testimony.

On November 26 the prosecution, feeling assured of a conviction, was successful in having Curtis taken back into custody. He was incarcerated in cell 31 on the first floor near the entrance to the city jail. In spite of being afflicted with a case of painful neuralgia, the ever-social Curtis was happy to speak with the *Examiner*. "This is a dreary place for a winter

Curtis tries to make the best of his time in jail, putting on his best face for a reporter. (The San Francisco Examiner, *November 27, 1892)*

resort but I've got to stand it, so I might as well stand it pleasantly. Besides, it is nothing new for me . . . I had about nine months of it after I was arrested . . . I can't complain at all. You see, I've got a front room and a lower berth [pointing to a pallet on the floor with his cigarette]."

Curtis did not hesitate to say that he was not worried about the prosecution's new witness.

> This surprise party chap, Cann, that they
> say they are going to surprise me with is, in
> my judgment, either a man who has been in
> trouble and is to be protected by the police for
> testifying, or else he simply is broke and is to
> be paid for his testimony. I know he is willing
> to be bribed for he has gone to attorneys and
> practically offered to ship out for money. Two

hundred and fifty dollars is what he asked of us, I understand. He has told people more than once that he was "out for the stuff." Naturally his testimony does not give me any great concern.

As to those Holden girls [two teenage girls who were prosecution witnesses and gave contradictory testimony about the murder in the first trial], I've been an actor so long that I am a pretty good judge of acting, and if those girls have not been drilled I never heard a prepared speech.

Whenever they are examined outside of their main story, they go all to pieces. They can't tell an inch from a rod. They have been drilled to say "I don't know" to all but certain questions, and they are not the sort to forget a lesson. There is another thing about them. When they first appeared against me in the Police Court, they were almost in rags; there was the evidence of poverty all over them. Did you see them yesterday? They wore nice dresses and their hair was put up by a hairdresser. I'd like to know the cause of this change of fortune.

When the interview was over, Curtis lit his cigarette and picked up the novel by May Agnes Fleming he had been reading in his cell. Fleming was Canada's most popular female writer of detective fiction at the time, and Curtis was quite likely immersed in learning about all the aspects of the type of situation that he currently found himself in.

Almost six months earlier, the *San Francisco Chronicle* of March 1, 1892, had agreed with the *World*'s claim that the jury was "packed," saying, "Indeed, this important information was what may be termed an open secret all over the town whilst Mrs. Johnson was still stumbling through her self-contradictions and Mrs. Holden was explaining how she and her daughters prepared themselves for bed and yet watched what was going on in the streets. And right here we must digress in order to ask a few pointed questions about these Holden girls. Their testimony was so peculiar as to cause any disinterested observer to hunt for a motive for it, and in that hunt to pause at the fact that they appeared at the police court in very shabby and threadbare attire, while in the superior court they blossomed out." They speculated, as did Curtis months later, that the taxpayers were the ones who furnished the girls new attire, as had been done in a prior case.

On November 29, 1892, John Cann testified at the trial. He was a hotelkeeper and Civil War veteran as well as a former policeman in Idaho. When Cann entered the courtroom, everyone strained to get a glimpse of the heretofore mysterious witness. He was more than six feet tall and weighed about 250 pounds. Possessing heavy eyebrows, a thick salty mustache, and steel gray hair, he shifted his eyes deliberately, which matched his very considered movements. After struggling to remove his rain-drenched coat, he draped it on the back of the witness chair and settled in for his examination.

District Attorney Barnes began the questioning with "While in the city at that time, was there anything to attract your attention?"

"Yes, sir. A shooting scrape that I happened to see." The

entire courtroom stiffened to attention.

"What time was this?"

"At twelve o'clock."

"Where had you been that night?"

"To see the panorama of the Battle of Gettysburg." (This was a museum at Tenth and Market streets.)

"Well, you go on and tell the story of what you saw that night in your own way."

"I went to the panorama of the Battle of Gettysburg and after I had been there for some time, someone told me of another panorama, and I started to go to it. It was rather late and I walked along Market Street two or three blocks, then I turned to the right for two or three streets and then turned again to the left. After the last turn, I heard someone coming along behind me, and turning I saw two men coming along. One seemed to have hold of the other sort of scuffling. They did not pass me on the sidewalk, but crossed diagonally to the other side of the street. One was a shorter man than the other. When they got to the other side of the street, I saw the shorter man reach with his left hand into his pocket, draw a pistol and shoot. The barrel of the pistol was a little up. The big man fell down. The little man fired again and then ran away."

Cann testified the men were speaking rather loudly when they came up behind him. He stated that he did not see any-one else around on that street but that there was a man selling something "a little back." He continued, "After the shooting, two men came back bringing a third."

By now, the jury must have been wondering how a veri-table crowd of "eyewitnesses" could have been on the street where Grant was killed and not have been seen by the other witnesses. When Foote cross-examined Cann and pointed out some discrepancies in his story, Cann ended up contradicting

all of the other witnesses for the prosecution when he swore
he heard only two shots. (There were two bullet holes in the
fence at the scene of the shooting and one bullet lodged in
Grant's skull.) Foote also called into question Cann's motivation for testifying, asking the witness about his allegedly
asking Henry Kowalsky for money. The *Examiner* summed up
the courtroom's reaction to the prosecution's surprise witness
on November 30, 1892. "When [Cann] had finished telling the
court what he knew about the case, the jury knew no more
than before."

The next witness called was Thomas Mullins, who had
claimed at the first trial to have witnessed the shooting and
found the pistol around the corner on Fifth and Folsom. Mullins was led over his previous testimony by the prosecution,
but when Foote cross-examined him in front of a large afternoon audience, Mullins ended up contradicting his previous
testimony on a number of points. After Foote was done with
him, Mullins was dismissed and hurried out of the courtroom
away from the large and colorful crowd of spectators.

Severe wind and rain had kept the morning audience to
a minimum, but the afternoon sun brought an eager crowd
rushing to the courtroom, including many actors and actresses
who arrived after afternoon rehearsals were completed. Local
newspapers consistently noted the attendance at the trial and
seemed rather taken by some of the theatrical people. "There
was one little blond in a fetching . . . costume of navy blue,
who came with a big fellow who seemed all cane, tweeds, high
collar, and yellow gloves," noted the *Examiner* on November
30, 1892.

The next witness called was George Alpers. His testimony
was consistent with the first trial, stating that he was in his
bar and heard three shots, went to the doorway, and saw a

man running up Folsom toward Fifth being pursued by three policemen. When Foote cross-examined him, Alpers testified that he did not see Mullins, Toomey, or Cann (three witnesses for the prosecution).

Officer Bode then took the stand and had to admit that he had been mistaken with some of his testimony at the previous trial. After Foote questioned him again on a particular point, the defense lawyer asked the policeman, "Then the other testimony is false?" Bode responded, "Yes, sir."

The following week, the prosecution rested its case, and Curtis's attorney George Knight made an opening statement for the defense outlining their version of events—that a third person had killed Officer Grant, that all the evidence against Curtis was circumstantial, and that no one had proved the murder weapon belonged to Curtis.

Knight seemed to particularly engage the attention of the jury when he relived Curtis's first hours in the police station and pointed out how Curtis had "broke forth in sobs and spoke so feelingly of his wife and the occurrences of that unhappy hour." Knight then did his best to discredit the testimony of Mullins, Toomey, and Cann, and his rebuttal was said to be "strong" by the *San Francisco Chronicle*.

Knight seemed confident when he wrapped up his opening statement, telling the jury that when the defense finished presenting its case, "We will be in a position to rest our case in your hands, and we do not fear for a moment as to what the verdict will be."

As soon as Knight called Curtis to the stand, the crowded courtroom crackled with excitement. The spectators were evidently riveted by seeing a nationally famous actor on trial for murder, and "a moment of surprise ran through the courtroom and many glances were bestowed on Curtis who sat by

Curtis's attorneys decide that he should take the stand and testify in his defense.
(The San Francisco Chronicle, *December 6, 1892)*

attorney Wilson looking rather ill at ease," according to the *San Francisco Chronicle* on December 1, 1892.

After Curtis finished testifying, District Attorney Barnes began a thorough cross-examination that started with his having Curtis tell the details of his life after moving to Berkeley in 1887. When Barnes got to the point of questioning Curtis about his being arrested by Officer Grant, Judge Murphy said that he felt too ill to continue and called for a recess for the rest of the day.

When the court reconvened on Friday afternoon, December 9, District Attorney Barnes walked in with an air of urgency and delivered a bombshell to the court, announcing that the juror whose case of tonsillitis had postponed the opening of the trial had died early that morning.

W. W. Foote then made a motion that the current eleven surviving jurors be retained and a new one be added to make the mandatory twelve, but Barnes made a motion that the jury be dismissed, which Judge Murphy quickly granted. Murphy then announced that he would be trying only civil cases in the future and that he did not want this case to interfere with his transfer to the civil division. Murphy told Barnes to assign the case to a new judge, adding that eight years of trying criminal cases was enough for him.

The case was continued until the following Saturday, when a date would be set for yet another trial. But the death of a juror wasn't the only bombshell to hit the San Francisco courtroom that day. Curtis's attorney George Knight interrupted the murmurings of the spectators to announce, "If it pleases the court, I am very anxious that some definite date should be set for the trial of the Harper case [another murder case before Judge Murphy in which Knight was involved]. The defendant as yet has had no trial and, to avoid all appearance of a conflict of interest, I now give notice of my withdrawal from the case of Mr. Curtis, who will no longer be represented by me in any capacity."

The shock of this one-two punch was felt throughout the courtroom, and many looked to Curtis to gauge his reaction. Wilson then submitted a request to continue the trial on Monday, December 12, as if to affirm to everyone in the courtroom that Knight's departure would not change a thing. The proceedings were continued to the following Monday, with the understanding that there would be an effort to find another judge to start the trial at that time.

When a reporter asked Wilson why Knight was leaving the defense team, Wilson replied, "I understand that he has had some trouble with Mrs. Curtis over his $750 fee."

When Knight was asked the same question by the *San Francisco Chronicle* on December 11, 1892, he replied, "I got out of the case simply because I won't allow anybody to play me. Foote and I were the first attorneys in the case and Wilson came in afterward. We were each to receive $5,000 for our services, and Mrs. Curtis now owes us $1,500 each on account. We have never received a cent, and only the other night I learned from Foote that Wilson had a contract with Mrs. Curtis for $10,000 in case of an acquittal. I inquired of Foote where we got off and he didn't know. I didn't either and so I got out."

The squabbling between Curtis's lawyers was further reported on by the *San Francisco Chronicle* on December 13, 1892.

> This business settled, Attorney Knight started
> to leave the courtroom, but he was stopped

at the reporters' table by Attorney Wilson,
who said: "I want it distinctly understood that
I have no contract with Mrs. Curtis and no
arrangement whatsoever for a contingent fee
in this case."

"Well," returned Knight, "I just told the
reporter what Foote told me."

Knight was asked if he expected to go back
into the case, and quickly replied: "No, sir:
when I leave a case once it goes for good."

Soon after Knight declared that he was no longer representing Curtis, rumors began circulating that Foote was not
happy with the case and that he might also leave — especially
after he announced that he would run for the U.S. Senate in
the Democratic primary. However, Foote's bid did not last long
as he dropped out of the race within a couple of weeks, and he
did end up representing Curtis in the later trial.

Henry I. Kowalsky, one of Curtis's attorneys in the first
trial, had not been part of the legal team in the second trial,
and one possible explanation for this was revealed at the end
of January 1893. The Bar Association had charged Kowalsky
with "grave dereliction of duty" involving the handling of an
underaged claimant on an estate case. Kowalsky supposedly
induced the minor to make a payment to him of $3,500,
telling his client that the judge had promised to make an
order of the payment the next day. The judge had made no
such promise and would consider it only in open court. The
bar found Kowalsky's statement was made for the purpose of
inducing the minor to pay him $3,500 and that the minor had
been deceived in the matter of another smaller payment. The
bar then recommended a committee present the charge to the

court. (*San Francisco Chronicle*, January 29, 1893.)

It was also later reported that, according to J. N. E. Wilson, the eleven surviving jurors in the second trial had signed affidavits to the effect that, based on the evidence submitted in the court, all eleven would have voted for Curtis's acquittal, according to the *Examiner* on August 26, 1893.

Curtis's third trial date was set for February 20, 1893, before Judge William Raymond Dangerfield, but the trial was trans-ferred back to Judge Murphy's court in spite of Murphy's efforts to rid himself of the criminal case, and the trial did not get underway until August 8, 1893, as new evidence was still being submitted almost two years after the murder. The se-lection of the jury took five and a half days, and then District Attorney Barnes gave his opening statement and recounted the history of the case. J. N. E. Wilson then opened for the defense and laid out all of the contradictions in the prosecu-tion's evidence.

District Attorney Barnes presented to the jury many of the same witnesses from the previous trials although there were prosecution witnesses "they never had the courage to produce again," according to the *San Francisco Call* on August 9, 1893. Those witnesses who were not physically present for the third trial had their earlier testimony read from transcripts, but Officer Bode appeared in person despite his being cross-examined roughly during the second trial. Bode told the jury about the soda bottle filled with whiskey that was in Curtis's pocket and the nippers that were on his right wrist.

And true to form, Foote tried to discredit Bode as a witness again, asking the policeman, "Were you not investi-gated by the Police Commissioners a short time ago for your connection with an alleged dice game conducted in your brother's saloon?"

"Yes."

"Didn't you send friends to the Commissioners in the endeavor to save yourself from being broke?"

"Yes."

"Weren't you kept on the force just to give testimony in this case?"

"No."

Then Foote brought up the name of Dan Shea, a criminal who had had trouble with Officer Grant, and then the defense attorney asked Bode if he had ever investigated the possibility that this Shea had committed the murder. Bode said no.

"You have simply taken it for granted that Curtis was the man?"

"Yes, sir."

As they had done in the last trial, the defense team kept claiming that a third man had been involved and that this man had done the shooting. They brought back their most important witness to date, W. E. Harrington, the carpenter who had stated that he was on the northeast corner of Folsom and Fifth streets the night Grant was murdered and saw three men coming across the street walking abreast. According to the *San Francisco Chronicle*, Harrington testified that as the men passed under his window the smallest man said, "Let me go. I've done nothing." He testified that the man on the right said, "Yes, let him go and I'll take him home." He then heard the man in the middle state, "Come along, you won't be hurt." After a moment's pause under the witness's window, the three men moved around the corner out of Harrington's sight as if to go down Folsom Street toward the police station.

"Two or three minutes later," Harrington testified, "I heard three shots, the first two close together and the third after a slightly longer interval. Then I heard someone run around the corner, pass under my window, and tear off up Fifth Street toward Market. I could not see, however, who it was."

Harrington was then grilled by Barnes, but the witness stuck to his original testimony. Barnes also questioned Harrington's vision, as some sort of malady was visible in the witness's eyes. Harrington said that his eyes were fine and that he saw quite well for someone his age.

At one point in the third trial, Marie took the stand to testify that she had given her husband $210 to pay a bill the night of September 10 although Curtis had testified the amount he had was $240. She also testified that when she went to visit her husband in jail she found bruises on his body. When she was shown the murder weapon, she said it was one "he had never carried, nor did she believe that he could have been hired to carry one of that character."

A constable from Berkeley named Daniel Meyer testified he met Curtis on the night of the shooting and that Curtis was "very drunk" and that he had to assist Curtis in getting on the train. Meyer said Curtis told him he was "going to take his wife to see Bernhardt that night, and showed his pockets full of twenty-dollar gold pieces."

In cross-examination, Meyer stated he did not testify at the previous trials as "he was not asked to," according to the *San Francisco Call* on August 19, 1893.

As the trial continued, detectives began actively looking for the mysterious third person who was supposed to have fired the fatal shot and escaped in the darkness. While no one had been able to trace this person beyond the scene, detectives did find an attorney who said he was approached by this third man. The attorney, A. Treadwell, was now reportedly willing to testify that the man had confessed to him that he had caused the quarrel and murdered Officer Grant.

Treadwell's statement, as told to an *Examiner* reporter, was published August 22, 1893.

> I was at my law office on Montgomery Street
> about 9:00 the morning of the murder when
> a shaggy and unkempt man of rough features
> bearing contusions of the face [burst] into my
> office in great excitement, almost breaking the
> glass door. I had seen the man on the Barbary
> Coast before, and I think he was once tried for
> burglary. Almost breathless, he said to me, "I'm
> in trouble and must get out of this."
>
> "What is the matter," I asked. He at once
> launched into his story. He said, as nearly as I
> can remember, "A policeman was killed down
> here on Fifth Street this morning, and I was
> in the scuffle and barely got away with my life,
> but the policeman is dead and he did not live
> long enough to tell any tales."
>
> My strange visitor was much perturbed
> during the entire interview, and he said again
> and again, "My god, I don't know what to do; I
> must get out of this at once or I'll be in dread-
> ful trouble myself." He then gave me many
> details of the scuffle, but he did not remain
> long enough to tell me how it began, and he
> glanced around nervously during his stay, as if
> pursued by someone, or as if in mortal fear of

arrest or great bodily harm. I was simply ap-
palled and I called my office mate in. I do not
care to mention his name now, but when the
proper time arrives, he and I can both make
oath to all I am telling you, and to even more.
The man finally said, "Do you doubt me? Then
look at this," and he pulled his trousers and
underwear up to his knees, saying, "Here is
where Grant and Curtis kicked me. They made
these bruises and knocked off these patches
of skin, and they did me these injuries on my
face, shoulders and arms."

Treadwell was asked if he knew the man. "Know him!
Why, his face was so hard that I'd recognize him in China.
In fact, I had often seen him consorting with low characters
before, and I had noted the fact that he had a very ugly-
looking physiognomy."

The lawyer was then asked if he knew where the man was
going. "He indicated that he would have to leave San Francisco
and that he had once lived in Southern California, and I in-
ferred from what he said that he would probably go that
way again."

The detectives who had heard Treadwell's testimony felt
they might know who this man was. He had been a suspect
already, and they were hoping to produce him before the jury
retired to decide the case.

But Curtis's defense team seemed to think they knew who
had visited Treadwell when they announced that there was
yet another potential new witness, a man named G. W. Rumble
of Syracuse, New York, who was expected to arrive in San
Francisco on August 21, 1893. According to Curtis, Rumble

actually witnessed the shooting of Grant but was not the
shooter himself. Curtis went on to explain in the *Examiner*
on August 22, 1893:

> Rumble is a man of very high standing at
> home, as will be shown by people who know
> him. He is the inventor of an electrical device,
> and at the time of the murder of Grant he
> had been busy several days prosecuting a suit
> against some people who had infringed his
> patent.
>
> On the night of the murder a friend had
> been showing Rumble around town, but left
> him at the Baldwin Hotel. Rumble was not
> sleepy and started for a walk. Near the corner
> of Fifth and Folsom Streets he saw Grant on
> his way to the station, having myself and the
> third man in custody. Rumble says that I was
> obstreperous and giving the policeman a great
> deal of trouble.
>
> He turned down Folsom Street behind
> me and heard me pleading with Grant to let
> me go. He says that I told Grant that I must
> catch the boat and that I offered him money
> to liberate me. He also says that the third man
> begged Grant to let us go, telling him that he
> knew me, that I was a good citizen, and that
> if he would let us go he would take me home.
> Grant refused to let us go, and pulled us along
> rather roughly.
>
> As we reached the station, says Rumble,
> the third man commenced to give Grant

trouble. He tried to pull himself away from the policeman's grasp. Then Grant called on Rumble to assist him. Rumble said, "Oh, I guess you can handle them all right."

As he uttered those words, the third man pulled his pistol and quick as a flash fired the shot that killed Grant. As the bullet struck him, Grant gave me a violent shove and I fell up against the fence. Then Rumble says the third man fired a second shot at me. His gun aim was bad and the bullet passed through Rumble's coat and then through the fence. The murderer then dropped flat on his stomach and fired a third shot, which was also intended for me, but again he missed me and the bullet went through the fence near the ground.

After firing the third shot, the murderer jumped to his feet and ran away, an example which, according to Rumble, I was quick to follow. Rumble was left alone with the dead policeman. He says that for a moment he was dazed, but as he recovered himself, the awful thought entered his head that if he was found there he might be accused of the murder. The idea of getting away came next. Acting upon the impulse, he scrambled over the fence into a vacant lot and hid himself under a wagon, where he remained for two hours . . .

When the last person had left the scene Rumble crawled from under the wagon and went home. The next day he met Treadwell and told him of his adventure.

After learning of my arrest, Rumble says
he determined to keep himself out of the case
unless he saw that I would be convicted. He
went East but changed his mind about keeping quiet and wrote to Foote saying that he
would come to San Francisco if his testimony
was required. He was in this city during my
first trial and would have been placed on the
stand but for the advice of a veteran lawyer
who argued that we had enough testimony
without him, and that it would be best not to
load down a good case with too much testimony.
He went East again, but returned and was
here when my second trial was interrupted by
the death of a juror. Again he returned home,
but he will be here to give his testimony now
when called upon.

While waiting for Rumble to arrive, the defense called
a W. R. Vice to the stand. He testified that on the night of
Grant's murder he was with the manager for Sarah Bernhardt
and ran into Curtis in the foyer of the Grand Opera House. He
testified that Curtis attempted to drag the manager and him
into the barroom to have a drink. Vice said that he resisted
Curtis's efforts and that there was a scuffle during which he
felt no pistol in Curtis's clothes, according to the *Morning Call*
on August 23, 1893.

This same article also detailed the testimony of Frank
Thompson, a Berkeley plumber, who confirmed that he had
given Curtis a bill for $240 and that he expected Curtis to visit
him and pay his bill on the day of the shooting, but that to his

surprise, Curtis hadn't turned up.

Curtis then took the stand and repeated his version of the events leading up to Officer Grant's murder, adding that he had fled the scene "just as a bird that is hurt tries to fly away." Curtis also answered the question as to why he borrowed money for drinks at the Tivoli if he had the $240 in gold coins in his pocket, saying that he had borrowed money to pay for his box seats at the Grand Opera House and was accustomed to running a tab at whatever bar he was drinking at.

Curtis's defense team then put Mark Abbott, a runner for the Cosmopolitan Hotel, on the stand who told of seeing the third man. According to Abbott, "I spoke to the police a few days later about what I had seen, but I was never called by them to testify."

After Abbott testified to seeing the mysterious shooter, Curtis once again entered the witness stand to testify in his own self-defense. When cross-examined, Curtis was asked about the chamois-skinned purse with the $240 in it and the bottle of whiskey in his pocket that seemed to replace it. "With dignity and indignation Curtis declared that he had not ordered the bottle of whiskey and placed it in his own pocket. 'I would not go to meet my wife with such a disreputable looking bottle,' he exclaimed with vehemence," as the *Examiner* reported on August 26, 1893.

Prosecutor Barnes then wanted to know if on September 9, 1891, Curtis had had a black pistol fall out of his pocket when he fell asleep in a chair at the Tivoli, as two employees of the theatre had testified to seeing. At this point Curtis began to lose the composure he had maintained throughout the questioning. He looked startled and glanced back and forth between Barnes and the courtroom as if he were trying to decide whom to address his response to.

Kreling and I have had a falling out. It all
comes from a lawsuit. When I was arrested,
he wanted me to make another defense, but I
would not do it. He advised me to admit that
it was my pistol and that the shooting was in
self-defense, but I wouldn't do it. I didn't do
it and I preferred to stand trial on a charge of
murder. Attorney Foote knows that this is so.

Curtis also testified that, under the advice of his attorneys, he did not tell anyone other than his attorneys that he had been robbed until the trial. With that, the prosecution finished their cross-examination of Curtis, and the actor displayed noticeable relief as he stepped down from the box.

The next day Barnes again brought up the two employees at the Tivoli who had testified that a gun resembling the murder weapon fell out of Curtis's pocket while he slept in a drunken slumber in a back room at the Tivoli a week or two before the murder. These men had not come forward with their evidence in the first two trials, and only revealed their knowledge a day or so previous to their testimony. When cross-examined, they said they were friends of Curtis's and did not want to get involved. One of these Tivoli witnesses, W. H. Leahy, was asked directly by Foote, "Were you a witness for Kreling in his lawsuit against Curtis?"

"Yes," Leahy admitted, adding that he had only come forward because he had been at the Tivoli when Barnes was there interviewing the staff and that he could not lie when directly asked a question.

Albert Palmer, the Tivoli barkeep, was next to testify. He was a stocky man and slow and deliberate in his answers. He, too, had not offered testimony in the two previous trials.

Palmer said Curtis was at his bar between nine and eleven the
night of the murder and ordered drinks and charged them to
his account. Palmer testified that Curtis said he had no money
and that the actor had borrowed one dollar for the ferry. Palmer
also said that he was the man who filled the soda bottle with
whiskey for Curtis that night, and he stated that Curtis got
testy when he was drunk.

Next Barnes called Officer Patrick Minehan to the stand
since the policeman knew the defense witness Mark Abbott,
the runner at the Cosmopolitan Hotel. Minehan said that he
had spoken with Abbott the day after the murder. "I asked him
if he knew anything about it. He said he did not, that he was
in bed or going to bed, and that he heard some shots. I met
him on the street several days later and he told me there was
no use asking him anything about the matter; that he knew
nothing about it." So, once again, the jury was left to decide
which witness was lying.

Interestingly enough, neither the defense nor the prosecution brought in the mysterious Mr. Rumble who supposedly
saw the murder even though Rumble was present in San
Francisco and ready to testify, having registered a few days
earlier at the Russ Hotel under an alias.

When interviewed by the *Examiner*, Rumble said, "I have
read the narrative of Mr. Curtis this morning, and I have nothing to say. I will not admit or deny that I saw Grant killed. If
the lawyers want to put me on the stand, I will tell all I know,
but not until then."

The reason Rumble was not called by either side might be
found in an article published in the *San Francisco Chronicle* on
December 18, 1895. It seems that Mr. Rumble had a reputation
of being a paid witness who would say whatever was requested
of him. He was also involved in a clock swindle and had

attempted to be a witness in another well-known case.

The next day, Thursday, August 24, Foote began his closing arguments. He carefully and meticulously spelled out the
details of the case. He noted that the police force had been
deeply involved in the testimony of many witnesses and that
they had fabricated falsehood and fraud to convince the jury
to convict Curtis. He asked for no hung jury, no mercy, but
demanded clear justice and a verdict of not guilty.

Curtis's attorney J. N. E. Wilson then spoke of the uncer-
tainty of the prosecution's testimony, closing his final arguments with "an eloquent reference to the marital love existing
between Curtis and his wife, and appealed to the jury to vin-
dicate Curtis and send him back to his home, his flowers, and
his pets," according to the *San Francisco Chronicle* on August
25, 1893.

Even though the brevity of his closing arguments surprised the courtroom, District Attorney Barnes was equally
eloquent when he described the funeral of Officer Grant
and urged the jurors, "Don't give a verdict on sympathy and
sentiment. Can you give a verdict on feelings for Curtis and
his wife when you have sworn here to do your duty as jurors?
Blind your eyes and weigh the evidence. Consider the cold,
cold facts. I beg you to decide this case on the law and the
evidence," the *San Francisco Chronicle* reported on August
26, 1893.

Judge Murphy then gave instructions to the jury for half
an hour, telling them they might find Curtis guilty of either
first- or second-degree murder. The jury began deliberating
on August 25, 1893, at around noon.

Three hours later they emerged from the jury room, and
court was called back into session. There was complete silence
when the judge asked the jury if they had reached a decision

The scene in the courtroom after Curtis's acquittal. (The San Francisco Examiner, *August 26, 1893)*

and the foreman responded that they had. When Judge Murphy asked what that decision was, the jury foreman responded, "Not guilty."

It turns out that there had been three ballots, with the first vote being 9–3 for acquittal, then 11–1, and the final holdout joining the majority opinion on the third ballot.

Surrounded by friends and the warm August air, Curtis and Marie made their way to the Occidental Hotel where bottles were waiting on ice for the celebration. In a *San Francisco Call* article on September 10, 1893, Curtis sounded like his old optimistic self again.

> I shall take up my old line of work just as soon
> as I can get my business affairs in the right
> condition. It is my intention to open in New

York about the first of October, though in the
meantime I may play here for a week or two.
I wouldn't want to have it seem that I feel
indisposed to appear in San Francisco, for the
people of the city have never been unkind to
me, and public sentiment has been in my
favor . . .

I shall take up *Sam'l of Posen* again, and
Hoyt & Thomas are now modernizing it for
me. On alternate weeks with that I shall present
a melodrama founded on the story of my own
case. I gave the order for it to Simms and Pettit
of London eight months ago, sending all the
evidence of my first trial. They have three acts
written, as they stated in a letter received this
week, and they are now concluding it with the
fourth. [There is no evidence that Curtis ever
performed a dramatization of his trial.]

In an undated article found in the Harvard Theater Collection, Curtis is further quoted as saying, "The melodrama
and *Sam'l of Posen* will be played on alternate weeks, and my
engagements at each theatre will be twice as long as before.
I received a telegram from Chicago today offering me $1,500
a week for forty weeks or more, but I do not expect to make
any contracts there . . . Mrs. Curtis will go through the season
with me, and she will continue to play *Camille* as the matinee
attraction."

There remains to this day a cloak of mystery over the events
that occurred in the darkness of the early hours of September

11, 1891. Although the verdict ended the trial, it did not answer all the questions surrounding the tragic events. Why did Grant arrest Curtis? Why did he need to put nippers on him? Whose gun was it? Why didn't the police pursue the third man from the beginning?

For the police department, pained by the loss of their comrade in such sudden and tragic circumstances, the anger and frustration would go on for decades.

The news of Curtis's acquittal was trumpeted in the New York papers the next day. They commented how the actor's lot is harder than others, as his face and personality are known by so many. They reported that there were some who used the trial to illustrate the depravity the acting profession brings into one's life. But the *Brooklyn Daily Eagle* pointed out on August 27, 1893, that "the number of stage people arrested in the course of a year is small compared to that of clerks, mechanics, politicians and professional men whose callings ought not to incite to evil. The actor rarely sins from the heart. He may be weak, but seldom wrong."

The *Albany Law Journal* reported on September 16, 1893, that "a good many people will be pleased to hear that the actor M. B. Curtis—more popularly known as Sam'l of Posen—has, at last, been acquitted of the charge of murdering Policeman Grant of San Francisco. He has had to endure three trials, and has spent in his defense about $50,000 . . . As the jury was out but two hours . . . it may be taken for granted that the verdict is strictly in accordance with the evidence, but Curtis's has been a fearful ordeal for an innocent man to be subjected to."

A Troubled Comeback

Audiences are not strangers to me.
They're the best friends I've got in my life.
—*Elaine Stritch*

⌐

Even though M. B. Curtis was now a free man after his acquittal in the third trial, his legal entanglements didn't end. The
San Francisco police could not accept their failure to convict
Curtis and the damage done to their reputation, and they
were still chewing over the case as late as 1910. Even more
troubling for Curtis was District Attorney Barnes's filing a
complaint in Superior Court of bribery against Frank "King"
McManus, a saloonkeeper and mobster, and William Dunn,
a former state senator, on October 10, 1893, less than two
months after Curtis's acquittal. The complaint stated that the
two had given $8,000 to an unknown John Doe to bribe jurors
in order to acquit Curtis. McManus submitted a statement that
jurors C. Shaw Coy, a clerk at the Security Savings Bank, and
T. M. MacFarlane were the ones he paid. Curtis's attorney J. N. E.
Wilson presented an affidavit to the complaint stating that
the two accused men had tried to extort money from him by

San Francisco gang leader Frank McManus on trial for attempting to bribe jurors. (The San Francisco Examiner, *November 2, 1893)*

claiming they had paid out $2,000 and suggesting that Curtis had "agreed" to give them $6,000 more.

The following day, Dunn and McManus were arrested for bribery and trying to extort money from Marie Curtis. After posting bond, the men were released. The San Francisco *Examiner* of October 21, 1893, noted, "Both men seemed to be unusually nervous and their attempts at joviality were evidently forced." On November 1, 1893, the preliminary examination of Dunn and McManus began with both men standing and fidgeting while the complaint was read. The charge was the attempted bribery of one to four jurors in the Curtis trial. When Wilson's affidavit stated that after Dunn and McManus found

out Mrs. Curtis had no money the men had asked for ten
lots in Peralta Park, laughter rose in the court, and McManus
smiled broadly and stared at Dunn proudly, as described by
a reporter for the *Examiner* on November 2, 1893.

According to newspaper reports, including one in the
San Francisco Call on October 21, 1893, other unsavory characters were also claiming they had bribed the jury and were
demanding payment and threatening the life of Curtis. He
had armed a number of employees at his Fresno ranch with
shotguns, and a sheriff was on duty there as well. While the
Nebraska State Journal's discussion of the current affairs in
San Francisco does smack of more than a touch of Midwest-
ern moralizing, their admonition to Californians is not off
the mark and does much to explain the situation Curtis now
found himself in.

> The discovery of the jury bribing in connec-
> tion with the Curtis murder trial is no new
> experience for San Francisco. One of the
> colossal disadvantages of living on the Pacific
> Coast, and especially in San Francisco, is the
> existence of corruption in public affairs. It is
> found in the courts, in the city governments,
> and the management of the schools, and will
> remain in all of them until the people of the
> West Coast awake to their duties as citizens.
> The cause of this unfortunate condition is to
> be found mainly in the lack of public spirit
> among the earlier settlers.

Subpoenas were issued for both Curtis and Marie—as
well as for MacFarlane, one of the jurors who supposedly was

bribed to vote in Curtis's favor. While it was feared by police that MacFarlane had already left the state, two detectives were sent to Curtis's Fresno ranch to track down the actor and his wife, but the two policemen could not locate Curtis or Marie even after spending two days looking for them.

Both the prosecutor and defense attorneys then began frantically trying to reach Marie to find out where her husband was, and they eventually found her in J. N. E. Wilson's office while she was there discussing Peralta Park business. Marie told the court that her husband was hunting in the country and couldn't be reached.

Despite the absence of its star witness, the trial began for the accused jury bribers with J. N. E. Wilson testifying that McManus and Dunn had visited Marie at the Occidental Hotel and had demanded money from her as well.

Marie then took the stand and described the visit in detail, saying that she had asked the men if Curtis had promised them money or had borrowed any cash from them. According to Marie, they answered, "No, but after we state what we've done, we think Mr. Curtis will be man enough to do what is right—this is, to pay us."

Marie was asked if she was afraid of McManus, and she responded that she was, even though the men had been polite when they had visited her at the hotel. This was no idle fear on Marie's part. McManus was known to be an extremely brutal individual. He once burst into a hospital operating room and tried to repeatedly club an unconscious patient on the head. McManus had also smashed the windows of St. Patrick's church on Mission Street and threatened to kill Reverend Peter Grey when the priest refused to say a mass in honor of McManus's brother, who had just been murdered by one of McManus's bartenders.

During Marie's testimony, a mysterious and rather bizarre fact emerged—MacFarlane, the main juror accused of taking bribes to acquit Curtis, had fled to Fresno after the complaint was filed, staying with the actor and his wife for ten days or so according to Marie's testimony. But Marie testified that MacFarlane had denied taking any bribes and had decided the case on its own merits. Why the juror briefly holed up in Fresno with the Curtises was never explained.

After Marie left the witness stand, District Attorney Barnes declared that he wanted Curtis to testify before the end of the case and that a subpoena was already at the Fresno sheriff's office. The next week, when the district attorney assured the judge that he believed Curtis could be "obtained" as a witness, the case was held over to the following week, according to the *Examiner* on November 8, 1893.

Curtis, meanwhile, had evidently boarded an eastbound train in Sacramento the day before hearing of his wife's court date. Using the many tricks of stagecraft and makeup he had learned during his career, the actor rode the train disguised as a tramp. As the train approached the California-Nevada border, Curtis took off his costume and began mingling with his fellow passengers, entertaining them with many funny stories without mentioning his current troubles. Several people on the train recognized Curtis and knew he was running from the court, and someone called the authorities from Truckee, providing the first public information on Curtis's whereabouts in months.

As the train continued east and crossed the California state line, Curtis must have breathed a sigh of relief, as he evidently no longer felt the need to keep a low profile. "On the contrary, he was boisterous in his contact and attracted attention by it." Two females, "one a young and handsome girl

and the other an elderly woman," were said to be "his com-
panions" and were in the same section of the sleeper car as
Curtis. The three attended a buffet together and drank heavily.
"One passenger of an observing turn of mind said that the
Curtis party had drank four quarts of beer and one of whiskey
between Grand Junction and Colorado Springs," according to
a November 4, 1893, article in the *Examiner*.

On the same day that McManus and Dunn were released
on bond, Curtis showed up in Boston, registering at the Parker
House Hotel under the name James Powers (the name of a
very successful comic actor at the time). Curtis was recognized
the following day and quoted as saying he had come east
as he was in need of rest. The *Nevada State Journal* printed
Curtis's statement on November 10, 1893: "It cost me $80,000
to defend myself in my trial for shooting a policeman in San
Francisco. And as for getting out of California to avoid arrest
for jury bribery, there is no truth in it."

On December 5, 1893, all charges against McManus and
Dunn were dismissed, and in New York Curtis's planned
return to the theatre was big news. Curtis called on the *Mirror*
and told them his stay would be for a long time. "My purpose
in coming? Well, I am tired of being a landed proprietor and
I think I shall go back into my legitimate work again. I began
as an actor, and although I have made a snug fortune by my
investments, I feel that I shall not be happy until I am once
more in harness."

There was some question, however, as to exactly how "snug"
Curtis's fortune was currently and when he would actually
return to the "harness" of his stage career. For, despite the failure of his Peralta Park Hotel project, Curtis was again playing

the role of grand hotelier, this time in the Lone Star State.

In early 1894, Curtis joined his brother Frank at Chicago's Grand Pacific Hotel, registering under the name of D. B. Anderson of Philadelphia to, no doubt, again avoid the prying press. But he was soon recognized and explained his current situation in an interview published in the *San Francisco Chronicle* on March 22, 1894.

> I am running my hotel at Austin, Texas, and
> am now on my way to New York to take to the
> boards again. I wish to say that the stories
> telegraphed from San Francisco that I had
> confessed to killing Policeman Grant, and that
> I had also confessed to jury bribing, are un-
> mitigated falsehoods. The Police Department
> of that city has followed me with relentless
> fury and with all the spleen of a set of Vidocqs
> [a French society dedicated to fighting and
> solving crime]. In no other city would I have
> received such treatment as I received there. It
> has been two years and six months since my
> arrest for murder, and in all that time I have
> suffered greatly.

The Curtises, no doubt needing to get some distance from their California troubles, had purchased the Driskill Hotel in Austin, Texas, in December of 1893. The Austin *Evening News* stated that Curtis paid $350,000 for the Driskill, much of it in cash, "some on time, and 1,280 acres of fine land near Fresno, Cal., 300 acres of which is in grapes, and ranks as the finest raisin vineyard in all Southern California."

Once again Curtis's optimistic dreams were not balanced

THE DRISKILL HOTEL · AUSTIN, TEXAS
1886

(Private collection)

by planning and prudence. He was either unaware or untroubled by the Driskill's difficult history. The hotel, the largest hotel in Austin, had been built in 1886 by cattle baron Jesse Driskill. Despite hosting the 1887 inaugural ball for Texas Governor Sul Ross and providing luxurious accommodations for the well-heeled, the hotel was closed in late 1887 after the Galveston Beach Hotel poached half of the Driskill's staff. After a cold winter killed 3,000 of their cattle, the Driskill family was forced to sell the hotel to Jim "Doc" Day, though legend has it that Driskill lost the elegant hotel to Day in a poker game. Day had no better luck than Driskill did in trying to keep the sprawling Romanesque-style hotel afloat. Despite his keeping the Driskill in the limelight by hosting visiting dignitaries and throwing parties for state officials, Day soon tired of the expense of keeping the hotel open and was only too happy to pass along his financial problems to the ebullient Curtis, who had been enamored of Austin since his first visit in 1881.

But Curtis had no better luck in the hotel business than

the previous owners. He was almost immediately forced to borrow money to keep the hotel running. The upkeep of the property was so costly that even with full occupancy and the rooms going for what then were top rates, Curtis was losing money. Soon after acquiring the Driskill, Curtis made another major real estate deal, estimated in the *New York Times* as worth about $800,000. He traded the Driskill Hotel to New York hotel magnate George H. Deller. In return, Deller gave Curtis 6,000 lots in Lakewood, New Jersey, where the Rockefellers and the Goulds were beginning to use their own properties as vacation retreats. It was also reported that Curtis received a country home and ten acres on Long Island as part of the deal. It was now time for the temporary Texan to head east and return to doing what he did best.

On April 30, 1894, an updated version of *Sam'l of Posen* opened at New York's Standard Theatre. Some of the new features in the play were a cable car scene and a tie-in to Jacob S. Coxey, who had led a protest group known as Coxey's Army to Washington, D.C., to demand government assistance for unemployed workers suffering from the effects of the Panic of 1893.

According to an undated and unsourced newspaper article in the Harvard Theater Collection, Curtis's return to the New York stage was greeted with warmth and enthusiasm.

> Mr. Curtis's appearance was the signal for a
> long-continued chorus of friendly welcome.
> He was recalled again and again after each
> act, and the audience did everything in their
> power to show him that old friends were still
> fast friends, and that they were heartily glad to

Sketches celebrating Curtis's return to the stage in a revised version of Sam'l of Posen *at New York's Standard Theatre.* (Illustrated Weekly Dramatic News)

renew acquaintances . . . The actor himself has
lost none of his old-time drollery or his won-
derfully clever power of character acting. He

was pestered for a speech after each fall of the
curtain, but he only replied to the vociferous
summons with bows and smiles that told how
he appreciated his reception.

An article in New York's *Spirit of the Times* said the crowds
did not believe he committed the murder in San Francisco, reporting that Curtis had a "prodigious welcome . . . when he made
his first appearance on stage since his unhappy experience
in San Francisco." The "demonstrative and receptive" crowd
arrived early, and the house was packed long before the start
of the play. Understandably, the play's murder scene had been
removed—a topic obviously fraught with disturbing reminders
since Curtis's trial. The *New York Times* predicated on May 1,
1894, that Curtis "will probably make a new fortune with his
revised play and afford much wholesome merriment to the
multitude." This prediction seemed prescient as Curtis and his
play were held over for a second month at the Standard.

For reasons that were not mentioned in the press, Marie
did not initially perform in the revived *Sam'l of Posen*, but she
eventually returned to portray Celeste, as she had done for so
many years. But the season that began with so much promise
began to flounder. The pressure on the still-traumatized Curtis
to return to his former career was apparently weighing on the
actor, and he began to drink heavily, which was now affecting
his performance. When Curtis reopened *Sam'l of Posen* in San
Francisco, as much to regain his reputation and pride as to
regroup financially, the actor was said to be hissed off stage.
His old friends were avoiding him, and Curtis was beginning
to get caught up in lawsuits that were a result of his mounting
debts. As the *Brooklyn Daily Eagle* observed on June 24, 1894,
"Mr. Curtis seems to be born to trouble."

In early September, Curtis announced his intention to re-work *Sam'l of Posen* once again, with the added attraction that he would precede it with a one-act farce called *The Irish Em-igrant* that would enlarge upon common immigrant themes. But it seemed that the actor could not quite escape his recent traumas. A B. Dolan, who claimed he was a witness at Curtis's murder trial, attached the scenery of *Sam'l of Posen* in St. Louis against payment of his $50 witness fee. Curtis declared that Dolan was a blackmailer and applied for a warrant for his arrest, and Curtis once again found himself in court.

By September, Curtis was performing *Sam'l of Posen, the Drummer Up-to-Date* at the Opera House in Decatur, Illinois. According to the September 8, 1894, *Decatur Daily Republican*, the script was not the only part of the production to be updated: "The drummer of today is always a stylish and well-dressed gentleman, and Mr. Curtis relegated his old plaids and stripes to the past, and in their place, will show all the latest fads in dress, not forgetting, of course, jeweled studs in his collars, which seems to be the latest craze."

As well as the new play was received in some parts of the country, Curtis and Marie were reportedly mistreating their company members during their comeback tour. And Curtis began keeping the whereabouts of his lodgings secret to dodge his many creditors. When approached by reporters, Curtis declined to comment on the state of his company or personal affairs, save to say he was doing everything he could to get back on his feet again. But the production of the often-revised *Sam'l of Posen* was beginning to stumble, and the cast blamed Curtis and Marie.

Curtis was said to have become "irritable, disagreeable and tyrannical," according to the *New York Times* on Septem-ber 10, 1894.

He demands more than one could possibly
do, and when his commands are not obeyed,
he flies into a terrible passion and insults and
abuses everyone with whom he has come in
contact. It is said he has forgotten all his wife
did for him in his great trouble and applies
epithets to her when in a drunken rage that
are too shameful for publication. He refuses to
even recognize those who worked hardest for
him during his confinement in jail, and when
his aged father . . . fell ill and, being in need of
money, asked his son for $50, the latter would
not recognize the appeal.

W. C. Le Tort, a member of Curtis's company, had some
insight into Curtis's mental state at the time. Le Tort, who had
played a "black face" part, was replaced by a black actor and
was refused the salary he felt was owed him. Le Tort said in a
September 24, 1894, interview with a Chicago newspaper that
he slept in a room adjoining one occupied by Curtis and that
he could not sleep because of the noise produced by Curtis
pacing the floor back and forth all night, "too nervous and
worried to sleep, he keeps up a weary tramp throughout the
long hours of the night, mumbling and talking to himself. He
is drinking hard and sometimes when intoxicated insults his
audiences from the stage."

On a recent St. Louis engagement, an intoxicated Curtis
had thrown so many insults at the audience that the manager
had threatened to lower the curtain if it did not stop. Reports
such as these only fueled the public's appetite for scandal,
and newspapers began printing every story and rumor about
Curtis they heard, including the dubious story about Curtis

refusing his father fifty dollars.

By now it was obvious that Curtis had lost control of his exhausted emotions and was slipping into rage, despondency, and despair. He had changed from an exuberant comic on stage to a tragic figure in his own life. His frustration, mixed with his past feelings of success and invulnerability, created a toxic mix not unlike the poisonous cigar that knocked out Sam'l in the gambling den. Only this time it was for real.

Of the sixteen members of his company performing in *Sam'l of Posen* since late August 1894, only five were still in the company two months later. Six of the actors who left told stories to the press of "unkind actions on the part of the star." Curtis's box office receipts were attached in New York, St. Louis, and Minneapolis. But despite these troubles, the play generally got favorable reviews. A theatre in Boston "rang with applause and Mr. Curtis must have felt his heart warm anew toward his true and tried New England friends." Marie had her share of applause as well. "She is a charming little woman, bright and vivacious, and very pretty," according to an undated and unsourced article in the Harvard Theater Collection.

After playing in Bangor, Maine, at the end of October, Curtis opened at the Park Theatre in Boston for a two-week run to strong advanced sales. The end of November 1894 found the actor and his company back in Brooklyn at the Bijou Theatre playing to large and appreciative audiences, though a reviewer for the *Brooklyn Eagle* noted on November 20, 1894, that "Curtis shows the effect of passing years and perhaps of his scrape in San Francisco, that came near retiring him from the stage for good."

In mid-December 1894, Curtis wrote to playwright William A. Brady asking him for the part of the Jew in Brady's Boston production of Sutton Vane's *Humanity*. According to the *Fort Wayne* (Indiana) *News*, Brady was said to have written NOT ON YOUR LIFE across the cover of the letter. This same article went on to say, "In the old Academy days, Curtis played to big houses in Fort Wayne in *Sam'l of Posen*, but he has been losing his grip everywhere since then."

Curtis unexpectedly closed his 1894–1895 season on December 19. His manager announced that the company would be reorganized and that Curtis would open in a new play, although many doubted if Curtis was in any shape to star in a new play anytime soon. The *San Francisco Chronicle* summed up Curtis's current state fairly succinctly on December 22, 1894: "He has displayed extreme nervousness and irritation, and numerous stories have appeared in print as to his difficulties with his managers and members of his company." Curtis was clearly suffering from the severe and unrelenting stress he had been under the past three years, and his theatrical and business responsibilities were being adversely affected. He had now reached the point that his "stage" needed an immediate change of scenery.

Curtis booked passage on the *Teutonic* on December 16, 1894, and set across the Atlantic soon after, heading for a German sanatorium accompanied by a physician. The December 28, 1894, *Daily Palladium* (Oswego, New York) was hopeful about Curtis's chances to recover his health and personal stability.

> Since his misfortune in San Francisco, Curtis
> has never been altogether rightly balanced,
> and his actions during this season in connec-
> tion with his employees must be put down to
> that cause. Curtis's financial transactions, too,

would have been enough to unbalance a stronger
man. A few years ago he was a semi-millionaire.
Now all he has got is unprofitable property . . .
While eccentric, Curtis is by no means a mad
man, and it is very likely that this sea voyage
and rest may restore him completely.

Marie also sounded upbeat when she spoke to a *Berkeley
Gazette* reporter on January 10, 1895.

Mr. Curtis is in London. I had a cablegram
from him in which he said that he had arrived
and was well. I shall join him in about six
weeks. Oh, I wish it were only ten days. He
has gone to London to endeavor to secure a
new play. We have been playing *Posen* now for
fourteen years, and I thought it went well last
season. One could hardly expect people to
come to see it again . . . I am here now settling
up our estate. You know, we are more or less
in debt, for we had great expenses. Fortu-
nately, that affair is now all settled, although
"they" tried hard to prevent it. Yes, it was a hot
encounter while it lasted, but I was in it all the
time. Yes, indeed, I was in the fight. Now we
intend to come back and live in California. I
am now in negotiation for a piece of property
in Berkeley, for which I intend to trade some
other property. We shall make our home in
Berkeley and shall probably be there during
the summers, for the rest of the time we shall
be on the road . . . We played twenty-nine

weeks in all and had a very successful season.
Our next season will probably open in October, that is, provided Mr. Curtis does not get an
opening in London. He had had many offers
to go there, and we may open in the great metropolis . . . There are many good comedies in
London and, if he does not find what he wants
there, he will go to Paris and to Berlin . . .
When we get what we want, we shall organize
a new company and open in New York . . .
Shall I appear with him? Oh, yes indeed, for
he would never think of opening without me.

The interviewer, obviously smitten with the charming
Marie, then added, "The actress who had stood off detectives
and deputy sheriffs during her husband's trial for his life
shook her head and smiled in a fond sort of way, which served
to denote that Sam'l of Posen would be but a half-hearted
young man without his partner."

While Curtis worked toward his first European performances,
W. J. Hurley's trial was going on in San Francisco, and Hurley,
one of the two jurors who voted for acquittal in Curtis's first
trial, claimed that Curtis was aware of the bribing of the
jurors. If this was proven, Curtis would face felony charges.
Though he could not be charged again for murder, Curtis
could go to prison if convicted of bribery. However, Hurley's
reputation as a witness was not good, and he was considered
by many to be a "professional" in the witness trade. The *San
Francisco Chronicle* had been digging into the never-ending
and very public spectacle, and published their concerns about

the present case on March 27, 1895.

> [Hurley] is or was only the tool of some person
> or persons much shrewder and sharper than he
> and equally unprincipled, and it should be the
> aim of the authorities to find out who such per-
> sons were and send them to the State Prison
> as well as Hurley . . . Curtis declared, so it is
> said, that his acquittal had cost him $80,000.
> Where did the money go? Who got it, and who
> were the distributing agents? It might be good
> policy for Judge Wallace and District Attorney
> Barnes to promise Hurley, not immunity for
> his crime, but a mitigation of his sentence, if
> he will tell who his principals were and supply
> the evidence for their conviction.

Three days later, Hurley was sentenced to five years in prison
without having implicated Curtis in the affair. In May 1895,
the *Times* reported that Curtis was with Marie in London
setting up a production of *Sam'l of Posen*. On July 4, 1895, he
produced a trial matinee of *Sam'l of Posen* at the Gaiety Theatre. Although reviews were mixed, one American newspaper
summarized the response of the British press that "opined in
a chorus of condemnation and express wonder at the fact that
the play was successful in the United States." One reviewer
argued that the cultured West End crowd would probably not
like the play but felt that many in the outskirts of London and
in the manufacturing districts would indeed like the performance as they enjoyed eccentric comedy even when it was
presented in conventional melodramatic form.

Sam'l of Posen's character and experiences were typically American and did not seem to appeal to British sensibilities. London of 1895 was not the immigrant destination that New York and America were, and Samuel Plastrick was beyond the grasp of London's playgoing cognoscenti who understood neither the drummer's Yiddish phrases nor his struggle to improve his lot in the world. Even though the first London performance of *Sam'l of Posen* was also its last, Curtis made a good impression on the reviewer for a London weekly newspaper, the *Stage*, on July 11, 1895.

> Mr. Curtis is a spruce, dapper little man with mobile features, big eyes, the whites of which he shows in a droll way, and many queer mannerisms, which have doubtless grown upon him during the long period of his connection with this play. The character which he sustains is not quite so unfamiliar over here as some people would have us believe, and it is at any rate a welcome variant upon the stereotyped stage Jew . . . Altogether, however, he was an amusing and original impersonation, and as such it was favorably received on Thursday.

In September 1895, Curtis was back in the States performing to overflowing houses at the Schiller Theatre in Chicago. And he was also back in the middle of his stew of financial troubles. On the night of September 23, deputy sheriffs went to the box office during the show to seize the night's take although Curtis's manager, Duncan Harrison, had already been there and taken the cash. By ten p.m., forty deputies had arrived, some at the stage door in the front, some at the door at the rear. They had been given instructions to seize any property belonging to Curtis due to a suit brought by the Academy Theatre Company in Milwaukee that alleged Curtis was booked to play a run at the Academy but did not honor his contract.

In December, Curtis's household furniture was seized against a $2,000 writ from a Mina Dalker. Dalker had, on September 20, 1894, traded to the Curtises her house at 720 St. Nicholas Avenue in New York City for a lot in Solano County, California, and some lots in Berkeley's Peralta Park, and there was a dispute as to the values of the properties.

The Dalker real estate episode continued into October of 1896 when Curtis took the stand in the suit. Curtis's testimony turned rather theatrical, according to the *San Francisco Chronicle* on October 17, 1896.

> Mr. Curtis was evidently suffering from a great attack of stage fright and made a very poor witness for himself. The first question the plaintiff's attorney asked brought Mr. Curtis to his feet in an instant and he made a speech which had a certain amount of melodramatic effect. The question was: "Did you ever speak to the plaintiff about the property in question previous to your trial for murder in San Francisco?"
>
> "Unfortunately for me," said Curtis, "the episode which I was connected with in San Francisco, and which has been the foundation of all my troubles, is cropping out at all times. On the charge of murder I was honorably acquitted, yet it seems on every occasion

possible my enemies cowardly draw that
episode into play. There is no real reason for
it. I was proved innocent of the charge, and
now I protest against the word murder being
brought into the present case. It has no bearing on the matter involved, and people who
hear of it only begin to ask questions and the
whole incident is unearthed again, and I ask
the protection of the court."

The plaintiff's attorney, who had asked the
question, apologized and asked to strike out
both his question and the actor's answer. This
the Judge agreed to. In answer to other questions, Curtis acknowledged that he had never
seen the ranch and lots traded for, and was
not a party to the transfer as the property all
belonged to his wife. The witness then began
to hesitate in his answers and the attorney of
the opposition said, "I want you to answer my
questions in a proper manner."

Curtis opened his eyes in astonishment at
the lawyer's attitude, and replied, "I am doing
that."

"You need not make eyes at me in that
manner," said the lawyer, "you are not on the
stage now."

This retort angered the witness, who
turned to the Court and said: "Your honor,
I am accustomed to talking in a big theatre,
where I am compelled to talk loud and use my
hands and face for proper expressions, and if I
used my eyes as the attorney says I did, it was

because I am used to it, and not as an insult as
the attorney would have you believe."

The Judge upheld the witness and the attorney
accepted the actor's excuse.

Curtis's testimony on the witness stand in this real estate
dispute wasn't the only drama that was occurring offstage. In
1895, Curtis purchased the American rights to a British play
called *Gentleman Joe* for $5,000 in advance royalties and 10
percent of the receipts. Curtis claimed to have exclusive American and Canadian rights to the play for ten years. According
to Curtis, at least two other American productions of the play
stole music or scenery and infringed on Curtis's rights. Curtis
met with one of the pirate producers and urged him not to go
forward with the theft of material. The producer gave his word
not to, but on opening night, to Curtis's surprise and disappointment, the man did not keep his word. Insulted by the
breach of trust, Curtis, who was in the audience, began to hiss
"like a steam engine" and successfully interrupted the stolen
performance, according to the *Dramatic Mirror* on December
28, 1895.

Curtis's *Gentleman Joe* opened at New York's Fifth Avenue
Theatre a week ahead of a third production of the same play
at the Bijou. Actor John T. Powers, in his book *Twinkle Little
Star*, regales readers with the story of what happened when
a sheriff, denied entrance at the stage door, bought a seat for
Curtis's second performance at the Fifth Avenue Theatre.

When Curtis strolled on stage and began to sing, "I'm
Gentleman Joe, I'm gay and free, as a bird in the air, or a fish
in the sea," the sheriff scrambled onto the stage and began his
theatrical career with the line "Oh, you think you are, eh?"

Curtis bested the sheriff by jumping into the private box

Curtis as Gentleman Joe. (TCS 1. Houghton Library, Harvard University)

stage right. A chase to rival a future Keystone Kops routine
ensued, with Curtis running up the aisle with the sheriff in
pursuit. In a flash, Curtis burst through the theatre door
and rounded a turn, flying down Broadway still in his stage

239

costume. Looking for an opening as he dodged his way through the stylish crowds of Broadway, Curtis spotted the Sturtevant House and plunged through the doorway. Circling the room with his eyes, he spotted a stairway to the basement and made a beeline for it. He flew down the stairs and made his way to the cellar, burrowing himself behind a huge steam boiler. The sheriff, who had been right on Curtis's heels, soon took the very warm actor into custody.

Meanwhile, the startled audience, not really sure of what was artifice and what was real, slowly straggled out of the theatre while having a lively discussion about what they had just witnessed.

Curtis ultimately lost the rights to *Gentleman Joe*, as he was playing the role of the lead character without written approval from the play's owner. When he was sued for breach of contract, Curtis prevailed in court on almost all parts of the suit, but the judge ruled that by playing Gentleman Joe himself without prior permission of the playwright he had broken his contract and forfeited his rights.

Even while Curtis's current difficulties were headline news in newspapers across the country, many people still admired the actor's resiliency. When Curtis went back to Atlanta's Lyceum Theatre after an eight-year absence from the city, a writer for the *Atlanta Constitution* opined on March 19, 1896, that "Curtis has endured much since he was last seen in Atlanta—his sensational trials on the coast and his recent fight for *Gentleman Joe* forming a combination that would have downed an ordinary man. But Curtis is no ordinary man. He is very much alive."

And the review published in the paper on April 1, 1896,

testified to the fact that there was plenty of life left in M. B. Curtis. "That Mr. Curtis is head and shoulders away beyond other actors of similar character on the stage it only requires a few minutes' observation to convince one. His comical walk across the stage is half the battle, while his plausible manner and audaciously conceived and boldly carried out explanations would wean a man away from a twelve month's worry."

Curtis's portrayal of Sam'l of Posen was now deeply imbedded in the national psyche. In May 1896, as Curtis was performing *Sam'l of Posen* at the Charlottesville Opera House in North Carolina, the proprietor of the Golden Rule Dry Goods Store in Chicago was shot dead in front of his store during a robbery. One of the robbers fired several shots at people on the street while he was escaping, wounding two bystanders. Police released a bulletin to apprehend two men, one of them nicknamed "Samuel of Posen."

In an effort to keep up with changing times and changing tastes, the Curtises were now experimenting with a shortened vaudeville version of *Sam'l of Posen*, which had drawn well at Chicago's Olympic Theatre the year before. Vaudeville dated back to the 1840s, when a Frenchman introduced a series of shorter musical acts into a longer dramatic show. In America, it developed into a series of short specialty acts strung together and the new format was gaining popularity with audiences.

As the new year of 1897 dawned, news reached Seattle and San Francisco that gold had been discovered in the Yukon, triggering a stampede of would-be prospectors headed for the Klondike. And Curtis and Marie proved to be no less susceptible to gold rush fever than the rest of the country. Later that year, the Associated Press announced that Curtis and Marie, along with six members of the *Sam'l of Posen* company, had organized a "joint stock concern" to mine gold in northern Canada. It was reported that they would start for Dawson City and the gold fields on the second steamer that left for Dawson City in the spring.

Even though the Curtises never made it to the Klondike, everyone was caught up in the rush to northern riches and a Dr. C. J. Mullins of Dawson City was updating *Sam'l of Posen* audiences about the frenzied activity in the Yukon.

When Curtis and Marie were performing at the New Grand Theatre in Salt Lake City, they shared the bill with Oscar Ellison, a twenty-seven-year-old magician known as the Great Dante. Ellison, who had begun performing at the age of sixteen, would figure more prominently than any gold mine in the next chapter of the Curtises' lives.

CHAPTER TEN

Down Under and Back Again

When you're a young man, Macbeth is a character part.
When you're older, it's a straight part.
—Laurence Olivier

⁓

M. B. Curtis, now forty-seven years old, faced a crossroads in his career in early 1898 after the vaudeville version of *Sam'l of Posen* didn't catch fire, the prospect of mining for gold in the Yukon didn't pan out, and his brief stint of playing second fiddle to Lillian Russell in *An American Beauty* had ended. Never one to rest on his laurels, Curtis, no doubt realizing that an aging actor had fewer opportunities for success on the stage, decided to get into managing other performers, a less grueling job. He now hitched his hopes on another performer—Oscar Ellison, son of the famous magician Professor Anderson, who had been performing to great acclaim for a number of years already. The twenty-seven-year-old Ellison, known as the "Mormon Magician" or the "Great Dante," had become famous by debunking a charlatan spiritualist in Salt Lake City, where

The magician Dante and his wife, Edmunda. (W. G. Alma conjuring collection. Photographs. State Library of Victoria)

he had performed alongside Curtis and Marie.

In mid-June of 1898, Curtis and Marie sailed to Honolulu from Victoria, British Columbia, accompanied by the young magician, whom Curtis was now managing. After three successful performances in Honolulu, the Curtises intended to continue touring with Dante to many places in the South Pacific.

But Curtis's tour with Dante soon met with predictable difficulties. The February 1899 run in Wellington, New Zealand, was canceled because of a dispute between the theatre and Curtis that revolved around Curtis's right to admit guests for free to the performances, a common practice known as "director's free seats." There were other allegations that Curtis had booked several halls (Stratford, New Plymouth, and Hawera) but had not played the dates and hadn't paid for the rental of the theatres.

While at Wananui on January 31, 1899, Dante was told that Curtis and Marie were letting people in for cash without giving them a ticket. Dante arranged for the box office to be monitored by a watchman who concluded that there was a difference of £54 between actual and reported revenue. Curtis denied the charge and closed the show, demanding that Dante show proof of the alleged deception.

Ellison's local manager (Curtis had been the general tour manager) stated that Ellison was telling the truth and that he, too, was suing Curtis for tour accounts in the amount of £104 that he believed were owed to him.

Even though Curtis was thousands of miles from home, he once again found himself in the familiar surroundings of a courtroom. The New Zealand judge saw the case as one man's word against the other and assigned the manager of the Palace Theatre to oversee ticket sales until the suit was actually settled. Evidently, the actual facts must have confirmed Curtis's account of the incident as published articles in America said that the suit was finally settled out of court, with Ellison paying Curtis $7,000.

Despite this rather rocky introduction to the Antipodes, Curtis and Marie must have found something to their liking in the southern hemisphere because Curtis was back in New York in early April of 1899 looking for artists to tour Australia.

And while he was on the hunt in New York for new performers to manage, Curtis found the time to play a part in the new revolutionary medium of film that was just beginning to emerge in the United States. It was four years before audiences would flee their seats in panic to avoid a train that appeared to hurtle toward them from the screen in *The Great Train Robbery* when Curtis visited a New York studio to make a very short film. The American Mutoscope and Biograph Company

Three surviving stills from the 1899 moving picture M. B. Curtis. *(Seaver Center for Western History Research, Los Angeles County Museum of Natural History)*

released a one-minute-and-forty-second black-and-white silent film entitled *M. B. Curtis* on May 13, 1899. The length of the film was limited by the technology and it appears that no copies of the 101-foot-long film survived. But one can't help wondering how Curtis viewed the nascent technology that would soon alter America's entertainment landscape forever. There are, however, a few stills from the movie that survived, and they are probably as close as audiences will come to "watching" this pioneering endeavor.

While in New York, Curtis also met with a reporter who wrote in an unsourced and undated article found in the New York Public Library for the Performing Arts, Billy Rose Collection, that "the last time I saw M. B. Curtis, somewhere about three years ago, he was in pretty bad shape financially. He had just made a ghastly failure with a wretched piece he had brought over from the other side of the water [*Gentleman Joe*], and his monetary fetters bound him hand and foot. He owned a lot of land away off in the West, but he could realize nothing upon that, and he had spent a long and harrowing evening with me wondering what he was going to do about it. Shortly afterward he disappeared from this neighborhood and I never heard anything more of him until a day or two ago, when I learned that he was in New York looking for an attraction to take with him to Australia."

No doubt already aware of Australians' fascination with African American performers and cognizant of the popularity of the Fisk Jubilee Singers (whose successful Australian tour helped Fisk University improve its finances) and familiar with the 1886 tour of O. M. McAdoo (who deeply influenced the man who adapted a traditional Zulu song "Wimoweh" into "In the Jungle the Lion Sleeps Tonight"), Curtis engaged a minstrel company for his second Australian venture. The

The multitalented Ernest Hogan. (Billy Rose Theatre Division, The New York Public Library for the Performing Arts)

company was led by Ernest Hogan, the era's leading African American comedian, singer, dancer, writer, and actor. The company also included the bandmaster N. Clark Smith, whose musical career was inspired by a personal meeting with Frederick Douglass. Although mostly forgotten by history,

Smith was arguably the most important teacher of music to the African American youth of his time as Earl Hines, Lionel Hampton, and Cab Calloway were among his students who helped chart the course of American music.

The troupe steamed to Vancouver where Curtis signed up the Criterion Quartette to join the tour. The company was to be known as M. B. Curtis's Afro-American Minstrels, and they departed British Columbia on the *Miowera*, arriving in Honolulu on the afternoon of June 12, 1899, after nine days at sea.

After several successful performances — headlined by Hogan since most audiences were already familiar with his famous song "All Coons Look Alike to Me," a song he later regretted composing — the troupe quickly packed up and was back on the *Miowera*, which was now bound for Suva in the Fiji Islands. They stepped off their ship on June 18, staying only six hours to perform. On June 27, the troupe arrived in Sydney and opened their show for a five-week run after a few days of rest and rehearsal.

Curtis must have enjoyed surveying the packed houses for the opening performances and reading reviews such as the one the Sydney *Referee* published about a week after the opening.

> There was a splendid house and most of the items on the very lengthy programme were encored. The duel scene, which concluded the first part, between Mr. Billy McClain and Mr. Ernest Hogan, aroused great merriment. The same couple of artists also kept the house in splendid humor by their antics in the "Rag Time Opera," while the former, who is practically the life and soul of the show,

contributed several coon songs and gags in
his own inimitable fashion. Miss Madah A.
Hyers, the "Bronze Patti" [a reference to the
most famous opera singer of the time, Adelina
Patti], was heard to great advantage in a couple
of operatic selections; the Kentucky Four did
some exceedingly clever buck and wing danc-
ing; the Lilliputian creole contortion danseuse
twisted and twirled in a risqué fashion. The
performance concluded with the laughable
Cake Walk in which the competition between
the various couples was very keen.

Despite being billed at the Criterion under the blatantly
racist title Hogan's Unbleached Coons, the company did, in
fact, enjoy their month's stay in Australia. It was a fresh and
welcome change from their daily experience as African Americans in the United States. Black Carl (the magician also known
as the Black Dante, who was every bit the equal of his white
counterpart, Oscar Ellison) remarked upon the strange experience of eating alongside whites. Billy McLain was able to drive
around town with a "pale lady" with no problems. In remarks
preserved in the New York Public Library for the Performing
Arts, Billy Rose Collection, Hogan is quoted on September 2,
1899, as saying, "We are treated as equals, and we know how to
conduct ourselves accordingly. The ladies of the company are
already great social favorites, while I, as a song writer and author, have received marked attentions from the best families.
A major of the British Army sat beside me at dinner to-day. He
opened a bottle of real champagne and we drank to an An-
glo-American alliance. He was very kind to me, and I expect to
visit the garrison as his guest tomorrow."

Nathaniel Clark Smith, who was a favorite of John Philip Sousa's.
(Private collection)

But despite the initial excitement, attendance began dropping off quickly. Sydney audiences were evidently getting their fill of this kind of entertainment. Curtis must have realized that he had made a strategic blunder in bringing his company to Sydney right after McAdoo's Georgia Minstrels had closed there. Curtis could have opened in Melbourne, where he would not have followed a competing company's run. Instead, he had chosen a deal where his troupe would receive all the profits from ticket sales rather than a set fee, and now the Criterion was almost empty.

McAdoo himself had anticipated the problem Curtis

now faced. After his arrival in Sydney, he wrote a letter to friends back home that was published in the *Indianapolis Freeman* on June 29, 1899.

> We arrived safe . . . into Sydney and found a
> most beautiful harbor and city with the most
> genial people to meet, and from our reception
> and courteous treatment, a man is a man here.
> There is no color line to fight. You are known
> for what you are. Since our arrival we have
> learned that a man named Curtis has gone to
> America after another colored show, and my
> advice to performers there is not to come here
> at present, as the country is too small for three
> colored companies. Besides, this man Curtis's
> reputation here is not the best.

After their disappointing run in Sydney, Curtis's minstrels left for New Zealand, where they received a warm welcome as recorded by the Wellington *Evening Post* on August 31, 1899. "This afternoon the city streets were enlivened by the parade of the band of the Curtis Afro-American Minstrels and Variety Company, which is to open its Wellington season in the Opera House to-night. The company arrived last night, and, besides being strong numerically, has some stars in their particular line."

After a good first week in Wellington, the troupe was again left lonely in the theatre. McAdoo's troupe was performing in the same city at the same time, and the community could simply not support two competing companies. Tension between the two groups mounted. There were acrimonious conversations between Curtis and his lead actors over money.

Friction mounted until Billy McClain and Curtis had what was described as a "violent scene." As the newspaper told it, Curtis entered the stage with a large pistol and asserted that he was in charge while pointing his handgun at the people he was trying to impress. The mention of a gun seems bizarre in the extreme after what Curtis had been through and, if a true account, indicates a desperate mental state. However, no record of any charges being filed against Curtis has been found. Back in the States, the September 23, 1899, *Indianapolis Freeman* reported on the events that ensued.

> Owing to bad business and worse manage-
> ment, the M. B. Curtis Afro-American Minstrel
> and Vaudeville Company [one of the many
> names Curtis's troupe went by] has been
> stranded. Curtis skipped the country owing
> salaries, and fifty of America's leading vaude-
> ville and minstrel stars are thousands of miles
> from their home in a bad financial way, many
> in the party being almost penniless. Friends in
> the country, upon learning of the Company's
> condition, provided financial aid and several
> returned to America, while others decided
> to accept offers from prominent managers in
> Australia.

News spread down New York's Seventh Avenue like rolling thunder and a collection was taken up to get the performers home after the Colored Professional Club received a cablegram from Hogan in Sydney asking for help.

STRANDED BY M. B. FROM HOGAN. CURTIS SNEAKED

OUT OF NEW ZEALAND. STRANDED HERE. CABLE
MONEY. FO' GAWD'S SAKE. LADIES SUFFERING.
HOGAN

The club swung into action. "Many a little soubrette failed
to receive her clean lingerie last night owing to the fact that
the lady who does the washing was hustling around the Ten-
derloin trying to raise subscriptions for the unfortunates," and
the president of the Colored Professional Club was quoted
as saying, "I never had much confidence in that man Curtis,
anyhow. He's a good for nothing, but Hogan thought he was
all right."

Immediately after Curtis's departure, the indomitable
Hogan rallied the members of the troupe and renamed them
Ernest Hogan's Minstrels. He became their manager as well as
their writer and star performer. The newly formed company
of now-familiar stars performed in Brisbane at the Theatre
Royal in January 1900 to large audiences. By mid-March they
traveled back to Honolulu, doing what they could not have
done back in the States—be a multiracial company managed
by a black man that performed for white audiences. The *Pacific
Commercial Advertiser* wrote that "Hogan and his minstrels,
from cream to chocolate, have made a decided and deserved
hit, and there seems no sign of a diminution of public interest
in them." Hogan then mounted a new production of *Uncle
Tom's Cabin* in April, proving to any doubters that, although he
was an incredible comedian, he could indeed move people to
tears with his portrayal of Tom.

But despite their somewhat idyllic Hawaiian sojourn,
some troupe members grew homesick and some of them also
needed to travel to the mainland for performances so the
group booked passage—and paid for the tickets in full—on

the *Miowera*. The twenty-nine members of the company arrived on the dock with their luggage and their health certif-
icates countersigned by the British consul only to be denied
entry by the steam ship company. Suspecting that racism was
at the heart of their dilemma, the troupe enlisted the aid of an
attorney to either recoup their $1,900 or be allowed to board
the *Miowera*.

Hogan's minstrels continued to perform in Honolulu
until their legal troubles were resolved in May when Hogan
was awarded a $2,250 verdict against the steamship company
that owned the *Miowera*. On August 7, 1900, the troupe's
remaining suits were aggregated and the twenty-nine-member
company was awarded $15,000.

Hogan and his minstrels finally said good-bye to the
island of Oahu at a farewell performance to an enthusiastic
crowd at the Orpheum. The house manager presented Hogan
with a fine gold watch that had Hogan's monogram engraved
on it and the Hawaiian coat of arms in raised enameling on
the back. Hogan was taken aback by the gesture and movingly
spoke of his feelings for the people there and promised to
return soon, according to the *Pacific Coast Advertiser* on May
28, 1900.

Meanwhile, Curtis, along with Francis and Lillian Boggs, had
boarded the steamer *Kinau* on December 26, 1899, bound
from Honolulu to Hilo and points beyond. Francis Boggs, an
actor at this point in his career, would go on to have a long
professional relationship with Curtis and would be instrumental in starting the film industry in Hollywood. Although
Boggs and Curtis might have met when they were both acting
at the Alcazar Theatre in San Francisco, their time at sea

together was the beginning of a deep friendship between the two men.

Still in the company of Francis and Lillian Boggs, Curtis and Marie arrived in San Francisco on February 2, 1900, on the steamer *Australia*, and the very next day they went to Berkeley. Frank Curtis arrived in town from Chicago less than a week later, no doubt anxious to see the brother he hadn't seen in four years. Three weeks later, Curtis gave a performance of *Sam'l of Posen* to benefit the Berkeley Volunteer Fire Department's Marston Hose Company. Within a month, Curtis engaged his local contractor, C. R. Lord, to build a home for Francis and Lillian as Boggs was now managing and acting in Curtis's new rendition of *Sam'l of Posen*, which had been refreshed for the Curtises by H. D. Cottrell, a young up-and-coming Oakland playwright.

Meanwhile, Curtis, from his quarters at the newly opened California Hotel, returned to the civic life of Berkeley with gusto. Curtis spoke of his new plans for the city at a meeting of the newly founded West Berkeley Improvement Club. He promised the cheering crowd that streets would be improved and that he would bring in the investors who had approached him about establishing both a savings and loan and a bank. And he promised to erect an auditorium greater than any theatre the West End had ever seen if a lot was donated for this purpose.

When the president of the club got up and said they had no money to make monthly expenses, such as rent and accounting fees, Curtis rose and offered to pay for them himself until the club got on its feet. This inspired a town trustee to offer free accounting services. Curtis and the trustee were referred to as angels, and Curtis was appointed to a committee to further the ideas proposed for the group's advancement, according to the *Berkeley Gazette* on February 28, 1900.

Curtis then proposed to the club's entertainment committee that they produce a benefit theatrical extravaganza at West Berkeley's popular Sisterna Hall that would feature local amateur talent as well as Francis and Lillian Boggs.

By March 2, Sisterna Hall was getting a face-lift of new paint and wallpaper for the grand occasion, and on March 10 the show went off as planned in front of the largest crowd ever assembled for an entertainment event in West Berkeley's history. Not only was every seat sold, but standing room was sold to the point that many people could not get in the door and were turned away.

The curtain opened with Curtis performing a comedic burlesque sketch called "The New Judge," a farce about police court—the actor, no doubt, enjoying the chance to vent and get in a few digs at his former adversaries—which was then followed by Francis Boggs and his wife performing an "exquisite" light comedy called "Retaliation." From all reports, the entire audience was delighted with the evening, and the show raised $134 for the West Berkeley Improvement Club.

While waiting for the northern circuit tour of the newly revised *Sam'l of Posen* to begin, Francis and Lillian Boggs took their performance of "Retaliation" that had premiered at Sisterna Hall to an engagement at San Francisco's Chutes Theatre. It was to be a short run, filling in time until they hit the road with Curtis and Marie. But the Chutes management offered the couple a permanent position at the theatre when they saw the public's reaction to the play. The actor and actress happily accepted the Chutes's offer and informed Curtis they would no longer be traveling with him on tour. Despite their fortuitous landing in the Bay Area, the couple never put down roots in San Francisco. Francis and Lillian apparently never moved into their new house in Peralta Park, and by 1903, the couple was either separated or divorced, and Francis was performing in local theatres in Chicago.

The tour of the newly modernized *Sam'l of Posen* began with a performance at Berkeley's Shattuck Hall on April 30, 1900—with both Marie and Francis Boggs listed as cast members. Even though the play was now twenty years old, the *Berkeley Gazette* gushed on April 26, 1900, that "a brighter and funnier comedy has never yet been seen, pregnant with laughs and capable of convulsing all who witness it. Nothing need be said of Mr. Curtis. He and the dashing Sam'l have long been identified as one in the same person."

Before leaving the Bay Area, Curtis and his company played *Sam'l of Posen* in Oakland's McDonough Theatre, and then they toured throughout California that spring, returning to Berkeley from Los Angeles in mid-June.

Even though the tour was reportedly profitable, the *Brooklyn Eagle* announced that M. B. Curtis had filed a petition in bankruptcy court in St. Paul, Minnesota, on October 6, 1900. The actor was claiming liabilities of $117,000, with the largest amount of money ($24,302) being owed to James Raymond of Austin, Texas, for his helping Curtis trade the Driskill Hotel to George Deller for land in New Jersey and New York (Deller was listed as the second largest creditor at $10,000). Curtis declared assets of only two scarf pins, which were valued at $25 total.

In an ironic juxtaposition, Madah Hyers (the phenomenal singer Bronze Patti whom Curtis had earlier abandoned in Australia) had made her way home and was now appearing with her *Colored Aristocracy* company in an open-air concert in front of the Berkeley Opera House a month after Curtis had declared himself bankrupt. Evidently, Miss Hyers had recovered from her Australian misadventure with Curtis while the actor never seemed to regain his equilibrium.

The Curtises were now struggling to find another new theatrical vehicle. In late January and early February 1901, Curtis and Marie successfully tested in Bridgeport, Connecticut, a new vaudeville version of their old play, now transformed into *Samuel at the Herald Square Hotel*. The new *Samuel* then went on to New York.

Curtis was trying, with his typical energy, to stay afloat, but Marie also had to file for bankruptcy on July 10, 1901, in St. Paul. Her filing claimed she had $175,171 in debts and assets of $275 in clothing, which were exempt from the proceedings by law. The largest creditors named were James H. Raymond ($25,000) and James H. Day ($12,000), both of Austin, Texas— more hangovers from the Driskill Hotel purchase. Marie owed money to around one hundred creditors, including dressmakers, bill posters, agents, doctors, and dentists.

But the Curtises seemed determined to persevere, despite their financial problems. Both Marie and Curtis traveled to Cincinnati in a minstrel and vaudeville review, and they were planning yet another vehicle that they hoped would vault them back into the limelight—and back into solvency.

A Long, Slow Fade

Every exit is an entry somewhere else.
— Tom Stoppard

In June 1902, it was announced that Curtis had signed with the Morris and Hall Agency and would star in a new play called *The Greenhorn of Breslau*. The play, written by Herbert Hall Winslow, was to be elaborately staged, and Curtis predicted that his new venture would surpass *Sam'l of Posen*.

The plot of *The Greenhorn of Breslau* involves a young immigrant who, while on board a ship to America, is robbed of all his money. At the same time, diamond smugglers on the ship hide their loot in the back of a painting owned by the young man, Mosche Petchke, played by Curtis. Mosche disembarks in New York with his luggage and the portrait. His lack of money causes the immigration officials to order him deported, but he bolts away and is chased by the diamond smugglers who are trying to get their diamonds back, but all ends well when the final curtain falls.

Characters from many ethnic backgrounds were introduced in the play, including a German American customs agent, a Swedish cook, a Cockney, an Irishman, and a French adventuress (played by Marie, of course). There was even a scene where an ocean liner and a fully rigged yacht sailed under the Brooklyn Bridge on stage.

And an old friend of Curtis's was also featured in the play. According to an unsourced, undated article in the Harvard Theater Collection, "In the first scene, the Statue of Liberty . . . forms the background of a scene which takes place on Ellis Island. Curtis was at one time instrumental in keeping the torch on the statue lighted at his own personal expense."

But despite having Curtis and Lady Liberty sharing the stage, the first opening of the play failed miserably. In November, the *San Francisco Chronicle* announced, "One of the most complete dramatic failures of the season has been scored by M. B. Curtis, an actor well known on the Coast. His starring tour in a play entitled *The Greenhorn* lasted just two weeks. Then he disbanded his company and burned the manuscript of the play."

Not one to stay down for long, Curtis was to perform on November 27, 1902, at the Grand in Paris, Kentucky, in a new play, *Sam'l of Posen's Brother*, also written by Herbert Hall Winslow. The new role was said to give him "more scope for the display of his ability as an impersonator of the German-Jew than any other role in which he has appeared," according to Kentucky's *Bourbon News* on November 21, 1902.

Curtis said, in responding to the reporter's questions that day, "I am the first man who ever played the part of the German-Jew on the American stage. On returning to this country and noticing how the other impersonators of the Jew were caricaturing him, I determined to revive my former creation and begin where they leave off. I consider my new play far superior to *Sam'l of Posen*, and my supporting company is the best I have ever had." Curtis reinvented the play yet again.

In January 1903, Curtis and company were back in Atlanta, a town that always gave him a warm and enthusiastic welcome, to do what one newspaper called "one of the cleverest sketches on the vaudeville stage." That same month, St. Joseph's Academy of San Francisco purchased the six-acre Peralta Hall property. Curtis's old magnificent almost hotel was about to become a boys' school.

In the middle of June, Curtis and Marie performed the old *Sam'l of Posen* in Oakland and "scored one of the most pronounced hits in Central Theatre history. The house was packed. In the audience were hundreds of theatre goers who had witnessed the production years ago, with the same star in the title role. That the actor lost none of his skill and the play none of its capacity to please was demonstrated by the immense success which characterized the production," according to the *San Francisco Chronicle* on June 16, 1903.

Perhaps buoyed by this enthusiastic reception, Curtis decided to give *The Greenhorn of Breslau* another shot and revived the supposedly immolated script on June 22 at the Central. This time the critical reaction was vastly different. According to the *Oakland Tribune*, "The laughter was almost continuous and there is a little love-thread woven in the plot, giving pathos and color to the lighter strains of the play." The *San Francisco Chronicle* claimed that "there is hardly any noticeable intermission between laughs" in the play they had panned the previous year.

However, Curtis's successful comeback was soon cut short by his failing health and a natural disaster. In June of 1904, Curtis checked into a health spa in Byron, California, in search of a "rest cure" from his hard life on the road and his heavy drinking. But Curtis was back in the Bay Area shortly

The Grand Opera House after the San Francisco Earthquake. (Private collection)

after the Great San Francisco Earthquake of April 18, 1906. He must have been horrified by the widespread devastation and saddened to see the entire theatre district where he had launched his career and returned to as a star so many times reduced to smoking rubble. But one can't help wondering what Curtis felt when he realized that the area where Officer Grant was murdered had been cleansed by fire as well.

Even though Curtis went back to performing only four months after the earthquake, appearing in the vaudeville version of *Sam'l of Posen* at Oakland's Novelty Theatre, his popularity was on the wane. And despite a 1905 New York State newspaper—the Hornsville *Weekly Tribune*—referring to President Teddy Roosevelt as the "only real political Samuel of Posen in public life," Curtis's influence on American culture was fading as well. On April 16, 1907, Berkeley City Trustee Christian Hoff made a motion to change the name of Posen Station to Bancroft Station. However, the motion was never approved and the station remained named for Curtis's famous character until 1916, when the Southern Pacific Railroad built a new depot at University Avenue and Third Street.

In an effort to reestablish himself in the Bay Area, Curtis became the manager of the newly built Richmond Opera House, located in the booming oil-refinery town of Richmond, California, just north of Berkeley. The elaborate theatre hosted vaudeville shows as well as the latest novelty in entertainment —moving pictures.

Part of Curtis's job at the opera house was to solicit advertisements from local businesses that would be placed on the theatre's front curtain. In August 1907, Curtis was again in Police Court, this time as a defendant in search-warrant proceedings instigated by his employer who believed that Curtis had made off with ten advertising contracts and an unknown number of letters that were the property of the opera company after a disagreement that resulted in Curtis's tearing down the front curtain of the theatre.

When police searched Curtis's Berkeley residence, they found the missing contracts. Curtis told the court that the contracts had been made out in his name and denied that the contracts were the property of the opera house company. Although the outcome of the case is unknown, it is probably safe to assume that soon after the trial, Curtis had to set off in search of a way to reinvent himself yet again.

Curtis's next opportunity to re-create his original success in a new medium came in 1909 from the still-nascent movie industry, an emerging art form that was struggling to find its feet. As the *Moving Picture World* proclaimed on December 3, 1910, "Artistically, the moving picture men do not know where they are going, but they are on their way."

While many people were optimistic about the future

of movies, which were touted as the workingman's theatre because they were less expensive and shorter than the traditional stage entertainment of the time, the critics were beginning to complain about the dime-store-novel plots that somehow always involved a beautiful and innocent country girl falling for an evil and untrustworthy city slicker. While the flood of westerns hitting the market at the time allowed ordinary moviegoers to "travel" to places that had heretofore taken much time and money to see, the dramatic scenery quite often seemed to be the best part of the movies as the plots, according to the *Moving Picture World*, were "so silly that they positively make your spine shrivel."

One critic complained that the producers of films were unwilling to pay for skilled writers and actors unless an occasion warranted special attention. Houses were paying $10–$15 for scenarios and the *Moving Picture World* believed that audiences were becoming bored with plots devised by underpaid writers who produced a "continual stream of sensational melodramas."

In an effort to move the industry forward, moviemakers turned to literary playwrights and began producing their established and successful works on film. The *Moving Picture World* heartily endorsed this "most encouraging tendency of the picture play business [to make films of] well-known plays and books." And this is when M. B. Curtis entered the soundstage.

William Selig, a former musician and minstrel performer in California, had founded a movie company in Chicago in 1896 that produced travelogues, industrial films, and a number of comedies that featured the standard slapstick of the day.

On November 29, 1909, Curtis signed an agreement for

Francis Boggs, to the left of the cameraman, directing the action in the 1910 movie The Girls of the Range. *(Private collection)*

$1,000 with the Selig Polyscope Company that gave the movie producer the rights to *Sam'l of Posen*, with Curtis playing the leading role. A number of the actors from the stage company were recruited for the movie, and filming was done at Selig's Chicago studio, where Curtis ran into his old friend Francis Boggs, who was now working for Selig.

Having returned to Chicago after filming the most important scene in *The Count of Monte Cristo*, Boggs made a number of westerns, including one starring Tom Mix and Hoot Gibson, in the same year that Curtis's movie was made and later oversaw the first film featuring Fatty Arbuckle, *Ben's Kid*.

Curtis's movie was released on March 3, 1910, along with Selig's $35,000 cinematic extravaganza of L. Frank Baum's *The Wizard of Oz*, and the film played everywhere from New York to Montana to California and Winnipeg. The *New York Dramatic Mirror* reviewed the movie on March 12, 1910, and seemed caught between the old world and the new.

This is one of the most notable of recent releases because it is an authorized adaptation from a prominent stage success and the chief part is played by the actor who originally made the part famous. M. B. Curtis played the part with all his old time stage effectiveness, but this reviewer is unable to grow enthusiastic over the picture on that account. In fact, there is too much the appearance of stage work about Mr. Curtis, especially toward the end. However, the film will no doubt prove popular and is strongly interesting.

After the filming of *Samuel of Posen*, Curtis was immediately offered a role in another Selig film, *The Sanitarium*, a comedy directed by Francis Boggs that featured Fatty Arbuckle. It wasn't the starring role, but it offered Curtis a chance to remain in the film business and reunite with fellow actors and

A photo of Curtis in Samuel of Posen *taken from a poster for the movie. (From the collections of the Margaret Herrick Library, Academy of Motion Picture Arts and Sciences)*

actresses from the Belasco stock company of San Francisco.
The movie portrays Fatty Arbuckle as a young man in debt
who house-sits his aunt and uncle's mansion while they vacation in Europe. Arbuckle's character, Charley Wise, turns his
relatives' house into a sanitarium to try and make some money
and hilarity ensues. It is not known what role Curtis played.

Why *The Sanitarium* was the last movie Curtis acted in is
unknown, but one possibility is that Curtis's declining health
and his battles with alcohol overwhelmed his movie career.
But his deteriorating physical condition didn't stop him from
making his usual enthusiastic grand plans for the future.
Encouraged by Francis Boggs, Curtis wrote to Selig from the
Colorado town of Hot Sulphur Springs, where the actor was
enjoying a bit of a rest. (The following letter is reproduced
courtesy of the Academy of Motion Picture Arts and Sciences.)

> My Dear Mr. Selig;
> I am in receipt of a letter from Mr. Francis
> Boggs asking me to write to you regarding the
> foreign trip which he wrote to you about . . .
> I would very much like to take this trip for
> you, and if you would let a first class operator
> accompany me, I think it would be one of the
> most profitable, as well as latest, advertise-
> ments you have ever had thus far. I could make
> industrial and educational films and in Hono-
> lulu, where there is always a company of ac-
> tors, I could with the assistance of the natives
> make you a splendid film of the landing and
> death of Capt. Cook, also the last and greatest
> battle ever fought there, in which King Kame-
> hameha vanquished his enemies by forcing

them over the Pali Pass where more than 2,000
of them were dashed to pieces 600 or 800 feet
below on the rocks.

Then I could make some good films of the
surf bathing, and of the pine-apple, taro, guava,
honey, rice and sugar industries, also the great
work now being carried on by the government at Pearl Harbor; the leper settlement at
Molokai, which is very interesting indeed, and
the volcano Kilauea and its burning lake of
perpetual fire and probably other numerous
subjects which I will be able to obtain while
on the different islands of Hawaii . . . Then I
should advise going direct to Japan as July and
August are the best months there. In Japan
I could get such reels as the silk industry . . .
[and] I may say that in all of the countries that
I might visit there are always strolling English
and American players that I might engage
cheaply to make films of comedies, dramas, etc.
At Kyoto the priests perform a classic drama
called the No Dance on historical subjects
which will make interesting films.

Then the best native Japanese Company
that they have is at Kyoto where I would be
able to get several interesting dramas as they
are clever actors and pantomimists. Then there
are the street scenes of the various countries,
water scenes and the volcano of Fujiama [*sic*]
and the coaling of the Japanese warships at
Nakasaki [*sic*], which is done by women. Then
there is the rice, tea, and fishing industry, the

cherry blossom and chrysanthemum festivals
and others too numerous to mention . . .
From Japan I could go to Manila visiting all
the different islands, thence to China and visit
Shanghai . . . thence to Eastern Siberia and
Vladivostock [sic]. In Pekin [Beijing] I could
get a very good film where the camel trains
with brick tea, perfumes and essential oils go
through Nankow Pass from Mongolia, sometimes 600 or 800 strong.

I simply give you these different ideas of
films to show you the possibilities of the subject . . . and think when I am on the different
grounds I could send you from 1 to 3 releases
a week should you want them . . . I am ready to
start at any time you may say the word, and I
will go for $150 a week and traveling expenses
. . . In the event of my going on this trip and if
you so desire it Mr. Boggs has my manuscript
of "Spot Cash" or "Sam'l of Posen on the
Road" and "Sam'l of Posen's Brother Isadore"
which I could do for you before starting on
the trip and you can have these two plays with
the rights thereunto for $1,500.

Trusting to hear from you soon on this
subject, I remain,

Sincerely yours,

M. B. Curtis

Curtis's creativity and enthusiasm are apparent in this
letter, and his knowledge of the world of his day is as impres-
sive as it is broad. A couple of days later, he wrote to Francis

Boggs to let him know of the letter to Selig. Curtis told Boggs that he had been at the spa in Colorado but that it was "too lonesome." Curtis then went to the Paso Robles Hot Springs in California, reporting that he might leave there soon as he was feeling "fit as a fiddle now" and that "Mrs. C." might join him in a week.

Despite apparently regaining his health—or taking a break from his heavy drinking—Curtis never made his proposed trip to the Orient. Whether Selig was interested in Curtis's proposal is unknown, but an event in suburban Los Angeles in 1911 might have had a major impact on Curtis's future plans. Selig, accompanied by his wife, had come for a three-week visit to the Los Angeles studio set up for the Selig Polyscope Company by Francis Boggs in Edendale (the early site of the silent-movie industry in Los Angeles that now contains the neighborhoods of Echo Park, Los Feliz, and Silver Lake). Selig and Boggs were in Boggs's office on October 27, 1911, discussing how to proceed with filming during a constant drizzle when the studio's janitor, Frank Minnimatsu, charged into the room clutching a pistol he had taken from an actor's dressing room. Without uttering a word, he fired five rounds into Francis Boggs and two at Selig. Boggs was gravely wounded and rushed to the hospital where he was pronounced dead. Selig, shot in the head and arm, was taken to his hotel room as his wounds were more superficial.

The janitor was apprehended by a number of actors and a mounted policeman who had been riding by the studio and heard the shots. When he was placed in a cell, Minnimatsu refused to utter a word. He later informed the police that Boggs "was always very nice to me. But a man told me he was evil and had to die."

The schizophrenic Minnimatsu was sentenced to life in

prison in San Quentin for first-degree murder where he lived
for twenty-six years, gardening and refusing parole twice
because he preferred to remain among his gardens on the
rocky promontory of San Quentin rather than be deported to
Japan. He died at the age of fifty-six of tuberculosis in 1937,
"the oldest prisoner in point of incarceration," according to
the *Ukiah Republican Press* on July 28, 1937.

With his budding movie career apparently at an end, Curtis
and Marie took over the lease of the Oxnard Opera House
in August of 1912. Erected around 1905, the Oxnard Opera
House was originally built as a skating rink. The skating craze
had subsided shortly after the hall's opening, and by 1907, the
rink was closed and the building was remodeled into a theatre.

After taking over the lease, Curtis immediately hired a
crew of tradesmen from Los Angeles and procured new seats
and gave the opera house a new coat of paint inside and out.
The floor was raised, the stage was enlarged, and the latest
in stage lighting was installed, with Curtis's brother Charles
offering to provide the new lighting equipment.

Despite Curtis's evident enthusiasm for his new venture,
which mirrored his Peralta Park Hotel efforts, the actor's
health continued to fail, no doubt due in part to his drinking,
and Marie had to step in to manage the new business. And the
business was not the only concern that was affected by Curtis's increasingly erratic behavior. His relationship with Marie
—his compatriot, his costar, his constantly loyal wife—was
now deteriorating as well. Soon after their move to Oxnard,
the Curtises were in court to settle a domestic dispute that
questioned Curtis's sanity. The *Oxnard Courier* reported the
results of the hearing on October 13, 1912.

The complaint had been brought earlier in
the week by [Curtis's] wife, who alleged that he
had made threats against her. When the case
came up for a final hearing his wife admitted
that she believed it was a case of a little too
much liquor, rather than insanity, and it was
suggested by the court that both of them be
put under probation, and they left the courtroom arm in arm.

Curtis, better known as "Sam'l of Posen"
to the theatrical world, agreed to go on probation not to drink, while his wife must scold
him no more, and the one who violates the
probation shall give up his or her half interest
in the Oxnard Opera House.

In order to determine his sanity, an insanity commission, composed of Drs. Cunnane
and Huning, was appointed. A large number
of Oxnarders were taken as witnesses . . .
[but] none of them got a chance to testify, and
attorneys state that it was a laughable matter,
as Curtis, presumably insane, gave a very sane
and logical talk to the court.

Perhaps in an effort to salve his disappointment over not going to Japan to make movies for William Selig, Curtis brought
Japan to Oxnard, booking a Japanese theatre company that
performed a very lengthy play that spanned two nights and
featured their own sets and costumes, including a 2,500-year-
old kimono. But in spite of their creative bookings, the Curtises apparently faced financial troubles as Marie soon had to

sublease the house.

On May 12, 1913, Curtis was again arrested and charged with "being addicted to liquors to such an extent that he was not accountable for his acts." Appearing in court as a refined gentleman (according to the *Oxnard Courier* on May 16), Curtis stated that "several months ago my wife brought just this kind of charge against me in Ventura county, but the court dismissed it within a few minutes. I admit I have been drinking somewhat, but I did so because I was suffering from ptomaine poisoning. She will not come into court and swear that I threatened to kill her. We have been married thirty-eight years and I have never killed her once."

Later that month, with yet another sublessee walking out on his debts, the *Oxnard Courier* noted how spotty attendance had been at the opera house. In this unstable environment, the opera house was subleased a few more times, never with much success and never for long. Sometime in 1914, Marie again took the reins of the operation. She hired a manager and opened the house as a movie theatre with occasional live productions. The pair ran the opera house to the best audience turnouts since its glory days of old.

An article in the *Ventura County Historical Society Quarterly* titled "There Was an Opera House in Oxnard" by Madeline Miedema outlines the acts that were brought in. A female wrestling champion came to the opera house, offering fifty dollars in gold to any man or woman who could last fifteen minutes with her. However, her defeat of big Frank Dominguez in five minutes was attended by only a "handful" of admirers. Later in 1914, Madame Le Zora hypnotized a man in the window of Lehmann Brothers Department Store and left him there for seven hours before carrying him into the opera house to be released from his trance while the attentive audience watched the proceedings. A female cobra dancer tried to woo the public, and Roshier and His Dog Bobby stunned the town when Bobby jumped from the top of the Lehmann Brothers Department Store, a distance of 104 feet.

By August, a new pair of managers tried awarding nightly prizes to boost attendance. Anything from cup-and-saucer sets to furniture were offered. In 1915, a Metz automobile valued at $555 was to be given as a grand prize. But even these efforts did not keep the new managers from skipping town in October (one wonders if they drove off in the Metz). Once again, Marie was forced back into managing the place herself.

On March 22, 1915, the Curtises must have felt a melancholy sadness as they read George Jessop's obituary in the newspaper. Jessop had died in London where he had gone to write *Shamus O'Brien* and other operas, as well as novels about Irish American life. The death of the writer of the original *Sam'l of Posen* must have given the couple pause to reflect on their earlier glorious success (and their own mortality) even as they were struggling to keep the Oxnard Opera House open against the massive weight of changing times.

At the end of December 1915, the Curtises completed a deal to sell the Oxnard Opera House, receiving as part of the transaction some Los Angeles property owned by the buyer, a Mrs. Anna A. Holst. Upon completion of the deal, the Curtises moved to Los Angeles, where Curtis seemed to drop out of sight for a while, according to the *Oakland Tribune*, which ran a piece on May 21, 1916, about the Peralta Park Hotel and Curtis. They said that Curtis had disappeared, moving about after his trials, and that it was rumored in Berkeley that he was in San Diego recently, planning once more to revive "the

Marie in Her Greatest Love. *(From the collections of the Margaret Herrick Library, Academy of Motion Picture Arts and Sciences)*

venerable *Sam'l of Posen.*"

But while Curtis's star was dimming to black, Marie was enjoying a resurgence of theatrical success after possibly separating from her husband at some point. Fox Pictures released the silent move *Her Greatest Love* on April 1, 1917, and it starred Marie, who played Lady Dolly, a social-climbing and manipulative mother who is living in sin with an aristocrat. Marie was in her fifties now, but she still had a ravishing quality that lent itself to her portrayal of villainesses.

Marie continued her successful performances on stage and film into the late 1930s, even starring in a play called *Nerves* with a young Humphrey Bogart.

One day in 1918, a poorly dressed elderly man came to Peralta Park and walked around the grounds of Saint Mary's College High School, formerly the Peralta Park Hotel. Someone approached the old man and asked him if he was looking for someone. The man replied, "No, I'm just looking around. I'm Maurice Curtis and I built this building." One wonders if Curtis's visit to the ghost of his past was prompted by the death of one of his lifelong friends, the actress Maggie Mitchell, who died at the age of eighty-three on March 22, 1918, in New York. Mitchell had visited Curtis while he was putting together Peralta Park in the 1880s, and the local newspapers had reported that she had purchased some lots in the park.

Two years after Curtis's visit to Berkeley, the aging and ill actor was being cared for by a William T. Wyatt of Los Angeles, a representative of the Actors' Fund. In a karmic twist of fate, the Actors' Fund was the organization that Curtis had helped to found in 1882. Curtis had only been sick a matter of days when he was taken to Los Angeles County Hospital. He died the following day on December 27, 1920, the cause of death listed as chronic intestinal nephritis. His brother Frank, a retired widower now living in San Mateo, California, was notified of his death. In a sad footnote to a grand theatrical partnership, Curtis's marital status on his death certificate was listed as "unknown."

Maurice Bertrand Curtis was laid to rest "surrounded by friends of his play-world." Services were held in the chapel of Bresee Brothers on Figueroa Street. The December 30, 1920, *Los Angeles Times* said of him, "From 'super' to a position of eminence on the American stage, then a manager-producer and reputed possessor of millions, and then back, inch-by-inch, fighting and struggling against ill fortune until death overtook him in the County Hospital—Mr. Curtis's life was itself a drama of surprising events."

In its obituary, the *Los Angeles Times* notes an event that
took place in San Francisco "several years ago" that the members of the acting and theatrical profession remembered him
by. It seemed to be "a Curtis," exemplifying his love of the
unexpected and intense. "Mr. Curtis, then at the height of his
fame, was seized by the craze then sweeping the country—the
mania for fancy vests. Following a discussion one evening in
the old Palace Hotel, he announced that he would startle the
town in the morning. He did. He visited a large number of
haberdashers the next day and bought seventy fancy vests of
various patterns."

The January 16, 1921, New York *Herald* called Curtis "an
historic figure in the American theatre, although entirely
unknown to the present generation . . . Mr. Curtis was the first
actor to put a modern Jew on the stage, and it was he who
was in reality the pioneer of all the swarm . . . He showed the
young Jewish immigrant who landed here as a comic greenhorn who made his way by his shrewdness and honesty . . .
It was the first attempt to put before the public any genuine
study of the Jew immigrant in this country."

The Berkeley *Daily Gazette* wrote on December 29, 1920,
"He had a brilliant mind, and numbered among his friends
here many people prominent in social, artistic and political
circles."

The same article said of Curtis's relations with Berkeley,
"He had, in fact, so many extensions of his personality that by
hook or by crook, he kept his fellow townspeople either excited, amused, or stupefied by day and by night."

Sam'l of Posen, the play, had led an amazing life as well.
As the *Oakland Tribune* pointed out on May 21, 1916, "Whenever everybody thought that *Sam'l of Posen* had outlived its

The Peralta Park Hotel being demolished. (SFNO District Archives of the De La Salle Christian Brothers)

usefulness and was ready to be shelved for good, it would suddenly bob up somewhere, and almost as many people would be going to see it as ever." Indeed, it was Curtis who made the work live and breathe.

On March 4, 1946, a fire destroyed the top two floors of Saint Mary's College High School, which was housed in the building formerly known as the Peralta Park Hotel.

The two remaining lower floors of the old hotel were utilized until September 16, 1959, when the building was razed as an earthquake hazard, thus erasing all traces of Curtis's dream palace.

On February 9, 1941, a note in the *Oakland Tribune* told of the recent death of Posen A. Johnson. He was the baby who won the $100 prize M. B. Curtis had offered to the first child born in Berkeley named Posen. His father, Rasmus Johnson, and his family had an apartment in the back of Posen Station. The passing of Mr. Johnson marked the end of an era, but nothing will close the book on M. B. Curtis and his Sam'l of Posen. Not now.

ACKNOWLEDGMENTS

In any endeavor, one relies on the previous works of others and the help of many people and institutions. This book would not have been possible without such help.

Many thanks to David Hough, who acted as a magician in editing this book; to Dan Janeck whose wizardry at proofreading seems to defy all belief; to Scott Smiley whose indexing was as top-notch as we had ever seen; and to Lisa Elliot for her talent, eye for design, and her ability to see what an author is trying to do and make it come alive in her design.

I would like to extend a very special and heartfelt thank-you to three very talented and dedicated professionals for their brilliant work: Thomas A. Smart, Robert Barnes, and Victoria Haje, all of the firm of Kaye Scholer LLP.

Additional thanks go: to David Strelinger and Daniel Zur for sharing family heirlooms; to the late Jerry Sulliger, the best historian I have ever met, for his inspiring generosity and friendship; to Barry Moreno from the Ellis Island Foundation for our many fascinating discussions; to Malcolm Margolin who had lunch with me years ago to discuss the book and suggested I forge ahead with my 1,200-page manuscript and publish a five-volume set on the topic . . . and open a museum; to Matt Whittman, Elizabeth Falsey, Luke Dennis, and Kathleen Coleman from the Harvard Theater Collection, Houghton Library, Harvard University; to Janet Lorenz, Faye Thompson, and Kristine Krueger at the Academy of Motion Picture Arts and Sciences, Center for Motion Picture Studies, Margaret Herrick Library; to the Mark Twain Papers curators at the Bancroft Library for sharing their expansive collection with

me; to the University of California's Bancroft Library, especially
Susan Snyder, Erica Nordmeier, David Farrell, Peter Hanff,
David Kessler, Dean Smith, and Iris Donovan, who have made
the research visits there more than useful; to the New York
Public Library and the Performing Arts Library, the Astor,
Lenox, and Tilden Foundations, and the Billy Rose Collection
for the collections they maintain and the help they offer and
to Thomas Lisanti, Louise Martzinek, and Alexandra M. Henri;
to Nicolette Bromberg and Rebecca Baker from the Univer-
sity of Washington Libraries; to the Seaver Center for Western
History Research, Los Angeles County Museum of Natural
History, and Betty Uyeda and John Cahoon; to the State Li-
brary of Victoria and Gregg Flegg, Dominique Dunstan, and
Mark Showalter; to Gary F. Kurutz from the California State
Library; to the Alexander Turnbull Library, National Library of
New Zealand; to the Performing Arts Collection, Arts Center
Melbourne and Lucy Spencer and Jeremy Vincent; to the staff
at the Newspapers and Periodicals Room of the Doe Library
of UC Berkeley, who make it possible for people like me to
navigate their collections; to Carole Louise Perrault from the
National Park Service who generously shared her research,
political cartoons, and conversations about the Statue of
Liberty with me; to the SFNO District Archives of the De La
Salle Christian Brothers and Jennifer Sturm and Saint Mary's
College High School of Berkeley and Jeanne Gray Lough-
man; to Anthony Bruce, director of the Berkeley Architectural
Heritage Association and Daniella Thompson, past president,
for their contributions of images, articles and advice; to Ken
Wayland who shared a theatrical poster reproduction; to Jack
Oso for his many months of help in organizing and cataloguing
articles so I could find them efficiently and his helpful early
editing; to retired Berkeley firefighter Michael Flynn, whose

generosity years ago in sharing the Berkeley Firefighters Association historical collection with me provided a rich resource; to Albany Fire Chief Marc McGinn and the Albany Fire Department for their accommodations and sharing of their history collections; to the Oakland Public Library History Room and the Newspaper Room for their fabulous collections and friendliness; to the San Francisco History Center, San Francisco Public Library, and Jeff Thomas and Christina Moretta; to the Berkeley Public Library History Room; to the Albany Library and Vivian Jaquette; to the California Historical Society's Linda F. Burton and Debra Kaufman; to the New York Public Library Digital Collections; to the Bohemian Club's Matt Buff; to Mary Lou Rooney for her steadfast support and belief and earlier editing and suggestions for this work; to Gale Garcia for sharing many newspaper articles on Curtis; to the Hampden Booth Library and Ray Wemmlinger; to Liz Stevens, former manager of Prudential California Realty in Berkeley; to Steve Zerbe, who has been of invaluable assistance; to Jeff DeFreitas for sharing his family's history and images; to the folks at Builders Booksource, George and Sally Kiskaddon, Travis Ash, Rex Carey, David Short, and Alan Dishman, for their support and generosity; to Greg Schmalz, the manager at Copy Central on Solano Avenue, and his staff; and to the people at Truitt and White Lumber Company, too many to name, who have been such good friends.

And thanks to T. Roush and the San Francisco Performing Arts Library and Museum; to Ben Crane; to the New Jersey Public Library in Ashbury Park; to John Bluey Brattle for his help in answering an important question; to Tom Boblitt and Vintage Non–Sports Card chat board; to Allen Cohen for conversing and sharing about Curtis; to the Tehama County Recorder's Office; to the Episcopal Diocese of Michigan; to the University of Michigan and Leonard A. Coombs; to Mark Nelson at the California Oil Museum; to Loretta E. Filon from the Central Nevada Museum; to Terry Ketelsen at the Colorado State Archives; to the Detroit Public Library and reference librarian Jeanne Salathiel; to Ashley Koebel from the Burton County Historical Collection; to the Free Library of Philadelphia Rare Book Department and Music Department and Jim LeFager, Joseph Shemtov, and Tee Quakhaan; to Ted Johnson from Independence National Park; to Mike Freeman; to the George Eastman House Motion Picture Department and Jared Case and Anthony L'Abbate.

And thank you to Midgeteyeball; to Ken Wayland for sharing the old theatrical posters he found in his house; to Vivian Kahn for sharing her Strelinger family research; to Bruce Kercher of UNSW; to Karl Gurcke from the Klondike Gold Rush National Park; to Glenna Dunning from the Los Angeles Public Library; to W. D. Barry and Christine S. Albert at the Maine Historical Society; to Marty Jacobs from the Museum of the City of New York; to the Masterpiece Marketing Group and Eric Amundson for his able assistance; to John Henry Loomis at the National Theatre in Washington, D.C.; to Roykaa's Auctioneers and Paul Roykaa; to the San Pedro Bay Historical Society and Doug Hansford for his research; to James Sanderson; to Deborah E. Cribbs at the St. Louis Mercantile Library at the University of Missouri–St. Louis; to the Quebec Family History Society; to Janet Birckhead at the Long Branch Free Public Library; to Betsy Dudas from the Ocean County Historical Society; to Molly Kodner at the Missouri History Museum Library and Research Center; to author Jill Dolan; to the St. Louis Public Library and Jean M. Gosebrink; to Lynne Landwehr; to Anna Porter at the United States Embassy in Papua New Guinea; to Denise Anderson and Kelly Grogg at the University of Iowa; to James Liversidge, Denise Anderson, and Lindsay Moen with the University of Florida; to Teresa Gibson, Robert Ray, and Charles Haddix for their help with the biography of N. C. Smith; to Helen Adair for help with various articles on Curtis and his plays; to the Utah History Research Center; to Sayre Van Young and Lisa Walker; to Bart White for sharing a letter that revealed much about early Berkeley history.

And special thanks are due to my friends for their deep and long friendship and support: to Mary Lou, Bob, Austin, and Dana Rooney, who are an example of the amazing stock of lifetime friends that the Philadelphia soil nourishes; to Bernie Strauss, who has been a solid friend and inspiration for forty years; to Susan and Ed Wheeler for thirty years of being right there; to all the Serotas and Bradins for being such amazing and unique families; to Bob Hawley for being a lover of books and history and jokes; to Dave Deppen for his support when it was really needed; to Judith Dunham and Charles Denson for their continual and rich friendship and support; to El Collie for sharing her amazing dreams with me; to the Burshad family, who were the greatest neighbors a Philadelphia row-house boy could have had; and to Eddie Burshad, who always rubbed my head for luck when I was a kid. I hope it worked, my friend. And to Rookie and Eddie, who provided a role model for a love that has lasted sixty-six years so far; to William E. Halpin, who has been a mentor, friend, and storyteller as well as a reader for earlier manuscripts; and to my late friend Maggie Newsome whose friendship I carry with me at all times. She met me with open arms and interest every single time I saw her and listened with an open heart and a smile. To Stefan, who took a moral stand at great personal expense to stand by me; and to Gary and Joan Herbertson, Gail

Ramsey, Beverley Hansen, Jim Herbertson, and their families, I am honored to be an adopted member of this proud and kind clan; to Stephen Edwards for his feedback upon reading an early manuscript on Curtis; to James and Laura Saunders for their support and friendship; to Carmen DeArcé, Eduardo Garcia, and Danny, Rosa, and Jessie Chen, who are always smiling and welcoming and excited about life; to the Mortenson family—John, Jan, Christopher, and Joseph—and John's incredible and inspiring persistence in the face of adversity; to the late Justin Burney, whose true kindness lingers with all those he graced with his friendship; to Robin Burney for her friendship, especially in times of need; to Dvir Baraka whose smile and support have been so valuable to me; to Irv Staats and Jane Ashland; and to Dan and Barb Wilcox.

And to my family, my brother-in-law, Tom Smart (who helped with reading and feedback), and my nephews, Cody Smart (who did photography and research for the project) and Zac Smart (who gave feedback).

Thank you all.

INDEX

Note: page numbers in *italics* refer to illustrations. Throughout the index, "MBC" refers to M. B. Curtis.

A

Abbott, Mark, 210, 212

Abbott, Mr., 175–176, 187

Abbott, Mrs., 171, 175–176, 187

Academy of Music, Brooklyn, 73

Academy of Music, Buffalo, 23–24

Academy Theatre Company,
   Milwaukee, 236

accents, 50

Actors' Fund of America, 62–65, *64*,
   278

Adler, Stella, 45

Albany, NY, 36, 67–68

Albany Argus, 36

Albany Evening Journal, 36

Albany Law Journal, 216

Albany Opera House, 36

Alcazar Theatre, San Francisco,
   105–107, *106*, 111, 118, 255

Alhambra Theatre, San Francisco, 28

"All Coons Look Alike to Me" (song),
   249

Allen, John, 155, 163, 168–169, 178

Alpers, George, 196–197

An American Beauty (play), 243

American Mutoscope and Biograph
   Company, 245–247

Arbuckle, Fatty, 267, 268–269

Arch Street Theatre, Philadelphia, 82

Arizona Republican, 162

Arkansas, 59

Around the World in Eighty Days
   (pantomime), 104

Asian trip, planned, 269–272

Atchison, KS, 68

Athens, GA, 35, 56–57

Atlanta, GA, 133, 240–241, 263

Atlanta Constitution, 18–19, 240–241

Austin, TX, 222–225

Australia (steamer), 256

Australian tour, 245, 247–252

B

Bacon, Mr., 78–79

Baldwin Theatre, San Francisco, 28

Baltimore, 35, 73

Bangor, ME, 230

Bank Nights lottery, 109

bankruptcy filings, 258–259

Barnes, William S., 191, 194, 199, 202,
   204, 210–213, 217, 221, 234

Barnum & Bailey's Circus, xi

Barrett, Lawrence, 19, 27

Bartholdy, Frédéric Auguste, 1, 2

Baswitz, Charles, 65, 66

Battery Park immigration depot,
   Manhattan, 7

Baum, L. Frank, 267

Bebus, Davenport, 89

Behrend, Gustav, 117

Beijing, 271

Belasco, David, 27–28, 46

benefits, 62–65, *64*, 73

Benny, Jack, 19

Ben's Kid (film), 267

Berkeley, CA

California Hotel, 256

Hopkins St. home (Peralta Park),
118, 118–119

intent to move back to, 232

Judson Powder Mills explosion, 140

MBC as promoter and civic
benefactor in, 113–115, 256–257

Peralta Park and Hotel, 111–113,
115–125, *118*, *124*, *139*, 139–141,
163, 189, 236, 258, 263, *280*, 281

Posen Station, xi, 114, *115*, *123*,
264–265

Shattuck Hall, 258

Sisterna Hall, West Berkeley, 257

Sixth Street cottage, 116

St. Joseph's Academy, 141, 263

St. Mary's College High School,
141, 278, 281

West Berkeley Improvement Club,
256–257

Berkeley Advocate

ad to sell Peralta Park residence
and lots, 160–161

anti-trespassing ad in, 119

articles and reports, 112, 113,
116–117, 119–129, 163–164

Boyd editorial, 156

on liquor, 150

reviews, 116

Berkeley Daily Gazette, 279

Berkeley Daily Herald, 190

Berkeley Gazette, 232–233, 257, 258

Berkeley Herald, 141

Berkeley Homestead Loan
Association, 124

Berkeley Light Company, 114

Berkeley Opera House, 258

Berkeley Station, 119

Berkeley Volunteer Fire Department,
Marston Hose Company, 256

Berlin, 233

Bernhardt, Sarah, 56, 76, 141, 143–145,
144, 147, 209

Bijou Theatre, Brooklyn, NY, 230, 238

birds, pet, 69–70

Bismarck Tribune (North Dakota), 76

Black Carl (aka the Black Dante), 250

Blazing Saddles (film), 66

Bode, Officer, 162, 168, 178, 186–187,
197, 202–203

Bogart, Humphrey, 277

Boggs, Francis, 255–258, 267–272

Boggs, Lillian, 255–258

Bohemian Club, 32

Booth, Edwin, 19

Booth, John Wilkes, 34

Booth, Rachel, 80, 92

Boston, 36–38, 65, 150, 222, 230

Boston Daily Journal, 46–47

Boston Globe, 83, 176

Boston Globe Theatre, 65

Boston Herald, 173

Bourbon News, 262

box office receipts, 65, 67, 130, 230,
235

Boyd, John E., 156

The Boy Detective (play), 20

Brady, William A., 230–231

Bridgeport, CT, 259

Briggs House, Chicago, 12

Brisbane, Australia, 254

British Columbia, 244, 249

Broadway Theatre, New York, 29

Brook, Peter, 31

Brooklyn Daily Eagle, 116, 216, 227, 230

Brooklyn Eagle, 59, 66, 258

Brooks, Mel, 66

Budapest, Hungary, 7–9, 104

Buff, Matt, 32

Buffalo Bill, 84

Buffalo Courier, 42–43

Burton, Clarence Monroe, 10

Bush, Frank, 48

Bush Street Theatre, San Francisco, 28, 29, 93, 97, 131–132

Byron, CA, 263

C

California. *See also* Berkeley, CA; San Francisco

Byron health spa, 263

Los Angeles, 112, 116, 258, 272, 276

Monterey, 143

Oakland, 258, 263, 264

Oxnard Opera House, 273–276

Paso Robles Hot Springs, 272

Richmond Opera House, 265

Sacramento, 221

Samlposen, planned town of (Tehama County), 107–109

San Diego, 276

Sanger Junction ranch, Fresno, 189–190, 219, 220, 221

Solano County, 236

touring, 97, 258

Truckee, 221

California Hotel, Berkeley, CA, 256

California Land Association, 108

California Stock Company, 26

California Theatre, 19, 27–28

Calloway, Cab, 249

Camille (play), 76, 80, 82, 141, 144–145, 147, 215

Canada

British Columbia, 244, 249

Dawson City, Yukon, 242

Fleming, May Agnes, 193

Klondike gold rush, 241–242, 243

Montreal, 14, 22, 95, 112

Quebec, 22, 95

Toronto, 17, 20

Cann, John, 191, 192, 194–196, 197

Carendon Hotel, New York, 33

Carlo (dog), xi, 122

Caught in a Corner (play), 3–4, 97–101, 103–108, 112, 116, 127

"Caught in a Corner" (article), 26

census (1870), 16

Centennial Exposition (Philadelphia, 1876), 1

Central House Hotel, Waterloo, IA, 96

Central Theatre, Oakland, CA, 263

Chaplin, Charlie, 19

Charlotte, NC, 35, 75

Charlottesville Opera House, NC, 241

Chestnut Opera House, 104

Chicago (*continued*)

Chicago (*continued*)

Briggs House, 12

Golden Rule Dry Goods shooting, 241

Grand Pacific Hotel, 222

Hooley's Theatre, 80

McVicker's Theatre, 12–14, *13*, 38, 47, 59

Olympic Theatre, 241

Schiller Theatre, 235

Selig Polyscope Company, 266–267

sheriff confrontation story, 96

Chicago Times, 14

Chicago Tribune, 12, 26–27, 103, 160

China, 271

Chutes Theatre, San Francisco, 257

Cincinnati, 20, 105, 259

Civil War, 11

Claremont, Branch and Ferries Railroad, 119

Clarendon Hotel, New York, 84, 91–93, 112

Cleary, Edwin, 89

Cleveland, Grover, 1

Cleveland, OH, 80

clock, stolen, 80–82

Colorado, 69–70, 133, 269, 272

Colorado Springs, 69

Colored Aristocracy company, 258

Colored Professional Club, New York, 253–254

Columbus, OH, 17

Columbus and the Discovery of America (pantomime), 104

Compendium of History and Biography of the City of Detroit (Burton), 10

Connecticut, 73, 259

A Connecticut Yankee in King Arthur's Court (Twain), 134–138

Connor, M. W., 163

contract conflicts, 67–68

Cook, Dr. and Mrs., 141, 145, 157, 173

Cook, L., 65

copyright infringement, 78, 238

Cosmopolitan, 45–46

Cosmopolitan Hotel, San Francisco, 210, 212

Cottrell, H. D., 256

The Count of Monte Cristo (film), 267

Courtaine, Mr. and Mrs. Harry, 29

Coxey, Jacob S., 225

Coy, C. Shaw, 217–218

Criterion Quartette, 249

Criterion Theatre, Sydney, 250–251

Crowley, Patrick, 152

Cunnane, Dr., 274

Curtis, Frank (brother; né Strelinger)

arrival in Berkeley, 126

in Chicago, 222

childhood, 7

health of, 60

as manager and producer, 35–36, 38, 60, 93

murder trial and, 163

name change, 14

Sam'l of Posen ownership interest, 127

in San Francisco, 256

in San Mateo, CA, 278

splits from MBC, 60, 108

theatres owned by, 126

Twain project and, 137

Curtis, George Washington (brother;
né Strelinger), 10, 14, 16, 82, 83
Curtis, Marie Alphonsine (née
Fleurange; stage name Albina de
Mer). *See also specific theatres and
locations*
background, 22, 95
backstage feasts, 76–78
bankruptcy filing, 259
bribery/extortion case and, 218–221
in *Camille*, 76, 80, 82, 215
as Celeste in *Sam'l of Posen*, 24–25,
38, *72*, 75–76, 80, 227
domestic dispute in court, 273–274
in *Elaine*, 90
grandmother, death of, 141
in *The Greenhorn of Breslau*, 262
health and illness, 73, 82, 111–112,
120
in *Her Greatest Love* (film), 277, *277*
as host, 78
hysterectomy, 120
interviews, 24, 83
jealousy of other actors, 92
Klondike gold rush and, 241–242
lucky ring, 25–26
on MBC in London, 232–233
in *Mr and Mrs. Peter White*, 23
murder trial and, 157–158, 160–162,
167, 173, *177*, 181–183, 185, 189,
214
in *Nerves*, 277
Oxnard Opera House and, 273–276
in *The Pearl of Savoy*, 24
pen-and-ink drawing, *23*
photographs of, ix

pregnancy rumors, 56
as Rebecca in *Sam'l of Posen*, 38, 56
in *Spot Cash*, 84
success of, 75–76
vacations, 58, 70, 78
wardrobe, 24–25, *25*
Curtis, M. B. (Maurice Bertram, né
Mortiz Bertram Strelinger). *See
also* murder trial, San Francisco;
*Sam'l of Posen; specific plays and
locations*
Asian trip planned, 269–272
bankruptcy filing, 258
childhood and youth, 7, 10–12
D. B. Anderson alias, 222
death and obituaries, 278–281
in Detroit, 16
domestic dispute in court, 273–274
early career, summary of, 29–30
early jobs, 12–14
"escape" on train disguised as
tramp, 221–222
family background, 7–10
firsthand accounts of talent of, 18–19
as first Jewish actor to portray male
Jewish character on stage, xiii
fisticuffs incidents, 70–71, 88–89
generosity of, 62
in German sanatorium, 231–232
health and illness, 91–93, 263, 269,
272
as host, 78
impersonation cases, 66, 124
James Powers alias, 222
mental state of, 97, 158–159,
228–230, 253, 273–274

Curtis, M. B. (*continued*)
    name change, 14
    number of roles played by, 19
    photographs of, ix, *15*, *18*, *21*, *86*, *268*
    plagiarism case, 101–103
    rusty nail in foot, 126
    Statue of Liberty, funding for
        lighting of, 3–6
    success and, 55–56, *58*
    training, 20
    vacations, 58, 70, 78
Curtis Afro-American Minstrels and
    Variety/Vaudeville Company,
    249, 252–253

D
Daily Alta California, 69
Daily Inter Ocean, Chicago, 38, 47–48
Daily Miner (Montana), 69–70
Daily Palladium (Oswego, NY), 231–232
Daily Sentinel, 96
Dalker, Mina, 236
Dante, the Great (Oscar Ellison), 242,
    243–245, *244*, 250
Davenport, Edgar, 67, 80
Davis, Mr., 138
Davis, Mrs., 185
Davis, Rev. W. W., 171, 174, 185
Dawson City, Yukon, Canada, 242
Day, Jim "Doc" (James H.), 224, 259
Dean, James, 7
Decatur Daily Republican, 228
Deller, George H., 225, 258
The Deluge (pantomime), 104
de Mer, Albina. *See* Curtis, Marie
    Alphonsine

de Mer, Felice, 26
Denison, Eli, 158
Denny, Joseph, 163
Denver, 69–70, 133
Denver *Tribune*, 69–70
Detroit
    family in, 15–16
    family settlement and businesses
        in, 9–10, 11
    fisticuffs incident, 70–71
    MBC's return to, 16
    Sam'l of Posen in, 36
    Sam'l of Posen revival in, 138–139
    vacation in, 70
    White's Theatre, 98–100
de Young, M. H., 107
Dickens, Charles, 47
Dickson, Charles, 33, 132
Doblin, Mr., 132
Dolan, A. B., 228
Dominguez, Frank, 275
Douglass, Frederick, 248
Driskill, Jesse, 224
Driskill Hotel, Austin, TX, 222–225,
    224, 258–259
drummer characters, *49*, 52–53, 95,
    136, 228. *See also* Sam'l of Posen
"A Drummer's Haven" (*Frank Leslie*
    Illustrated Newspaper), 95
Dumas, Alexandre, 76
Dumont, Frank, 65
Duneka, F. A., 98–100
Dunlop's Stage News, 130
Dunn, William, 217–222

E

Early Days in Detroit (Palmer), 11–12

earnings. *See* income and salaries

economic depression (1870s), 28

Edmunds, Leslie (Edmund Law
    Rogers, Jr.), 87–90

Edmunds, Mrs. Leslie, 87–90

Egypt (ship), 78

Elaine (play), 90

Ellison, Edmunda, *244*

Ellison, Oscar ("the Great Dante"),
    242, 243–245, *244*, 250

Emmett, Joseph Klein, 29

Episcopal Church, 14, 174

Erdman, Harley, 66

Ernest Hogan's Minstrels, 254–255

ethnic roles of MBC, 19–20

Eustache (play), 14

Eyre, Sophie, 130

Eytinge, Harry, 80, 83

F

Fagin (Dickens character), 47

15th Michigan Infantry, 11

Fifth Avenue Theatre, New York, 87,
    238–240

Fiji, 249

film, 245–247, *246*, 265–273

Fiske, Mr., 102–103, 109

Fisk Jubilee Singers, 247

fistfights, 70–71, 88–89

Fitchburg Daily Sentinel
    (Massachusetts), 78

Fleming, May Agnes, 193

Fleurange, Marie. *See* Curtis, Marie
    Alphonsine

Florence, W. J., 19

Fonzo, Fred, 173–174

food backstage, 76–78

Foote, W. W., 152, 162, 164–165, 167–168,
    172, 175, 178–179, 186–187, 189,
    191, 195–203, 211, 213

Ford, John T., 34–35

Ford's Theatre, 34

Fort Wayne, Indiana, 90, 231

Fort Wayne Gazette, 71

Fort Wayne News, 231

Foy, Mr. and Mrs. John, 122

France, 78, 141, 233

Frank Leslie Illustrated Newspaper, 95

Franklyn, Lester, 78

Fredericktown, PA, 81

Freeburger, Constable ("Uncle Free"),
    10–11

Fresno, CA, 189–190, 219, 220, 221,
    223

Fritchie, Barbara, 81

Fun on the Pacific (play), 34

G

Gaiety Theatre, London, 234–235

The Galley Slave (play), 91

Galveston Beach Hotel, 224

Gardner, J. W., 92

General Depot (play), 97

Gentleman Joe (play), 238–240, *239*, 247

Georgia
    Athens, 35, 56–57
    Atlanta, 133, 240–241, 263
    touring, 59

German sanatorium, 231–232

Gibson, Hoot, 267

Gif (play), 28, 38

Ginsburg (newsboy), 151

Golden Rule Dry Goods, Chicago, 241

A Gold Mine (play), 66

gold rush, Klondike, 241–242, 243

Goodwin, Nat, 32, 66

Gorman, Dick, 65

Grand Opera House, Denver, 133

Grand Opera House, Philadelphia, 137

Grand Opera House, San Francisco, 127, 145, 147, 170, 209

Grand Opera House, St. Louis, 81

Grand Opera House, Toronto, 20, 28–29

Grand Pacific Hotel, Chicago, 222

Grand Theatre, Paris, Kentucky, 262–263

Grant, Alexander, 145–155, *159*, 163, 216. *See also* murder trial, San Francisco

Grau, Robert, 75

The Great Train Robbery (film), 245

The Greenhorn of Breslau (play), 261–262, 263

Greenwalk, Ikie (character), 99–100

Grey, Rev. Peter, 220

Gulick, Joseph, 86–87

H

Hampson & Co., 2–3

Hampton, Lionel, 249

Hanna & Co., 12

Harcourt, Walter, 139

Harrington, W. E., 174, 187, 203–204

Harrison, Duncan, 235

Harte, Bret, 101–102

Haverly, Jack J. H., 62–64

Haverly's Brooklyn Theatre, New York, 59–60

Haverly's Fourteenth Street Theatre, New York, 3–4, 35–36, *54*, 59–61, 80, 100–102

Havlin's Theatre, Cincinnati, 105

Hawaii, 244, 249, 254–255

Hearst, William Randolph, 109

Henry Taylor Lumber Yard, Berkeley, 122

Her Greatest Love (film), 277, *277*

Hinckle, Walter, 179–180, 191

Hines, Earl, 249

Hoboken, NJ, 133

Hoff, Christian, 264

Hogan, Ernest, *248*, 248–250, 253–254

Hogan's Unbleached Coons company, 250

Holden, Mrs., 194

Holden girls, 193

Holder, Jennie, 153

Holst, Anna A., 276

Honolulu, 244, 249, 254–255, 269–270

Hooley's Theatre, Chicago, 80

Horan, Edward, 79

Hornsville *Weekly Tribune*, 264

Hotel Del Monte, Monterey, CA, 143

Hot Sulphur Springs, CO, 269

Howard, Frank, 112

"How Curtis Came to Fashion It into a Play," 14, 34

Howe & Hummel, 91

Hoyt & Thomas, 215

Humanity (play), 230–231

Humpty Dumpty (pantomime), 104

Hungary, 7–9, 15–16, 104

Huning, Dr., 274

Huntingdon, PA, 94

Hurley, W. J., 185–188, 233–234

Husband, R., 188

Hyers, Madah A. (the "Bronze Patti"), 250, 258–259

I

Illinois, 59, 80, 83–84, 97. *See also* Chicago

Illustrated American, 12, 20

Illustrated Newspaper, 4

"In Celeste's Dressing Room" (*Boston Globe*), 83

income and salaries, 14, 35, 36, 39, 55, 78

Indiana, 38, 59, 90

Indianapolis Freeman, 252, 253

Iowa, 95–96, 97

The Irish Emigrant (play), 228

Irvine Hotel, Waterloo, IA, 96

Isadore, the Commercial Tourist (play), 34–35

Isadore Plastrick (play; later *Sam'l of Posen*), 31–32, 33. *See also Sam'l of Posen* (play)

Isère (steamer), 1

J

Jacobs, Augusta (later Strelinger), 17

Janssen, B., 66

Japan, 270–271, 274

J. C. Blair Company, 94

Jean Baptiste (play), 95

Jefferson, Harry, 173–174

Jefferson, Joseph, 17, 96

Jeransen, Henry, 161

Jersey City, NJ, 138

Jessop, George H., 31, 33, 38–39, 66, 276

Jewish actors, 46

Jewish audiences, 48

Jewish characters on the stage, 45–53, *49*

Johnson, Mrs. Annie, 153, 176, 194

Johnson, Posen A., 281

Johnson, Rasmus, 281

Judson Powder Mills, Berkeley, 140

K

Kahn, Gustave, 138–139

Keegan, Charles, 73

Kentucky, 59, 262–263

Kentucky Four, 250

Kinau (steamer), 255–256

Kiralfy, Bolossy, 104

Kiralfy, Imre, 104

Kline, Charles, 40

Klondike gold rush, 241–242, 243

Knight, George A., 152, 162, 165, 172, 176–178, 197, 199–200

Kowalsky, Henry I, 152, 154, 169, 172–173, 180, 186, 196, 201

Krantz, Julien (character), 29

Kreling, William, 125, 145, 147, 148, 151, 211

Kyoto, Japan, 270

L

Lady Scales (ship), 7

Lakewood, NJ, 225

Lancaster, PA, 80–82

lawsuits, 78, 92–93, 138, 236–238, 245

Lazarus, Emma, 5

Leahy, W. H., 211

Leburie's Theatre, Memphis, 95

"Left His Pistol At Home," 169

Lehmann Brothers Department Store, Oxnard, 275–276

Leland, Mrs., 67–68, 78

Leland Opera House, Albany, NY, 67–68

Leslie, Frank, *4*

Le Tort, W. C., 229

Leuder, Alfred, 125

Levick, Gustavus, 105

Levy Cohen (play), 66

Levy the Drummer, or Life on the Road (play), 66

Lewis, Joseph (character), 129

Lewis, Sarah, 189

Le Zora, Madame, 275–276

Life on the Mississippi (Twain), 136

Lighthouse Board, New York, 5, 6

Lilliputian creole contortion danseuse, 250

Lincoln, Abraham, 34, 122

Locke, Mr., 138

London, 232–233, 234–235, 276

Long Branch, NJ, 58

Longfellow, Henry Wadsworth, 122

Long Island, 225

Lord, C. R., 120, 124–125, 256

Lord & Boynton, 118

Los Angeles, 112, 116, 258, 272, 276

Los Angeles County Hospital, 278

Los Angeles Times, 278–279

Louisiana, 59, 78, 115

Louis XIII, 19

Lowenthal, H. H., 152

Lyceum Theatre, Atlanta, 240

M

MacFarlane, T. M., 217–218, 219–221

"The Major's Story" (*New York Dramatic Mirror*), 101–103

Manila, Philippines, 271

Manitoba Daily Free Press, 161

Mansfield (Ohio) *News*, 33

Marble, Edward Stevenson, 39, 190

Marcoval, Augustine, *166*, 167, 176, 191

Mardi Gras, 78

Marie Antoinette, 25–26

Massachusetts, 66, 73. *See also* Boston

M. B. Curtis (film), *246*, 247

"M. B. Curtis Disappears," 91–92

"M. B. Curtis Famous for 'Drummer Characterization,'" 112–113

M. B. Curtis's Sam'l of Posen Company, 61, 67, 83

McAdoo, O. M., 247, 251–252

McAdoo's Georgia Minstrels, 251

McCarthy, James P., 163

McClain, Billy, 249–250, 253

McCullough, John, 27

McDonough Theatre, Oakland, CA, 258

McManus, Frank "King," 217–222, *218*

McVicker's Theatre, Chicago, 12–14, *13*, 38, 47, 59

Melbourne, Australia, 251

Memphis, TN, 95

The Merchant of Venice (Shakespeare), 51

Mestayer, W., 32

Michigan. *See also* Detroit
  15th Michigan Infantry, 11
  touring, 59, 80, 98

Miedema, Madeline, 275

Miller, Arthur, 53, 75

Milliken, J. F., 102–103

Milwaukee, 236

Minehan, Patrick, 212

Minneapolis, 230

Minnimatsu, Frank, 272–273

minstrel companies, 247–255

Miowera (ship), 249, 255

Missouri, 59, 80. *See also* St. Louis

Mitchell, Maggie, 17, 23–24, 58, 122–123, 278

Mix, Tom, 267

Mongolia, 271

Monterey, CA, 143

Montreal, 14, 22, 95, 112

Moore, Maggie, 27

Morgan, Hank (character), 135–137

Morning Call, 162, 209

Morris, William, 84

Morris and Hall Agency, 261

Morris Cohen, the Commercial Drummer (play), 65

Morrison, Lewis, 129–131

Moses Levy (play), 65

The Mother-in-Law (play), 28

moving pictures, 245–247, *246*, 265–273

Moving Picture World, 265–266

Mr and Mrs. Peter White (play), 23

Mullins, C. J., 242

Mullins, Thomas, 154, 169–170, 173, 176, 186, 196, 197

murder trial, San Francisco
  1st trial, 164–188
  2nd trial, 190–199
  3rd trial, 202–214
  acquittal and celebration, *214*, 214–216
  bail, 163–164, 189–190
  coroner's inquest, 152–155
  defense team, 152, 164–165, 199–202
  events, shooting, and arrest, 143–152
  Examiner interview, 191–193, 207–209
  Grant's funeral, 160
  Hurley bribery trial, 233–234
  later threats and demands against MBC, 219
  McManus & Dunn bribery trial, 217–222
  murder weapon, 155–156, *156*
  planned melodrama about, 215
  preliminary hearing, 161–163
  preparation for trial, 160–161
  public opinion on, 156–159

Murphy, John, 190–191, 199–200, 202, 213–214

My Hebrew Friend (play), 65

N

Nagy Selmetz, Hungary/Slovakia, 8

Nebraska, 84

Nebraska State Journal, 219

Neihaus, Mr., 116

Neihaus Planing Mill, Berkeley, 114

Neilson Lithographic Co., 139

Nerves (play), 277

Nevada, 97

Nevada State Journal, 222

"The New Colossus" (Lazarus), 5

New Grand Theatre, Salt Lake City,
   242

New Jersey
   Hoboken, 133
   Jersey City, 138
   Lakewood lots, 225
   land debts, 258
   touring, 80

"The New Judge" (burlesque sketch),
   257

Newman, Officer, 162–163

New Orleans, 78, 115

New York City
   Academy of Music, Brooklyn, 73
   Actors' Fund benefit, 62–64
   arriving in, before *Sam'l of Posen*, 32
   Battery Park immigration depot, 7
   Bijou Theatre, Brooklyn, 230, 238
   Broadway Theatre, 29
   Clarendon Hotel, 33, 84, 91–93, 112
   close of first run of *Sam'l of Posen*,
      58
   Colored Professional Club, 253–254
   Dalker real estate trade, 236–238
   Fifth Avenue Theatre, 87, 238–240
   Haverly's Brooklyn Theatre, 59–60
   Haverly's Fourteenth Street
      Theatre, 3–4, 35–36, *54*, 59–61,
      80, 100–102

   intention to return, after trial,
      214–215
   land debts, 258
   MBC's planned return to theatre,
      222
   Niblo's Garden, 65, 90–91
   Park Theatre, 87
   plans for new company in, 233
   Standard Theatre, 225–228, *226*
   Star Theatre, 33, 127–128
   Statue of Liberty, 1–6, *4*, 100, 262
   Strelinger family arrival in, 7–9
   Sturtevant House, 240
   Third Avenue Theatre, 126
   touring, 38, 230
   Windsor Theatre, 65

New York Clipper, 20, 22, 28, 29, 65, 139

New York Daily Graphic, 51–52

New York Daily Mirror, 87, 88–89, 93

New York Dramatic Mirror
   articles and reports, 3–4, 90, 97,
      136, 238
   citing of notices, 75
   interviews, 128, 133
   "The Major's Story," 101–103
   reviews, 84, 98, 101, 267–268

New York Herald, 24, 39–40, 279

New York Mirror
   on Actors' Fund, 62
   ads for *Spot Cash* in, 84–86
   articles and reports, 10–11, 36, 48,
      55–56, 58, 61, 65, 67–68, 70–71,
      97
   interviews, 48
   MBC letter to, 83–84
   reviews, 60, 64–65, 100, 103–104

Samlposen town (planned) and, 109

New York State

Actors' Fund, incorporation of, 65

Albany, 36, 67–68

Dunkirk, 93

touring, 66, 73, 82

New York Times

articles and reports, 86–87, 88, 92, 225, 227–229, 234

reviews, 129–130

New York World, 1–3, 5–6, 55

New Zealand, 244–245, 252–253

Niblo's Garden, Manhattan, 65, 90–91

Nicholas Nickleby (play), 20

North Carolina, 35, 75, 241

Norton, John W., 81

nose of Jewish characters, 48–50, *49*

Novelty Theatre, Oakland, CA, 264

O

Oakland, CA, 258, 263, 264

Oakland Daily, 125–126

Oakland Enquirer, 113, 146, 151, 157

Oakland Evening Tribune, 22

Oakland Theatre, 116

Oakland Tribune, 105, 130, 140, 263, 276–277, 279–281

obituaries, 279–281

Occidental Hotel, San Francisco, 122, 189, 220

O'Hara, Arthur, 16

Ohio

Cincinnati, 20, 105, 259

Columbus, 17

touring, 59, 80, 98

Olivier, Laurence, 243

Olympic Theatre, Chicago, 241

100 Years on the Road: The Traveling Salesman in American Culture (Spears), 52–53

Orpheum Theatre, Honolulu, 255

Osbourne, George, 130

Osbourne & Stockwell's Comedy Co., 105

Oscar Hammerstein I, 46

Our American Cousin (play), 101

Our Cousin Fritz (play), 29

Oxnard Courier, 275

Oxnard Opera House, 273–276

P

Pacific Commercial Advertiser, 254, 255

Palace Hotel, San Francisco, 122, 279

Palace Theatre, Wellington, New Zealand, 245

Palmer, Albert, 211–212

Palmer, Friend, 11–12

pantomimes, 104

Paris, France, 78, 233

Paris, Kentucky, 262–263

Parker, John A., 191

Parker House Hotel, Boston, 222

Park Theatre, Boston, 36–38, 150, 230

Park Theatre, New York, 87

Paso Robles Hot Springs, California, 272

Passett, Mr., 112

Pateman, Robert, 26

Patti, Adelina, 250

The Pearl of Savoy (play), 23–24

Pennsylvania

clock stolen in Lancaster, 80–82

Pennsylvania (*continued*)
Huntingdon, 94
Philadelphia, 65, 73, 82, 137
Pittsburgh, 91, 92
touring, 38, 73, 80, 82, 89, 136
Williamsburg, 60
Peralta, Domingo, 117
Peralta Building and Loan Association
of Berkeley, 125
Peralta Park and Hotel, Berkeley,
111–113, 115–125, *118*, *124*, *139*,
139–141, 163, 189, 236, 258, 263,
280, 281
Perrault, Carole, 5
Petchke, Mosche (character), 261
Petersburg, VA, 35
Petowsky, Myer (character), 129
Pettit, Mr., 215
Philadelphia, 65, 73, 82, 137
Philadelphia Bulletin, 50
Philadelphia Enquirer, 158
Piper, F. E., 150
pirated plays, 78–79, 238
Pittsburgh, 91, 92
Plagiarism (Salzman), 19
Plastrick, Samuel. *See* Sam'l of Posen
(character)
Porter, S. C., 185–186
Portland, ME, 35
Posen Station, Berkeley, ix, 114, *115*,
123, 264–265
Powers, John T., 238
Protestantism, 53
Puck, x
Pulitzer, Joseph, 1–2

Q

Quebec, 22, 95. *See also* Montreal

R

Raleigh, NC, 35
Raymond, James H., 258–259
Read, Buchanan, 81
Reno Evening Gazette, 148
"Retaliation" (comedy sketch), 257
Richmond, VA, 34
Richmond Opera House, Richmond,
CA, 265
Riddell, Walden, 92
The Rivals (play), 96
Rix, Alfred, 162
Rogers, Edmund Law, Jr. (aka Leslie
Edmunds), 87–90
Roosevelt, Teddy, 264
Rosenquest, J. W., 3
Roshier and His Dog Bobby, 276
Ross, Sul, 224
Rumble, G. W., 206–209, 212–213
Russell, Lillian, 243
Russ Hotel, San Francisco, 212

S

Sacramento, CA, 221
Salt Lake City, 69, 242, 243–244
Salzman, Maurice, 19
Sam'l of Posen (character)
accent and slang, 50
cartoons and drawings of, *x*, *54*, *63*
Detroit's interest in, 36
impact of, x–xii, 94–95, 135
as Jewish character, 46–53, *54*
mannerisms and costume,

description of, 18–19

origins of, 31–39

photographs, *xii*, *37*, *94*

pirated by Lester Franklyn, 79

products named after, xi, 94

robbery suspect nicknamed after, 241

wax nose for, 48

Sam'l of Posen (film), 267–268, *268*

Sam'l of Posen (play). *See also specific theatres and cities*

    Actors' Fund benefit, 64–65

    broken contract at Niblo's, 91

    close of first New York run, 58

    farewell performance, San Francisco, 127–128

    film rights to, 267

    financial attachments on, 228

    first tour, 57–59

    Frank as producer of, 35–36, 38

    French Canadian version of, 95

    as *Isadore, the Commercial Tourist*, 34–35

    as *Isadore Plastrick*, 31–32, 33

    Jewish audiences for, 48

    in London, 234–235

    Marie as Celeste in, 38, *72*, 75–76, 80, 227

    Marie as Rebecca in, 38, 56

    origins of, 31–39

    ownership interests in, 127

    pamphlet cover, *63*

    pirated version of, 78–79

    plot, 40–42

    posters, *42*, 51, *54*

    revivals, 138–139, 225–228, *226*, 256,

258, 263

    rewrites of, 39–40, 190, 215

    rights for, bought from Jessop, 38

    Sam'l meeting Rebecca (drawing), *41*

    success of, 39, 48, 55–56

    vaudeville versions of, 241, 243, 259, 264

Sam'l of Posen, the Drummer Up-to-Date (play), 228

Sam'l of Posen at King Arthur's Court (planned), 135–138

"Sam'l of Posen on the Road" (proposed film), 271

Sam'l of Posen's Brother (play), 262–263

"Sam'l of Posen's Brother Isadore" (proposed film), 271

"Sam'l of Posen's Varied Career" (*New York Herald*), 39–40

Samlposen, planned town of (Tehama County, CA), 107–109

Samuel at the Herald Square Hotel (play), 259

San Diego, CA, 276

San Francisco. *See also* murder trial, San Francisco

    Alcazar Theatre, 105–107, *106*, 111, 118, 255

    Alhambra Theatre, 28

    arrival from Honolulu to, 256

    Baldwin Theatre, 28

    Bernhardt in, 143–145

    Bush Street Theatre, 28, 29, 93, 97, 131–132

    California Stock Company, 26

    California Theatre, 19, 27–28

San Francisco (*continued*)
    Camille in, 141, 144–145
    Chutes Theatre, 257
    corruption in public affairs, 219
    Cosmopolitan Hotel, 210, 212
    development of character Sam'l of
        Posen and, 31–32
    farewell performance of *Sam'l of
        Posen*, 127–128
    Grand Opera House, 127–128, 145,
        147, 170, 209, *264*
    Julien Krantz performance, 29
    Klondike gold rush and, 241
    MBC's first visit to, 26–27
    Occidental Hotel, 122, 189, 220
    Palace Hotel, 122, 279
    Russ Hotel, 212
    Sam'l of Posen revival, 138, 227
    St. Luke's Episcopal Church, 174
    St. Patrick's Church, 220
    Tivoli Theatre, 125, 145–148, 170–171,
        210–212
    touring, 66, 92
San Francisco Call, 148, 149, 183, 184,
    202, 204, 214–215, 219
San Francisco Chronicle
    articles and reports, 108, 113–114,
        140, 231, 233–234, 236–237
    interviews, 24, 127
    on murder trial, 166–167, 175–176,
        189, 194, 197–203, 212–213
    murder trial sketches, *177*, *187*, *198*
    reviews, 105–106, 128, 132, 262–263
San Francisco Earthquake (1906), 264,
    264
San Francisco *Examiner*

    articles and reports, 28, 29–30, 132
    on murder trial, 146–147, 149–151,
        154–155, 178–186, 188, 190–193,
        196, 202, 205–210, 212, 219,
        221–222
    murder trial sketches, *156*, *159*, *166*,
        192, *214*, *218*
    reviews, 24
San Francisco Post, 108
Sanger Junction ranch, Fresno, CA,
    189–190, 219, 220, 221
The Sanitarium (film), 268–269
San Mateo, CA, 278
Saturday Evening Observer, 93
Savage, F. O., 87
Schiller Theatre, Chicago, 235
Schmidt, George, 112, 114
Schofield, John M., 3
The School for Scandal, 28
Scotchler, J. L., 124–125
Scouts of the Prairie (play), 84
Seattle, 241
Selig, William, 266–272, 274
Selig Polyscope Company, 267, 272
Selkie, Albertine, 16
Shakespeare, William, 45–46, 48, 51
Shakespearean roles of MBC, 19, 20
Shamus O'Brien (opera), 276
The Shatchen (play), 127–134, 138
Shattuck Hall, Berkeley, CA, 258
Shaw, W. J., 100
Shea, Dan, 203
Sheridan, Richard Brinsley, 96
Sherlock, Charles B., 45–46
Shylock (Shakespeare character), 46,
    51

Siberia, 271

Simms, Mr., 215

Sinden, Donald, 17

Sisterna Hall, West Berkeley, 257

Siter, Augusta, 16

Sketch, 26, 31–32

slang, 50

Slovakia, 8

Smith, Nathaniel Clark, 248–249, *251*

Smith, Reverend, 160

Smithsonian Institute, 81

Solano County, CA, 236

Sothern, Edward, 101

Southern Pacific Railroad, 114, 120, 265

Spears, Timothy B., 52–53

Spencer, Frank, 173

Spirit of the Times, 38, 50, 227

The Spirit of the Times, 90

The Sporting Life, 190

"Spot Cash" (proposed film), 271

Spot Cash (play), 84–90, *85*, *86*, 92, 93, 97, 127

Stage, 235

Staging the Jew (Erdman), 66

Standard Theatre, New York, 225–228, *226*

Star Theatre, New York, 33, 127–128

Statue of Liberty, 1–6, *4*, 100, 262

stereotypes of Jewish characters, 45–52

Sternroyd, Vincent, 105

Stianvnica, Slovakia, 8

St. Joseph's Academy, Berkeley, 141, 263

St. Louis, 38, 81, 229–230

St. Luke's Episcopal Church, San Francisco, 174

St. Mary's College High School, Berkeley, 141, 278, 281

Stoppard, Tom, 261

St. Patrick's Church, San Francisco, 220

St. Paul, MN, 84, 258–259

Strelinger, Augusta Jacobs (stepmother), 17

Strelinger, Bertha Schultz (mother), 7–8, *8*, 15–16

Strelinger, Charles (brother), 7, 9, 16, 273

Strelinger, Frank (brother). *See* Curtis, Frank

Strelinger, George Washington (brother; later Curtis, 10, 14, 16, 82, 83

Strelinger, Gisella (sister), 7

Strelinger, Julien (né Gyula) (father), 7–10, *9*

Strelinger, Moritz Bertram. *See* Curtis, M. B.

Strelinger, Rosalie (sister), 8

Strelinger saloon, Detroit, 11

Stritch, Elaine, 55, 217

Struck Oil (play), 27

Sturtevant House, New York City, 240

Sullivan, J. P., 92

"Summing Up for Curtis," 176

Sun, 102

Sunday Morning Constitution (Chillicothe, MS), 131

Swett, Edward C., 60–61, 67, 78–79, 82, 127

Sydney, Australia, 249–252

Sydney *Referee*, 249–250

Syracuse, NY, 206

T

Tabor, Horace, 69–70

Taylor, Howard P., 134–138

Tehama County, CA, 107–109

Tennessee, 59, 97

Teutonic (ship), 231

Texas

    Driskill Hotel, Austin, 222–225, *224*, 258–259

    Galveston Beach Hotel, 224

    touring, 32, 59, 60, 66

Theatre Royal, Brisbane, Australia, 254

"There Was an Opera House in Oxnard" (Miedema), 275

Third Avenue Theatre, New York City, 126

Thompson, Frank, 209–210

Tivoli Theatre, San Francisco, 125, 145–148, 170–171, 210–212

Toomey, Edward, 153–154, 169–170, 173, 176, 186, 197

Toronto, 17, 20

traveling salesmen. *See* drummer characters; Sam'l of Posen (character)

Treadwell, A., 205–206

Troutt, James Morris, 163–166, *164*, 169, 175, 180–185, 189

Truckee, CA, 221

Twain, Mark, 134–138

Twinkle Little Star (Powers), 238

U

Ukiah Republican Press, 273

Uncle Tom's Cabin (play), 13, 29, 254

U.S. Circuit Court, Chicago, 78

V

Vancouver, BC, 249

Vane, Sutton, 230

vaudeville, 241, 259. *See also* minstrel companies

Venice in London (pantomime), 104

Ventura County, CA, 275

Ventura County Historical Society Quarterly, 275

Verner, Charles, 88, 92

Vice, W. R., 209

Victoria, BC, 244

W

Wallace, Judge, 234

Wananui Theatre, Wellington, New Zealand, 245

Warner, John, 32

The Wasp, 93

Waterloo (Iowa) *Courier*, 95–96

The Wave, 162, 164–165

Wellington, New Zealand, 244–245, 252–253

West Berkeley Development Association, 114

West Berkeley Improvement Club, 256–257

White's Theatre, Detroit, 99

Wild West Show, Buffalo Bill's, 84

Williamsburg, PA, 60

Williamson, J. C., 27

Wilson, J. N. E., 162, 164–165, 169,
    175, 185, 191, 199, 200, 202, 213,
    217–218
Windsor Hotel, Denver, 69–70
Windsor Theatre, New York, 65
Winslow, Herbert Hall, 261, 262
Wires, Rodney, 32
Wisconsin, 59, 80, 236
The Wizard of Oz (film, 1910), 267
Wolf, 32, 33
Woods Theatre, 20
The World, 134, 194
Wyatt, Carrie, 38
Wyatt, William T., 278

Y
Yiddish, 51
Yukon, Canada, 241–242, 243

Z
Zimmerman, Henry, 16
Zouaves, 11